Dolls and Accessories of the 1950s

Dian Zillner

Photography by Suzanne Silverthorn

Schiffer Publishing Ltd

4880 Lower Valley Rd. Atglen, PA 19310

Dedication

This book is dedicated to Marge Meisinger whose interests are so varied that her collections include dolls, paper dolls, movie memorabilia, Native Americana, music boxes, and, of course, Shirley Temple. Marge has been collecting since the late 1950s and she has amassed a wonderful treasure trove of items which interest collectors in diverse fields.

Not only does Marge have a massive collection, her generosity in sharing with writers has been tremendous. Marge's collections have been featured in over eighty-five books.

In the doll world, particularly, not only is she willing to share her collections with people interested in learning about "something," she also shares her time by helping organizations with their "get togethers" and conventions.

Marge once again proved invaluable by providing dolls, catalogs, advertising, etc. to be used as reference materials and in photographs for this book.

Published by Schiffer Publishing Ltd.
4880 Lower Valley Road
Atglen, PA 19310
Phone: (610) 593-1777; Fax: (610) 593-2002
e-mail: schifferbk@aol.com
Please write for a free catalog.
This book may be purchased from the publisher.
Please include $3.95 for shipping.

In Europe, Schiffer books are distributed by
Bushwood Books
6 Marksbury Avenue
Kew Gardens
Surrey TW9 4JF England
Phone: 44 (0)181 392-8585; Fax: 44 (0)181 392-9876
e-mail: bushwd@aol.com

Please try your bookstore first.

We are interested in hearing from authors
with book ideas on related subjects.

Author's Note

All of the items in this book are from private collections. Grateful acknowledgment is made to the original producers of the dolls and materials photographed. The maker and/or copyright holder has been identified for each item whenever possible. If any omission or incorrect information is found, please notify the author or publisher and it will be amended in any future edition of the book.

The prices listed in the captions should be used as a guide only, and should not be used to set prices for dolls and their accessories. Prices vary from one section of the country to another and also from dealer to dealer. The prices listed here are the best estimates the author can give at the time of publication, but prices in the doll field can change quickly. Neither the author nor the publisher assumes responsibility for any losses that might be incurred as a result of consulting this price guide.

Contents

Introduction

I have been a doll collector since 1960. It is hard for me to imagine that the lovely hard plastic dolls of the 1950s were less than a decade old at that time. In those days, few collectors were interested in the dolls from that time period.

Times have changed! Hard plastic dolls in original excellent condition have become ever more popular in the last ten years. Perhaps it is because of the high prices fine bisque dolls are bringing or the age damage that has occurred to many composition dolls. Whatever the reason, current prices reflect this new popularity with the cost of most excellent hard plastic dolls dressed in original clothing more than doubling over the last decade. Also during the last ten years another phenomenon has occurred. For most collectors who can afford the best, only excellent to mint dolls, complete with their original tags and/or boxes are preferred. Although there are still some collectors who purchase a doll just because it is appealing, it seems that more and more collectors of hard plastic dolls see their collections as investments. Hard plastic is a field in the doll collecting hobby that still offers an abundance of dolls if a collector is willing to pay a top price. Dolls with replaced clothing, worn or replaced wigs, or other non-original features are presently not selling well while dolls that are in near excellent condition with original clothing are desirable even without tags and boxes.

Even the vinyl and/or hard plastic dolls of the later 1950s have also increased in their appeal to collectors. This is especially true of the fashion dolls like Alexander's Cissy and Ideal's Miss Revlon. Other fine dolls from the era representing Betsy McCall, comic characters, personality figures, and the large 30"-36" dolls also have become very collectible.

The price of a doll depends on the condition, popularity, and rarity of the doll. The prices in this book reflect the doll as it is pictured. If clothing has been replaced, this information will be included in the caption and the price given will be for a doll with replaced clothing. If the doll pictured includes the box, the price noted will reflect that extra addition. No price is listed for dolls pictured only in catalog advertisements in order not to confuse the reader about the condition of the doll (box or no box, tag or no tag, etc.). Some of the photographs in this book have been supplied by collectors who are very knowledgeable in their own field of expertise, i.e., Alexander, Terri Lee, Betsy McCall, etc. In this way we hope to show the reader which of these various dolls are the most unusual and therefore would be priced higher than like dolls dressed in more common costumes.

The many pictures in this book are intended to illustrate the wide variety of items which are available to today's collectors. Included in this book is a bibliography of materials used to research this volume. This will provide helpful sources for those collectors who want to continue to explore the field.

I wish to thank the many collectors who have been so helpful in sharing materials, photographs, dolls, and knowledge with me so this book could become a reality. Included are: Kelly Anderson, Mark W. Carpenter, Dorothy Cassidy, Jan and Darek Clanton, Patty Cooper, Denver Doll Emporium, Bob and Elaine Ehnisz, Judith Izen, Sidney Jeffrey, Carol J. Lindeman, Marge Meisinger, Peggy Millhouse, Connie Neal, Betty Nichols, Sue Peck, Dora and Al Pitts, Paula Reding, Leslie Robinson, Nancy Roeder, Marian Schmuhl, Rhonda Schoenick, Jim Shivers, Mary and Werner Stuecher, Carolyn and Dana Sharp, Jo Ann and Jason Walters, and Edith and James Wise.

I also would like to extend continued appreciation and thanks to my daughter, Suzanne Silverthorn, who again took many of the photographs for this, my seventh book. A special "thank you" is also given to my son, Jeff Zillner, who helped with editing once again.

Acknowledgement and recognition is also extended to Schiffer Publishing Ltd., and its excellent staff, particularly to Sue Taylor, layout editor, and editor Dawn Stoltzfus who helped with this publication. Without their support and extra effort, this book would not have been possible.

Alexander

The Alexander Doll Company was founded by Beatrice Alexander Berhman in 1923. At first the dolls were made of cloth and the operation was mostly an "at home" kind of enterprise. After Beatrice persuaded her husband Phillip Behrman to join her in her new business it began to grow. By the 1930s the company was marketing composition dolls dressed in the lovely clothes that became an Alexander trademark. The firm secured licensing in 1935 to make dolls in the images of the famous Dionne Quintuplets and these dolls proved to be nearly as popular as the Ideal Shirley Temple models. Other famous Alexander composition dolls were those representing Jane Withers, Margaret O'Brien, Sonja Henie, and Scarlet from Margaret Mitchell's *Gone With The Wind*.

The Madame Alexander firm continued its success through the 1940s and they were among the earliest doll companies to use hard plastic in their doll production. By 1948 many of their dolls were made of this new material. The firm continued producing the high quality doll costumes and was awarded the Fashion Academy Gold Medal in 1951, 1952, 1953, and 1954.

By the late 1950s the company was running three factories, two in New York and one in White Plains, New York. Hundreds of people were employed to make the dolls and clothes.

The dolls marketed by the Madame Alexander Company during the 1950s continued to enhance the firm's reputation as a maker of fine quality dolls. Although the Alexander firm did not produce a block buster seller like the Ideal Toni dolls, their excellent hard plastic dolls from the era now bring higher prices than those from any other company.

As the decade of the 1950s began, the Alexander Doll Co. was already producing the fine quality hard plastic dolls that would be their trademark for the next few years. The **Little Women** series (based on Louisa Alcott's book of the same name) was a staple for the company during the entire decade. Each year brought new changes in the costumes. The dolls of the late 1940s and the early 1950s used the hard plastic Maggie and Margaret faces and were 14" tall but by the later years of the decade smaller dolls were marketed as "Little Women."

The Alexander Co. always relied on fairy tales for inspiration and two **Cinderella dolls** were marketed in 1950. It is likely that "Poor Cinderella" did not sell as well as the Cinderella model wearing the fine ball gown. A **Prince Charming** doll was also sold the same year. Since all of the Alexander dolls use the same few face and body models, the company relied on the lovely Alexander clothing to transform the dolls from one character to another. All three of these dolls used the Margaret face and 14" bodies.

Alexander also produced the series of lovely ballerinas throughout the hard plastic era. At least one model of a ballerina was offered each year of the decade. The doll called **Nina Ballerina** was sold in 1950.

Bride dolls were also found in the Alexander catalogs. The bride from 1950 came in sizes of 14", 17", and 21", and was made with the Margaret face. The **Babs Ice Skater** from the same year was also made with the Margaret face. The Maggie faced dolls were offered in 1950 as walkers dressed in school dresses and as **Alice in Wonderland**. The Maggie face was also used on the **Polly Pigtails** dolls with the name taken from the *Polly Pigtails* magazine then being published for young girls.

The Alexander firm offered one of their fine personality dolls in 1950 when it honored **Mary Martin**. The star had made a big hit in the *South Pacific* Broadway show and the dolls were dressed in outfits based on costumes from the musical. At least three different outfits were made for the dolls which came in sizes of 14" or 17". See the Personality section for more information.

Although all of the Alexander dolls from the year 1950 are very collectible, the most sought after are the beautifully dressed **Godey** dolls which used the Margaret faces. Nearly every year the company produced dolls of a special nature which were usually portrait dolls.

In 1951, most of the Alexander dolls were still being made with Margaret or Maggie faces. The Margaret faced dolls included a ballerina, bride, majorette, and several of the Little Women. The Maggie faces were used on **Alice in Wonderland**, **Rosamund Bridesmaid**, **Kathy**, **Maggie Teenager**, and the other Little Women dolls.

But 1951 also brought some new faces into the Alexander line. **Violet** was a head turning walker made in the 18" size. Her face was later used on the Bennie and Winnie Walker dolls and still later as popular Cissy's face.

A 34" tall doll called **Penny** was also for sale in 1951. She had a soft cloth body and a stuffed vinyl head and limbs. She was based on a comic strip character of the same name. (See Comic Chapter).

Several new baby dolls were added to the line in 1951. They included **Slumbermate**, a soft baby with a vinyl head and closed eyes, **Honeybun**, also made of vinyl and cloth, **Littlest Cherub**, a small baby 9" tall, **Bonnie and Bitsey**, with hard plastic heads, and **Sunbeam**, modeled after a newborn infant.

There was also a personality doll sold in 1951 which represented **Sonja Henie** (see Personality section.)

Although all of these Alexander dolls are very collectible, the Portrait dolls of the period are the most desirable and expensive of any of the Alexander dolls. At least six of these dolls have been identified by Polly and Pam Judd in their book *Hard Plastic Dolls, II*. The dolls were all made in the 21" size and have lovely costumes. Collectors have given them names to help in identification. The dolls include the following known models: **Deborah**, a beautiful 21" ballerina with the Margaret face. Her costume was of white satin, tulle, and lace. **Kathryn Grayson**, a doll given this name by collectors because of her resemblance to the famous singing movie star of that name. The doll was 21" tall and also used the Margaret face. Her dress was made with a lace bodice trimmed in rhinestones and a tulle skirt. She wore tear drop earrings and flowers in her hair. She also carried a purse.

The doll called **Pink Champagne** was also 21" tall and used the Maggie face. Her costume was made of silk organza and was decorated with flowers and rhinestones down the right front of the dress as well as on her left shoulder. The beautiful doll called **Victorian Bride** was also 21" tall dressed in a costume based on styles of the 1870s. The bridal dress was made of white satin and lace. **Judy**, also known as the Godey Lady, was also 21" tall and was made with the Margaret face. She was dressed in an old fashioned costume of lace and taffeta. She wore a straw hat, and carried a purse. The 21" **Champs-Elysees** doll is also called the Lady with the Rhinestone Beauty Mark by some collectors because of the rhinestone set in the upper part of her left cheek. She was dressed in a black lace dress over a pink satin underdress. She came with bracelets and a black lace headpiece.

All of these dolls must have been very expensive when they were made and probably not too many were sold. Perhaps they were marketed to compete with the Style Show dolls produced by the Nancy Ann Storybook Co. They are very hard for today's collectors to find, and sell for a premium price at shows or auctions.

New dolls offered by the Alexander Co. in 1952 included the unusual 18" **Madeline**. Her head was made of vinyl while her fully jointed body was hard plastic. This doll was supplied with sixteen different outfits that could be purchased separately. She was also sold in 1953. Another important Alexander product from 1952 was the black **Cynthia** doll. This doll was actually a regular Margaret faced doll with black coloring added. She came in 15", 18", and 23" sizes and remains a very collectible doll.

Other dolls from the Alexander catalog from 1952 include a Margaret faced bride, ballerina, and **Snow White** plus a Maggie walker. The Little Women dolls were still being made with a combination of Margaret and Maggie faces. A three doll set of **Little Men** using the same faces was also offered.

A personality doll called **Annabelle** was marketed as being the little girl of the same name on the Kate Smith television show. The doll was actually a Maggie wearing a costume labeled Annabelle.

The baby dolls for the year were made of vinyl and cloth and were called **Bud**, **Rosebud**, and **Dolly Dryper**. Another unusual doll was **Barbara Jane** in a large 29" size. She had a soft body with a soft plastic head, arms, and legs.

In 1953 the new **Winnie Walker** dolls made their appearance in the Alexander catalog. The dolls were all hard plastic and came in sizes of 15", 18", and 25". The faces of these dolls are similar to the later Cissy doll. Another new doll was **Miss Flora McFlimsey**. Her head was made of vinyl and she had a plastic body. She was dressed in a Victorian style.

Margaret faced dolls included a bride, Margot Ballerina, **Wendy** (from Peter Pan), and the black Cynthia. Maggie faces were used on a **Peter Pan**, Rosamund Bridesmaid, and a Maggie Walker. Both faces were used on the Little Women Series.

The nicest and most collectible of the Alexander dolls for 1953 were the **"Beaux Arts Creations"** and the **"Glamour Girls."** These dolls were all 18" tall and used the Margaret and Maggie faces. Some of these dolls were inspired by the coronation of Queen Elizabeth which took place in 1953. These dolls were beautifully dressed and were expensive dolls even in 1953.

The 18" walking **Glamour Girls** included the following:

No. 2001A—Dressed in black taffeta and lace with a pink ostrich feather on her bonnet. She had black lace gloves and wore a pink embossed cotton gown.

No. 2001B—This doll wore a long party dress of blue print with tiny rosebuds which was trimmed in lace. The costume also had a straw lace bonnet and white gloves.

No. 2001C—Her print dress featured green leaves on strawberry pink with a wide sash. She also wore a big straw hat trimmed with pink roses.

No. 2010A—Dressed in a Godey Lady outfit of red taffeta for her gown and bonnet. She also wore a grey fur cloth cape stole and carried a red hat box.

No. 2010B—This doll wore a dress made of white taffeta with a wide sash and a big bow of red. The dress was also trimmed with red rosebuds and she wore a hat of white horsehair braid.

No. 2010C—Dressed in a gown of pink taffeta with a bodice of black velvet. Her puff sleeves were also trimmed in black. Her skirt featured streamers of black velvet, pink roses, and pink satin. She wore a black straw lace bonnet.

No. 2020A—The Queen doll was dressed in a court gown of white brocade and the blue Sash of the Garter. She also wore a jeweled coronet, earrings, a bracelet, and long white gloves to add to her glamour.

Beaux Arts Creations
#2025—Queen Elizabeth. The doll was dressed in a white brocade court gown and blue Sash of the Garter order. She also wore a long velvet robe trimmed in white fur cloth and silver braid. Her accessories included a jeweled tiara, earrings, bracelets, and long white gloves.

#2020B—Princess Margaret Rose. Dressed in a court gown of pink faille taffeta decorated with iridescent sequins. Her accessories included a jeweled tiara and bracelet, pearl earrings and necklace, and long white gloves.

#2020C—This doll wore a gown of pink satin and a long brocaded satin coat of blue (also came in pink) which was trimmed with rhinestones. Her accessories (tiara, bracelet, earrings) were also set with rhinestones. Collectors sometimes call this doll Lady Churchill but there is nothing in the Alexander catalog to indicate that the doll was made in the image of anyone special.

#2020D—Dressed in a gown of aqua taffeta draped with a flowing stole of nylon net embroidered with flowers and jewels. Also wore a jeweled tiara and bracelet and a necklace of pearls.

#2020E—This doll wore a gown of chartreuse taffeta trimmed with rosebuds and a big sash of green taffeta. Her tiara was gold with green brilliants.

#2020F—Dressed in a white satin ball gown and red taffeta evening cape. She carried a muff covered with red roses.

These dolls were all beautifully dressed and were expensive dolls even in 1953.

Besides all of these wonderful dolls, the Alexander company began to make the small 7.5" dolls they called **Alexander-Kins** in 1953. These hard plastic dolls remain as part of the Alexander doll production even today. The first dolls were straight leg non-walkers. Their clothing has always been beautifully made and these dolls offered an alternative to the cheaper Vogue Ginny and Nancy Ann Muffy dolls. At least thirty-two different dolls were marketed in 1953. Some of the dolls from that year included Peter Pan, Little Southern Girl, and Victoria. Only one basic doll was used but the outstanding clothing made each of the named dolls different. One doll was unusual, however. It was called **Quiz-Kin** and the doll had two buttons on the back which could be pushed so the doll could move its head to answer yes or no. In 1954 a walker mechanism was added to the Alexander-Kins to better compete with the other similar dolls on the market. One of the frequent names used for these small dolls was Wendy Ann (after Madame Alexander's granddaughter). This doll was usually dressed in a frilly little girl outfit reflecting the style of the 1950s. The real Wendy Ann died in 1954 and the name Wendy Ann was discontinued.

In 1955 the Little Women dolls were produced in the Alexander-Kins 7.5" size and these dolls continued to be sold in various costumes throughout the years.

In 1956 bending knees were added to the small dolls in keeping with what was happening to many other models of 8" dolls. The popular **Scarlet** doll from *Gone With The Wind* was added to the Alexander-Kins line in 1956 as a 7.5' doll and it continued to make frequent appearances in this small size for many years. The Alexander-Kins were sometimes sold with a variety of clothing in special boxes and additional outfits could be purchased separately. Furniture was also carried in some of the Alexander brochures to provide these dolls with beds, tables, and chairs.

The Alexander catalog for 1954 featured a series of dolls called **"Me and My Shadow."** There were seven different models of dolls made in matching 18" and 7.5" sizes. The larger dolls used Margaret, Maggie, and what was to become Cissy faces. These dolls are the most collectible Alexander dolls from 1954. Included were:

#2015—Blue Danube Waltz. Dressed in a dancing dress of blue taffeta with a side drapery of blue and gold striped taffeta. Also wore a gold coronet, necklace, and jeweled bracelets.

#2030A—Queen Elizabeth. Wore a white court gown decorated with a blue sash of the garter and a white orlon ermine cape. Her jewelry included a tiara, earrings, and bracelets. The costume was completed with long white gloves.

#2030C—Victoria. This doll wore a costume based on the styles of the 1850s. The dress was made of blue faille taffeta with side panniers and bustle drapery. Her hat was of white lace trimmed in flowers.

#2035D—Mary Louise. Wore a dress based on the Godey style. The gown was made of faille taffeta the color of burnt sugar. Her jacket was green wool felt and she wore yellow kid gloves.

#2030B—Cherie. Dressed in a gown of white satin trimmed in pink roses. Also wore a full length lined opera coat of pink taffeta and carried a rose trimmed satin bag.

#2035F—Agatha. Wore an Edwardian gown of rose iridescent taffeta trimmed with braid, flowers, and ruffles. The dress also had a short train in back. Further accessories included a necklace, hat, white kid gloves, and a parasol.

#2035E—Elaine. The doll was dressed in a garden party dress of blue organdy trimmed with lace ruffles. Her underdress was made of pink taffeta and her hat was made of white straw lace. The dress stood out by means of a hoop skirt.

The regular line of dolls was mainly a continuation of dolls of the past with an emphasis on the **Binnie Walker** dolls which had earlier been called Winnie Walker. Various outfits were used on the dolls in both the 15" and 18" sizes. The specially named Binnies were **Story Princess** (18"), **Flower Girl** (15", 18", 25"), and **Sweet Violet** (18").

Margaret faces were still being used on the Margot Ballerinas and the Wendy Bride dolls as well as several of the Little Women dolls.

A hard plastic doll called **Mary Ellen** was new in 1954. She was 31" tall and was sold in three different outfits. The Alexander baby dolls were still beautifully dressed in 1954 but the all vinyl models were not as attractive as the babies in years past. Kathy was the name chosen for most of these dolls.

The Alexander-Kins continued to sell well in many different costumes. A drink and wet baby was added to this line in 1954.

The Alexander dolls for 1955 concentrated on the new grown up **Cissy** doll. The doll was made of plastic except for her arms which were vinyl. Cissy's feet were arched to wear high heel shoes and she was a full figured fashion doll. Cissy was sold in four different ball gowns, a bridal dress and as Queen Elizabeth in the series called "A Child's Dream Come True." The more inexpensive Cissys were outfitted with up-to-date street length fashions. Other individual pieces of clothing could also be purchased to fit Cissy.

The other dolls sold that year were all repeats of the previous years with changes of costume. Included were a Margaret faced bride and ballerina, various Binnie Walkers dressed as a bridesmaid, the Story Princess, and a skater. The Mary Ellen dolls were updated with new formals and the baby dolls wore new costumes but basically included nothing new. The Little Women dolls and the Alexander-Kins were also a part of the Alexander line for 1955.

The offerings of the Alexander company for 1956 again relied heavily on the Cissy doll and her costumes. These dolls in the **"Cissy Fashion Parade"** wore fashions depicting a bride, bridesmaid, Queen Elizabeth (white brocade), long gowns made of black velvet, satin, pink taffeta, nylon tulle and pink taffeta, and a garden party dress of organdy. Cissy was also sold in street length dresses in a variety of styles. Additional clothing was also available which was sold separately. Maggie and Margaret faced dolls were still being marketed in various sizes and costumes. These included a Wendy Bride, Margot Ballerina, and McGuffey-Ana. The newly designed **Lissy** doll in the 11.5" size appeared for the first time in 1956. She came in many different costumes including a bride, bridesmaid, ballerina, coat and hat, and casual and party dresses. She was made of hard plastic and had arms joined at the elbow and legs jointed at the knee. Her feet were shaped for high heeled shoes. The doll was also sold in a boxed set with a nine-piece trousseau.

The baby dolls offered in 1956 were all repeats of the Kathy dolls dressed in different outfits. The Story Princess and Little Women were also repeats from previous years.

The Alexander-Kins dolls were restyled with bending knees in 1956 and over seventy different costumes were available for these dolls. Several package sets were also offered. The company catalog also featured furniture for these small dolls. Included were an upholstered divan and chair, costumer with six hangers, tea table and two chairs, bed, and a vanity and bench. New in the line was a baby doll called **Little Genius**. The drinking and wetting baby was 8" tall and came with a jointed vinyl body and a saran wig. Approximately seventeen costumes were available for this doll.

In 1957 Cissy was still the top doll in the line of Alexander dolls. In the series **"Cissy Models Her Formal Gowns"** she was dressed in gowns of black velvet, gold brocade (queen), nylon net and pink taffeta, purple velvet, lace and faille, taffeta with a large picture hat and as a bride, and Lady Hamilton. The doll also could be purchased dressed in six different street length costumes.

Although Cissy was still very popular in 1957, another similar doll was introduced in that year. The doll was named **Elise** and she was 16.5" tall. She came with a hard plastic body and soft vinyl jointed arms and she also had jointed ankles which allowed the doll to wear high or low heels. Another joint at the knees allowed the doll to kneel. Elise came dressed as a bride, ballerina, or bridesmaid or in simpler street length clothes.

Other dolls from years past included Lissy in four different outfits (additional clothing could also be purchased), and various Kathy babies. The Lissy dolls were also used for the Little Women series beginning in that year.

A new doll called **Dumplin' Baby** was introduced in 1957. She was 23.5" tall and was sold with either a wig or with molded hair.

The small doll Alexander line continued to offer the Alexander-Kins as well as the Little Genius dolls in 1957. The big news of the year in this line was the introduction of the new **Cissette** doll in the 10" size. She was made of plastic and was jointed at the knees, hips, shoulders, and neck. Her feet were molded to wear high heel shoes. Over thirty costumes were produced for this doll in 1957. The Alexander catalog offered furniture made of metal finished in brass to be used by Cissette. Included were a table and chairs, arm chair, vanity set, bed, and side chair.

Cissy still led the parade of dolls in the Alexander catalog for 1958. She was featured in a series of dolls called **"Dolls to Remem-**

ber." Costumes included a bride, Queen (gold brocade), satin cocktail dress, flowered gown, red taffeta gown, and a print dress featuring camellias with a velvet cape stole. She was also pictured in six street length dresses.

In the 1957 catalog Elise was shown in six different costumes, Lissy in four outfits plus the Little Women series, and Kathy and Dumplin' Baby still were being sold in the baby section.

New dolls for the year were **Kelly** and **Lovey-Dove**. Kelly came in two sizes, 15" and 22". She was made of rigid vinyl except for her head which was soft vinyl. She was a little girl model and came in five different outfits. In addition she was sold dressed as "Edith, The Lonely Doll." This doll wore a costume based on the outfit worn by Edith in the book by Dare Wright.

The catalog which pictured the small dolls offered by Alexander in 1957 showed over twenty different 8" dolls including several male dolls called **Billy**. The Little Women series continued to be offered in the 8" size in 1957. Cissette was dressed in twenty-two different costumes including a bride and queen (gold brocade). Little Genius (now called Baby Genius) was still being sold and he was pictured in eight different outfits.

There was no big news in the doll line for the Alexander company in 1959. Although there were new costumes for older models of dolls and several new dolls were introduced, there was no new line of dolls like the earlier Cissy, Elise, Lissy, or Cissette. The firm did break precedent that year when the **Shari Lewis** doll was first produced. Instead of using an existing doll and adding a new name, the Shari Lewis doll was an entirely new model. The doll came in 14" and 21" sizes. (See Personality Chapter for more information). Another new doll was **Sleeping Beauty** offered in 10", 16.5", and 21" sizes. The larger dolls were made of hard plastic with soft plastic arms and were dressed in blue satin trimmed in gold. Another successful doll for Alexander was "**Mary-Bel** the Doll Who Gets Well." This was the earlier Kelly doll packaged in a box containing dark glasses, spots for measles, leg casts, crutches, band-aids, adhesive tape, and gauze bandage. She was 16" tall. Also new in the Alexander line was the **Kathleen** Toddler doll. She was 23" tall and was made of vinyl. She came with either molded or rooted hair and was pictured in three different outfits.

Other dolls featured in the 1959 catalog included Cissy dressed in three different costumes, Elise in five outfits, Kelly in five costumes plus Edith the Lonely Doll, and various Kathy babies. The Kelly dolls were also offered in a 12" size in 1959. These dolls were the Lissy dolls made with flat feet instead of being shaped to wear high heel shoes. The body of this doll had no elbow or knee joints.

Cissette was still being featured by the company and was pictured in ten different costumes. These included a queen (white brocade), bride, bridesmaid, ballerina, formal, and several street dresses. The 8" dolls were pictured in only eight outfits and a male Billy was also still being sold. The 8" baby was called Genius and was shown in four different costumes. The Little Women series came in either the 8" or 12" sizes. Additional clothing for the various dolls was also sold separately.

By the end of the 1950s, fashion dolls were no longer the best sellers they had been earlier and doll companies concentrated on larger 36" dolls. Alexander introduced their big doll called **Joanie** in 1960. A smaller 30" model called **Betty** was also produced. Although the fashion dolls continued to be made, other dolls received more emphasis and the era of Cissy and Cissette type dolls dominating the market was over.

The Alexander Doll Company has continued to produce fine dolls decade after decade. After the death of Alexander's husband and her semi-retirement, the company was headed by her son-in-law Richard Birnbaum and her grandson William Alexander Birnham. The company was sold to Ira Smith and Jeffrey Chodorow in 1988. Madame Alexander died in 1990.

The Alexander Company produced many fine dolls during the decade of the 1950s that have now become classics. Some of these dolls have been reissued by the new owners of the Alexander firm. Collectors who cannot locate an old original Cissy doll can purchase one of these new releases and experience again the fine craftsmanship and beauty of the Alexander dolls.

14" hard plastic Nina Ballerina using the Margaret face. Circa 1950. She has sleep eyes, closed mouth, and applied wig. The doll is mint with her wrist tag. Her dress is tagged "Nina Ballerina/By Madame Alexander." ($600-800). *Doll and photograph from the collection of Nancy Roeder.*

14" hard plastic Little Women dolls circa 1948-1949 using the Margaret and Maggie faces. Left to right: Amy (Margaret face), Beth (Maggie face), Meg (Margaret face), and Jo (Maggie face). All of the dolls are mint with their wrist tags. Each outfit is tagged "Louisa M. Alcott's/Little Women/'Amy' [or Beth, Meg or Jo]/By Madame Alexander, N.Y. U.S.A./All Rights Reserved." ($1800-2000 set). *Dolls and photograph from the collection of Nancy Roeder.*

14" hard plastic Godey Bride and Groom and rare Godey Lady with original dark green dress. All are mint and original. (Groom $1200-1500, Bride $1500-1700, Woman in green dress $1500-1800). *Dolls and photograph from the collection of Nancy Roeder.*

21" hard plastic Babs Skater circa 1949. She has sleep eyes, closed mouth, and applied wig, and used the Margaret face. She is marked "Alexander" on the head. Her clothes are tagged Madame Alexander, etc. She is mint with her original wrist tag. ($900 and up). *Doll and photograph from the collection of Nancy Roeder.*

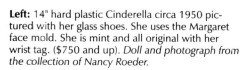

14" hard plastic Godey Lady dolls circa 1949-1950. These dolls all have sleep eyes, closed mouths, applied wigs, and use the Margaret face mold. The dresses are tagged "Godey Lady/Madame Alexander." The dolls are beautifully dressed and are very hard to find in this mint condition. ($1500-1800 each). *Dolls and photograph from the collection of Nancy Roeder.*

14" hard plastic Margot Ballerina circa 1950. She uses the Maggie face mold and has sleep eyes, closed mouth, and applied wig. She is mint with her wrist tag. ($500-700). *Doll and photograph from the collection of Nancy Roeder.*

Left: 14" hard plastic Cinderella circa 1950 pictured with her glass shoes. She uses the Margaret face mold. She is mint and all original with her wrist tag. ($750 and up). *Doll and photograph from the collection of Nancy Roeder.*

15" Baby Genius dolls circa 1950 with hard plastic heads, cloth bodies, and vinyl limbs. The dolls have sleep eyes, closed mouths, and are all original. The dolls were made with both molded hair and applied wigs. The dolls are marked "Alexander" on the backs of the heads and the clothes are tagged "Little Genius/Madame Alexander N.Y. U.S.A./All Rights Reserved." ($125-150 each).

21" hard plastic portrait doll circa 1951 known to collectors as the Kathryn Grayson doll. She has been given this name because of her resemblance to the famous Metro-Goldwyn-Mayer singing star of the 1940s and early 1950s. Her face uses the Margaret mold. This beautiful doll is unmarked. (Not enough examples to determine a price.).

The "Kathryn Grayson" doll is dressed in a dress with a lace bodice trimmed in rhinestones and a tulle skirt. She wears her original tear drop earrings but she is missing her original purse.

21" hard plastic portrait doll circa 1951 called "Champs-Elysees" or "Lady with the Rhinestone Beauty Mark." She has a rhinestone set in the upper part of her left cheek. (Not enough examples to determine a price.) *Doll and photograph from the collection of Nancy Roeder.*

The "Lady with the Rhinestone Beauty Mark" is dressed in a black lace dress over a pink satin underdress. She came with bracelets and a black lace headpiece. *Doll and photograph from the collection of Nancy Roeder.*

23" hard plastic Maggie Walker doll #2315 with the Maggie face circa 1952. She is mint with wrist tag and original curlers in the box she is carrying. The doll also came in sizes of 15" and 18". ($800 and up for this size and in this condition). *Doll and photograph from the collection of Nancy Roeder.*

14" and 18" hard plastic Kathy Skater dolls circa 1951 and 1950. The dolls use the Maggie face and are in mint original condition. (14" $500 and up, 18" $750 and up). *Dolls and photograph from the collection of Nancy Roeder.*

17" hard plastic Mary Martin doll offered in 1949-1950. The doll came dressed in several costumes including a formal and a sailor outfit. This costume is less frequently seen. It has her name done in embroidery on her denim shirt. She wears the saddle shoes then popular for many of the Alexander dolls. Her clothing is tagged "Mary Martin/of South Pacific." See personality chapter for more information. ($750 and up for dressed doll, costume only $125 and up).

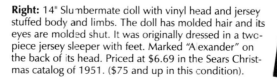

23" hard plastic Maggie Walker circa 1951-1952. She is mint with her original tag and box of curlers. ($800 and up for this size and in this condition). *Doll and photograph from the collection of Nancy Roeder.*

14" and 18" hard plastic Polly Pigtails dolls circa 1951 (doll on left) and 1950 (doll on right). The dolls use the Maggie face mold and are all original with tags and curlers. (14' $500 and up. 18" $750 and up). *Dolls and photograph from the collection of Nancy Roeder.*

Right: 14" Slumbermate doll with vinyl head and jersey stuffed body and limbs. The doll has molded hair and its eyes are molded shut. It was originally dressed in a two-piece jersey sleeper with feet. Marked "Alexander" on the back of its head. Priced at $6.69 in the Sears Christmas catalog of 1951. ($75 and up in this condition).

17" Honeybun with a stuffed vinyl head, applied wig, vinyl limbs, and cloth body. She has sleep eyes and an open/closed mouth with two teeth. She is all original with her tags and box. Her dress is tagged "Madame Alexander N.Y. All Rights Reserved." Her wrist tag says "Fashion Academy Award/Mde/Alexander/Dolls/N.Y." Circa 1951. Her original price tag reads $13.95. ($150-200).

18" hard plastic Bride from 1952 using the Margaret face #1850. The doll is mint and all original. The doll was also made in 15" and 23" sizes. ($750 and up). *Doll and photograph from the collection of Nancy Roeder.*

15" hard plastic Snow White #1535 with the Margaret face from 1952. The doll is mint and all original. ($600 and up). She was also made in 18" and 23" sizes. *Doll and photograph from the collection of Nancy Roeder.*

Right: 15" black hard plastic Cynthia from 1952. Alexander's term was "colored." She is all original with her tag. The doll came in sizes of 15", 18", and 23". She has the Margaret face. She has sleep eyes, closed mouth, and an applied wig. ($800 and up). *Doll from the collection of Sidney Jeffrey. Photograph by Peggy Millhouse.*

Left: 18" Madeline made in 1952 and 1953. The body is made of hard plastic and includes extra joints at the knees, elbows, and wrists. She has a vinyl head, sleep eyes, applied wig, and a closed mouth. The doll is all original. ($600 and up). *Doll from the collection of Jan Clanton. Photograph by Darek Clanton.*

TC-11A—**WINNIE WALKER** by Madame Alexander. Your favorite little girl will thrill to this beautiful doll wearing a party dress of fine Swiss organdy trimmed with tiny pearl buttons and imported val type lace. Lace-trimmed taffeta underwear, white straw lace bonnet, black slippers. Hat box has curlers and comb to wash, curl, and arrange her hair. 25" tall..................16.95

TC-11B—**WINNIE WALKER** by Madame Alexander walks when held by the hand. Moving eyes; wig that can be washed, combed, curled. Red rayon taffeta dress 'neath a smart navy cloth coat; with hat to match. White gloves; hat box with comb and curlers. 15" tall...9.98

TC-11C—**MADELINE** by Madame Alexander, fully jointed walking doll; of fine unbreakable plastic. Washable hair; elegantly dressed in red-trimmed bouffant white taffeta with matching bonnet. Includes beauty kit: red slippers; story book.18" tall..................14.95

Mail and phone orders filled . . . see convenient order form at center spread.

eet the *John Wanamaker* **Doll Family — lovable, life-like d**

Madeline and her marvelous wardrobe — Created by Madame Alexander, she's a gem by herself — completely jointed at wrist, ankles, elbows! Takes the realest poses — and holds them. She'll stand, sit, even go to sleep . . . and her hair is shiny saran any little mother will love to shampoo.

2N — Dressed in slip and panties, she's only 12.95. Complete with her fashion wardrobe and trunk, 39.95.

Here's what Madeline can wear: If purchased separately:

2E — Scarlet taffeta redingote, white party dress......3.95
2F — Taffeta-lined flannel coat and velvet beret.......3.95
2G — Chic hats in 3 assorted styles, each...............1.95
2H — Rayon satin or terry cloth housecoat...............1.95
2J — Rayon tricot or printed cotton nightgown...........1.50
2K — Organdy-trimmed, cotton morning dress.............1.95
2L — Sequinned cotton circle skirt, lacy blouse........3.95
2M — Denim slacks and checked cotton blouse............1.95
2O — Imported Swiss embroidered Val lace, satin sash...4.95
2P — Plastic hangers, set of 6..............................35
2Q — 19" Fibre travel trunk, with hangers...............5.50

Catalog page from The Dayton Company in Minneapolis, Minnesota, in 1953 picturing several Alexander dolls. Madeline sold for $14.95, and Winnie Walker, made of all hard plastic, sold for $16.95 in the 25" size and $9.98 in the 15" size. *Catalog from the collection of Marge Meisinger.*

Madeline was also advertised by John Wanamaker in New York. Along with the doll, the ad pictured several Madeline outfits priced from $1.50 for a nightgown to $4.95 for a party dress. A trunk to hold the wardrobe was priced at $5.50. *Catalog from the collection of Marge Meisinger.*

Right: Besides selling beautiful dolls, the Alexander firm also sold many individual clothes for their dolls of the 1950s. These 15" Alexander Little Women Beth and Amy dolls are modeling two of the dresses purchased for them in the early 1950s. The jumper was pictured in the Alexander catalog in 1953 and is #214. The lavender dress opens down the back showing a purple ruffled underskirt. No hat was included with the jumper but several styles of hats, shoes, and accessories could have been purchased separately. The dresses are marked "15" Doll/Madame Alexander/All Rights Reserved/ New York, U.S.A."and they also came in 18" sizes. (Dresses only $40-50 each).

Three more of the Alexander dresses that were purchased individually are pictured. They are shown on a 15" Binnie Walker doll, an 18" Maggie Walker, and a 15" Maggie. The blue and white checked taffeta redingote over a sleeveless white taffeta dress is pictured in the 1953 catalog in red and white. The middle outfit is a two-piece garment. It has a removable skirt covering a playsuit with shorts. The dress on the right is tagged "Maggie" but it was purchased without the doll. Neither dress came with a hat. (Clothes only $40-50 each).

Although this raincape is not tagged as an Alexander garment, it was probably purchased through the firm because it was with the dolls and all the other clothing. The boots were contained in an Alexander shoe bag but both the boots and the raincape may have been purchased by Alexander from another source to include with their clothes and accessories. (Raincape and boots only $40-50).

Two more 15" tagged Alexander outfits, purchased for these dolls in the early 1950s, are shown. The pink robe covers a nightgown trimmed with beading and ribbon #103 in the 1953 catalog. The ballerina costume on the right included satin panties as well. All the clothes are tagged with the Alexander name and were for 15" dolls. ($40-50 for each outfit).

Right: This boxed Alexander shoe bag was also found with the 15" clothes and dolls. Included are saddle shoes, dress shoes, house slippers (made of felt), and rain boots. (As pictured $75 and up).

Besides issuing the beautiful Beaux Arts Creations dolls, 1953 was also the year for the Glamour Girls Walking Dolls. Pictured is #2001B. She wears a dress of blue with tiny pink rosebuds and green leaves. She also is fitted with a white straw lace bonnet, white gloves, and a hat box containing curlers and a comb. She is a hard plastic walker. ($1600-1800). *Doll from the collection of Jan Clanton. Photograph by Darek Clanton.*

18" hard plastic Beaux Arts Creations doll from 1953. The doll was listed as #2020C in the catalog for 1953. She wears a gown of satin with a long brocaded satin coat over it. The coat is trimmed with rhinestones. She also has a tiara, earrings, and bracelet set with rhinestones. She has the Margaret face. Many collectors call this doll Lady Churchill but the catalog does not designate her as representing any real person. ($2,000 and up). *Doll from the collection of Jan Clanton. Photograph by Darek Clanton.*

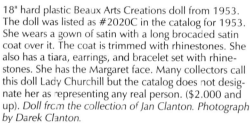

18" hard plastic Queen Elizabeth #2020a from the Glamour Girl Series from 1953. She uses the Margaret face mold. She is dressed in white brocade with the blue Sash of the Garter order. She wears a tiara, earrings, bracelets, and long white gloves and is all original. A more expensive version of the doll came with a long velvet robe with a border of white fur. ($1500-1900). *Doll from the collection of Jan Clanton, photograph by Darek Clanton.*

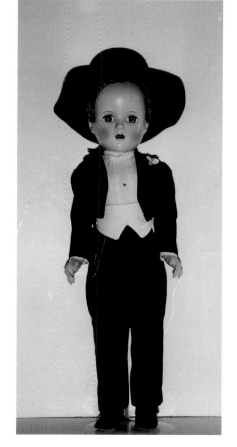

Left: 18" hard plastic male doll circa early 1950s. Although he has been called Winston Churchill and/or Prince Phillip by collectors, there is no known information to indicate that he was meant to be anyone but a groom to be sold with a bride. He is still a very collectible doll. ($1000-1200). *Doll from the collection of Jan Clanton. Photograph by Darek Clanton.*

Right: 18" Glamour Girl Walking Doll from 1953. She is #2010A in the company catalog but sometimes called Gody Lady by collectors. Her dress and bonnet are made of red taffeta and she has a grey fur cloth cape stole. She is missing her red hat box. Otherwise she is all original and mint. ($1800-2000). *Doll from the collection of Jan Clanton. Photograph by Darek Clanton.*

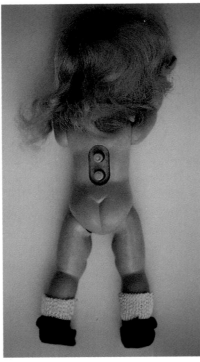

7.5" hard plastic Southern Girl circa 1954. The small Alexander dolls had walking mechanisms added in 1954. This doll is all original in mint condition. ($600-800). *Doll and photograph from the collection of Nancy Roeder.*

7.5" hard plastic Quiz Kin circa 1953. She has sleep eyes, closed mouth, an applied wig, and straight legs. She is dressed in tagged Alexander clothing marked "Alexander-kins/ Madame Alexander." Her body is marked "Alex" on the back. ($300-350).

The Quiz Kin doll had two buttons on its back that made the doll shake its head yes or no when the buttons were pushed.

This page from the Alexander small doll brochure from 1955 pictures the Queen #499, Lady in Waiting #487, Groom #466, Wendy Bride #475, Baby Angel #480, Wendy #488, Wendy's Bridesmaid #478, and The Best Man #461.

7.5" hard plastic Queen Elizabeth #499 from 1955. The doll is dressed in a gown of white brocade with a red velvet robe. She also has a tiara and blue garter ribbon. She is all original and mint. ($600-800). *Doll and photograph from the collection of Nancy Roeder.*

Left: Hutzler's department store of Baltimore, Maryland, issued a catalog circa 1955 which featured Alexander 8" dolls called Barbara Lee in the store material. The furniture offered with the dolls was made by Richwood Toys, Inc. The undressed doll sold for $1.98 while the clothes were priced at $1.98 to $3.98. *Catalog from the collection of Marge Meisinger.*

Two of the hard plastic Alexander-Kins Wendy dolls circa 1955. Both dolls are straight leg walkers. The doll on the left is #428 "Wendy helps mummy serve luncheon" from 1955. Both dresses are tagged "Alexander-Kins/by Madame Alexander." Her dress is made of navy blue taffeta trimmed in red rick rack and her panties are red and white stripe. The catalog says she is wearing red slippers but these shoes appear to be original. The doll on the right is from the same period and may have originally worn a slip with lace edging which showed beneath the dress although her panties match the dress. Both dolls are marked "Alex" on their backs. ($175-250 each).

8" hard plastic Alexander-Kins Wendy Bride #615 and Bridegroom #577 from 1956. Both dolls have bending knees. The dolls are mint and all original. ($400-600 each). *Dolls and photograph from the collection of Nancy Roeder.*

START-A-HOME FOR ALEXANDER-KINS

Below: 18" hard plastic Elaine #2035E from the "Me and My Shadow" series from 1954. The doll uses the Binnie Walker face. There were seven sets of these "Shadow" dolls issued. Each doll came in both 7.5" and 18" sizes. This doll is mint and all original. ($1500-1800). *Doll from the collection of Jan Clanton. Photograph by Darek Clanton.*

The 1956 Alexander brochure, "Dolls Are Little People," featured a page of furniture that was the right size for the Alexander-Kins dolls. Included were a divan and chair covered with velveteen, a wood round tea table with two chairs, a bed with a dust ruffle, a vanity with mirror and bench (vanity skirt matched the mattress cover) and a costumer with six hangers. *Brochure from the collection of Marge Meisinger.*

8" Wendy #591 from 1956. The catalog says this doll is "Oriental influence in miniature." Bending knees were introduced for the Alexander-Kins dolls in 1956. She is all original and mint. ($600-800). *Doll and photograph from the collection of Nancy Roeder.*

18" hard plastic Victoria #2030C another doll from the "Me and My Shadow" series from 1954. Her dress is of blue faille taffeta and she wears a hat of starched white lace tied with fuchsia ribbon. Her purse is also fuchsia. ($1500-1800). *Doll from the collection of Jan Clanton. Photograph by Darek Clanton.*

This advertisement of Alexander dolls was included in a catalog issued by The Emporiam in San Francisco in 1954. Dolls pictured include the baby dolls Bonnie and Kathy. The Bonnie doll came in several sizes including a 30" model priced at $25.95. The Mary Ellen hard plastic doll was 31" tall and sold for $29.95. The Binnie Walker hard plastic dolls came in sizes of 15", 18", and 25" sizes. The Flower girl is also pictured. *Catalog from the collection of Marge Meisinger.*

18" hard plastic Flower Girl walking doll from 1954. The doll came in sizes of 15", 18", and 25" and used the Binnie Walker face. She sold for $16.95 in 1954. Her dress is tagged "Madame Alexander/All Rights Reserved." She originally came with gloves and a hat box which contained curlers. ($250-300).

31" hard plastic Mary Ellen #3135 from 1954. She is a walker with sleep eyes, closed mouth, and an applied wig. She is wearing a long party dress just like the Flower Girl. She is missing her circlet of flowers for her hair, her white kid gloves, and her hat box of curlers. ($400-500).

A WHOLE FAMILY OF DOLLS FROM CRY-BABIES TO WALKERS

The Rhodes department store in Seattle advertised the new Alexander Cissy doll in their catalog in 1955. She was #2084 and was 20" tall with a fashion body and sold for $17.95. Her dress was of navy taffeta with a removable short jacket and she wore a straw hat of blue to match her outfit. Other dolls pictured include Kathy, Binnie Walker, Wendy Bride, and Margot Ballerina. The ballerina came in 15" and 18" sizes. Catalog from the collection of Marge Meisinger.

20" plastic and vinyl Cissy doll from 1955. She was part of series "A Child's Dream Come True" for that year. She is wearing #2100 a long torso gown of mauve taffeta with a bow as trim. She has drop pearl earrings and a bracelet. She is mint with her original tag. ($800-900). Doll from the collection of Jan Clanton. Photograph by Darek Clanton.

Two Alexander Cissy dolls were advertised in a catalog issued by Pomeroy's in Reading, Pennsylvania, in 1956. The dolls were priced at $15.95 and $16.95 each and were wearing outfits #2014 and what appears to be a variation of #2012. Catalog from the collection of Marge Meisinger.

Left: 20" plastic and vinyl Cissy doll from 1956. She was part of Cissy Fashion Parade from that year. She is wearing #2025, a nylon tulle dress over pink taffeta. She is all original. The Cissy dolls had hard plastic heads and bodies with vinyl arms. They had extra joints at the elbows and knees. Their feet were molded to wear high heels. Cissy had sleep eyes, closed mouth, and an applied wig. ($600-800). Doll and photograph from the collection of Carol J. Lindeman.

21" Cissy from "Cissy Models Her Formal Gowns" in 1957. She is #2171 and is described as being dressed in a court gown with no reference to Queen Elizabeth. She is wearing a gown of gold brocade with a golden tiara. The costume also features long white gloves, earrings, and bracelets. The doll is in mint condition with her wrist tag. ($800-900). *Doll and photograph from the collection of Nancy Roeder.*

Besides issuing many different designs of clothing to be sold with their dolls, the Alexander company continued to sell individual outfits for their dolls throughout the decade of the 1950s. Many of today's collectors try to assemble a collection of the clothes as well as the Alexander dolls. Pictured are two Cissy fashions that probably were sold as individual dresses although the one on the left is shown in the Alexander catalog on a dressed doll as #2014 in 1956. It has a replaced belt and tie. The dress on the right is made of polished cotton and is trimmed in lace and rhinestones. The hat is not original. (Dresses only $50-75 each). The shoes on both dolls are not original.

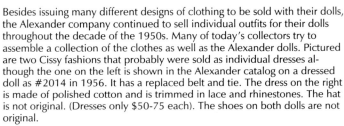

Three other outfits for Cissy are pictured. The one on the left is composed of two pieces and includes a satin overskirt that fits over a dress with a straight skirt. The nylon pink and white dress is trimmed with lace and dates from 1958. It is shown in the catalog on a dressed doll in that year. The dress has rhinestone buttons. The two-piece navy blue taffeta dress on the right dates from 1955 and is pictured in the Rhodes catalog. (Dresses only $50-75).

21" Cissy from 1958 dressed in #2211. The doll is in mint condition with her original tag. The information in the catalog describes the outfit as a polished cotton dress with a white straw hat and costume jewelry. There is no mention of a fur stole. ($550 and up). *Doll and photograph from the collection of Carol J. Lindeman.*

Left: 21" Cissy from 1958 dressed in #2252 in the Dolls to Remember series. She is in mint condition with her original tag. She is wearing a cocktail dress of satin trimmed with flowers and she is wearing shortie gloves. ($900-1,000). *Doll and photograph from the collection of Nancy Roeder.*

Catalog page from Mihlbaugh's of Sharon, Pennsylvania, from 1957-1958 featured several of the current Alexander dolls. Pictured is the Cissy Queen doll priced at $25, the 16.5" Elise ballerina priced at $12.00, Lissy Ballerina for $9.00, Wendy dressed doll in Sunny Day outfit $4.00, dressed Cissette in cotton dress $6.00, Kathy baby for $11.00, Lark baby with tub $7.95, and Cissy in flowered dress for $16.00. *Catalog from the collection of Marge Meisinger.*

15" hard plastic Margot Ballerina #1580 from 1956. She has the Binnie Walker/Cissy face. The doll also came in the 18" size. She bends above the knees. The doll is original except she is missing her tights. ($300-400).

11.5" Lissy hard plastic doll first introduced in 1956. Her arms are jointed at the elbow and her legs are jointed at the knee. Her feet are arched to wear "low" high heel shoes. She has sleep eyes, a closed mouth, and an applied wig. The doll pictured is #1234 from 1956. She is wearing an organdy dress and a wool cardigan and hat lined to match the dress. ($300-350). The doll is all original and mint. *Doll and photograph from the collection of Nancy Roeder.*

11.5" Lissy #1247 from 1956. She is wearing a bridal gown of white nylon tulle with a lace bodice over taffeta. Her tulle head-dress is trimmed with flowers to match her bridal bouquet. She is all original and near mint. ($300-350).

Right: As with their other dolls, the Alexander company also provided extra clothes for the Lissy doll. This dress is among several pictured in the company catalog for 1957. The extra clothing is shown hanging on a clothes rack. Also included were a nightgown, robe, fur coat, hat and muff, straw hat, long summer formal, party dresses, and cotton frocks. (Dress only $45-55).

Left: 8" tall Little Genius introduced to the Alexander line in 1956. The baby doll has a hard plastic head, vinyl body with curved baby legs, open mouth to take bottle, sleep eyes, and an applied wig. The doll is mint with its box, tag, and bottle. ($175-250).

8" Little Genius in mint original condition including its bottle, tag, and rattle. The dolls wore booties instead of shoes. ($175-250). *Doll and photograph from the collection of Nancy Roeder.*

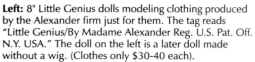
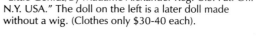

Left: 8" Little Genius dolls modeling clothing produced by the Alexander firm just for them. The tag reads "Little Genius/By Madame Alexander Reg. U.S. Pat. Off. N.Y. USA." The doll on the left is a later doll made without a wig. (Clothes only $30-40 each).

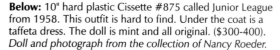

Below: 10" hard plastic Cissette #875 called Junior League from 1958. This outfit is hard to find. Under the coat is a taffeta dress. The doll is mint and all original. ($300-400). *Doll and photograph from the collection of Nancy Roeder.*

Left: 10" hard plastic Cissette doll introduced to the Alexander line in 1957. She has jointed knees, arched ankles for high heels, a closed mouth, sleep eyes, and an applied wig. This doll is #943 and is the childhood doll of Carol J. Lindeman. Her dress is made of lilac taffeta and it has a removable jacket. She also wears a hat of straw and carries a handbag. ($275-300). *Doll and photograph from the collection of Carol J. Lindeman.*

10" Cissette #842 called Afternoon Tea from 1958. She is dressed in a black velvet sheath, a pink chiffon hat, and wears a pink quartz necklace and earrings. The doll is mint and all original. ($350-400). *Doll and photograph from the collection of Nancy Roeder.*

16.5" Elise first introduced in the Alexander line in 1958. She is made of hard plastic with vinyl arms. She has extra joints at the ankle, knee, and elbow. The doll has sleep eyes, closed mouth, and an applied wig. She is pictured in a ballerina outfit made of nylon tulle with a satin bodice. She also wears long nylon tights and ballet slippers. This costume was pictured in the Mihlbaugh catalog shown earlier. It is circa 1958. Her clothing is tagged "Elise." Her back is marked "MME./ALEXANDER." Her head is marked "ALEXANDER." ($325-350).

10" Cissette wearing what appears to be #905 from 1957. The outfit shown in the catalog has pearl buttons instead of rhinestone as this one does. The Toreador pants are black velvet and she also wears a lace blouse and sash. Also shown are two extra outfits provided for Cissette. The clothes are marked "Cissette/c Madame Alexander/New York U.S.A." and they appear in a Cissette clothing box although it is not original with this clothing. (Doll $175-200, clothing $35-45 each).

Right: Additional clothing was also provided for the Elise doll. Pictured is Elise modeling a pink nylon dress tagged "Elise." This later doll has pierced ears. The hat and the jewelry are added. (Dress only $50-75).

Elise models a nightgown made of nylon trimmed in lace and a bed jacket of lace tied with a ribbon. Also pictured is a tagged red sleeveless dress made of red cotton and trimmed in white, her original chemise, hose, shoes, and an Elise box not original to this doll. Both outfits are tagged "Elise." (Clothes $45-60 each, shoes $18-20, hose $5-7, box $25 and up).

16" Marybel used the Kelly face and was a new product for Alexander in 1959. She was called "The Doll Who Gets Well." She is made of vinyl, with sleep eyes, closed mouth, and rooted hair. The doll was supposed to get the measles and chicken pox and had supplies for a broken arm and leg. She came with casts, crutches, sunglasses, band-aids, adhesive tape, and gauze bandage. The dolls were offered for several years in similar sets. ($300 and up).

22" Kelly doll introduced by Alexander in 1958. The larger doll is made of rigid vinyl except for her head which is made of soft vinyl. She has sleep eyes a closed mouth, pierced ears, and rooted hair. She is all original and has her tag. The smaller 12" Kelly was introduced in 1959. She used a Lissy face but this doll does not have the arched feet nor the extra joints as Lissy did. The doll is all original and very hard to find. See Montgomery Ward advertising from 1959. (Large $300-400, small $400 and up). *Doll and photograph from the collection of Carol J. Lindeman.*

Marybel was pictured for sale in this catalog page from the May Co. in Los Angeles in 1959. She was priced at $12.95. Other Alexander dolls shown are Elise ballerina for $11.95, 12" Little Women dolls (Lissy) for $9.95 each, Kathy Tears for $12.95, Elise Bride priced at $11.95, and 16" Kathy for $11.95. Tiny Tears and Toodles from American Character are also shown. *Catalog from the collection of Marge Meisinger.*

21" Shari Lewis doll from 1959. She was based on the famous ventriloquist. The doll is all original with her tag. The doll is all hard plastic with high heel feet. She has sleep eyes and an auburn wig. Her head is marked "ALEXANDER." Her dress is tagged "Shari" and she is #2430 in the company catalog. The doll also came in the 14" size. ($600-700). Also pictured are two of Lewis' puppet characters copyright Tarcher Productions, Inc. *Doll and photograph from the collection of Dorothy Cassidy.*

10" Sleeping Beauty circa 1959. Although the doll looks like Cissette, the feet are flat instead of being arched for high heel shoes. The doll was sold by Disneyland but it has also been seen in catalogs from the era, including the Spiegel Christmas catalog of 1959 where it sold for $4.95. The clothing tag reads "Madame Alexander/Presents Walt Disney's/Sleeping Beauty Reg. N.Y." ($250-300).

This page from the 1959 Montgomery Ward Christmas catalog pictures many of the dolls offered by Alexander that year. Shown are Kathleen Toddler, Kathy in Cool e Hat, Kathy, a Baby Princess, Elise Bride, Elise Ballerina, Cissette Ballerina, Cissette Bridesmaid, and Kelly in 12" and 16" sizes. *Catalog from the collection of Marge Meisinger.*

American Character Doll Co.

The American Character Doll Co. had its beginning in 1919. The firm produced many popular composition dolls during the 1920s and 1930s. Many of these early dolls were marketed under the trade name "Petite." The company manufactured composition Campbell Kids, Puggy, Chuckles, and many more baby and little girl dolls in the 1920s and 1930s. The most prolific period for fine quality American Character dolls came during the decade of the 1950s.

The firm's **Sweet Sue** dolls from those years were very popular with little girls. These dolls were produced from approximately 1950 through 1957 with several changes made to the designs. The first models were made of all hard plastic and had mohair wigs. By 1952 the Sweet Sue dolls had become walkers and their hair was synthetic. They came in sizes from 15" to 23" in ten different outfits. By the mid-1950s, some of the dolls had a set in wig cap so the hair could be rooted. Other companies used regular doll wigs on their hard plastic dolls. Sweet Sues were priced from $7.98 to $15.75 in 1952, depending on size and costume. By 1953 the large Sweet Sue doll was 25" tall. In 1955 another change was made in the Sweet Sue dolls when joints were added to the knees and elbows. The arms were then made of vinyl while the rest of the doll was still made of hard plastic. By 1956, the largest Sweet Sue was 31" tall and she retailed for $34.98 when dressed in a bridal costume. By 1957 the Sweet Sue dolls had again been restyled. In order to compete with Ideal's Miss Revlon and Alexander's Cissy, the doll was changed to a full figured fashion doll. Arched feet were added so Sweet Sue could be dressed in adult clothing. These dolls were made of vinyl instead of hard plastic. Most of the dolls in this series were 20" or 25" tall. The Sweet Sue was still being advertised as a walking doll.

Another big winner for the American Character Doll Co. during the 1950s was **Tiny Tears**. This baby doll was originally made with a hard plastic head and a rubber body. Its popular features included the ability to drink and wet as earlier baby dolls had done, but this doll was also able to cry real tears. Although there were variations on its clothing, the doll was usually sold dressed in a white romper trimmed in pink or a pink and white dress. The dolls were produced with either molded hair or hair that was rooted into a skull cap. Later dolls were made with vinyl bodies instead of rubber. The babies came in sizes of 11.5", 13.5", 16", or 20". Most of the Tiny Tears dolls were packaged in suitcases or boxes that contained a layette. The later dolls could also blow bubbles. Additional accessories included a play pen and a car bed. Although American Character continued to make the Tiny Tears dolls for many years, the later all vinyl models are not as attractive or as collectible as the earlier dolls.

Another popular baby doll made by the American Character Co. was **Toodles**. The dolls came either with molded or rooted hair and were made of vinyl. In 1956 the dolls were sold in sizes of 21" or 24".

By 1959 there were several different models of Toodles dolls and "follow me eyes" had become their special feature. Dolls included a 16" infant model, a 22" baby doll with a wig, a 23" walking doll with molded hair, and a 23" wigged toddler doll. The Toodles dolls were priced from $12 to $16.

American Character was also responsible for several character dolls during the 1950s. The most sought after is the **Annie Oakley** doll issued in 1955. The doll was a regular Sweet Sue doll dressed in cowgirl clothing which was labeled "Annie Oakley." **Little Ricky** from the CBS "I Love Lucy" show was also a popular personality doll for American character. The doll was issued in several different models including a Tiny Tears type (before he was born), a vinyl infant, and a toddler.

Another personality based doll was a departure for the American Character Doll Co. because it was an all cloth doll. It was based on the **Eloise** character created by Kay Thompson in her books about the mischievous little girl who lived in New York's Plaza Hotel. (See Personality and Comic chapters for more information and photographs of these dolls.)

American Character secured the license to make **Betsy McCall** dolls from the McCall Corporation in 1957 and they continued to produce Betsy dolls until 1962. Ideal had manufactured 14" Betsy McCall dolls earlier in the decade. The dolls were based on the character which appeared in the *McCall* magazine as a paper doll beginning in May 1951. The original paper dolls were drawn by Kay Morrissey. The first American Character Betsy McCall doll appeared on the market in 1957. The 8" hard plastic doll was jointed at the knees in addition to the neck, shoulders, and hips. The doll sold for under $3.00 and the many fashions designed for her make this doll even more popular with today's collector than she was with little girls of the 1950s. The costumes for the first year included eighteen different designs. This Betsy was made until 1960 and nearly one hundred outfits were produced for the doll.

In addition to dolls, Betsy furniture was also sold. This wood furniture was made by Strombeck-Becker Manufacturing Co. It was the same furniture as in their regular line, except the McCall furniture was painted white and decorated with decal designs, while the regular Strombecker furniture was finished in a light wood finish. The white furniture promoted by *McCall* included a rocking chair, twin/bunk beds, canopy bed, table and chairs, wardrobe, and three drawer chest. *McCall* magazine advertised the Betsy McCall furniture in their November 1958 issue. The pieces listed in the ad included a rocker for $2.00, a wardrobe for $3.50, and a four poster bed for $4.50. The ad stated the furniture was made by Strombeck-Becker and that other pieces were also available. The furniture was marked on the bottom "c McCall/Made by Strombeck-Becker."

Another model of Betsy McCall was produced in 1958. These dolls had soft vinyl heads with rigid vinyl bodies. They were 14" tall and several outfits were included which sold separately. In 1959 a more grown-up 20" Betsy McCall doll was issued.

A large 36" Betsy McCall doll was manufactured in 1959 along with a 38" boy doll called Sandy McCall. In 1961 a 30" Betsy was also made.

By 1958 most doll companies were concentrating on producing full bodied fashion dolls and the American Character Co. followed this trend when they secured the license to produce Toni dolls formerly held by the Ideal Toy Co. Their popular 10.5" **Toni** doll was marketed in that year. The doll had a hard vinyl body and a soft vinyl head. The doll was also supplied with lots of costume changes. A larger Miss Toni doll in the 20" size was also produced. It was called a walking doll and looked very much like the earlier Sweet Sue dolls from 1957. The new Toni dolls were marketed shortly before the arrival of Mattel's Barbie™ dolls in 1959 and were soon discontinued.

The company name was changed to American Doll and Toy Co. around 1960 but by 1968 the firm was no longer in business.

The decade of the 1950s provided the "golden years" for the American Character Doll Co. Dolls from the firm reached their peak, both in quality and popularity, during those years and collectors will continue to seek out fine examples from the era.

Advertisement from the Montgomery Ward Christmas catalog for 1952 picturing several Sweet Sue dolls which were sold under the "Pla-Mate" name. The hard plastic walking dolls ranged in size from 15" to 23" tall and were priced from $7.98 to $15.75 each. *Catalog from the collection of Marge Meisinger.*

15" hard plastic Sweet Sue doll with sleep eyes, applied wig, closed mouth, in her original clothing including her hat. She is a non-walker and unmarked circa 1950. ($175-200).

15" Sweet Sue doll wearing the same costume as one pictured in the Montgomery Ward catalog in 1952. The doll in the catalog was called "Sweetheart Waltz." The dolls carried hat boxes containing a hair braid by "Charles of the Ritz." ($275-300). *Doll from the collection of Jan Clanton. Photograph by Darek Clanton.*

Advertisement from the Sears 1955 Christmas catalog pictures two different Sweet Sue dolls. #A was called Sweet Sue Coed and #B was Sweet Sue Cotillion. The ad says the dolls are new jointed walkers with joints at the knees, hips, elbows, and shoulders. The dolls came in 18", 22", and 25" sizes.

18" hard plastic Sweet Sue walker with sleep eyes, closed mouth, and applied wig. She originally sold or $12.95 in 1952. She wears her original clothing but is missing the flowers that were on her head on top of the veil as well as her bridal bouquet. ($175-200).

Right: 20" Sweet Sue circa 1955-1956 is dressed in a red and white nylon dress trimmed in black velvet bows and flowers. Most of the Sweet Sue dolls were unmarked. ($175-200).

24" hard plastic Sweet Sue circa 1953. She is all original and is pictured with her box. ($350 and up). *Doll from the collection of Jan Clanton. Photograph by Darek Clanton.*

20" Sweet Sue doll dressed in the "Sunday Best" outfit as pictured in the American character catalog for 1956. The doll has rooted hair (in a skull cap), sleep eyes, closed mouth, and is jointed at the elbow and knees. The arms are vinyl. These dolls came in sizes of 15", 18", 22", and 25" and were priced from $9.98 to $17.98. She is all original except she is missing her purse. The same dress was also used on the 31" Sweet Sue that sold for $29.98. ($200-225).

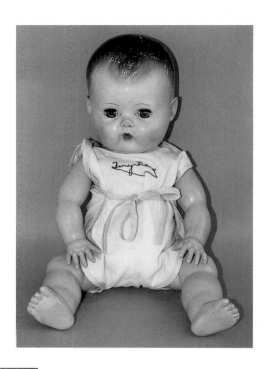

Right: 11.5" American Character Tiny Tears doll with hard plastic head and a rubber body. It has molded hair (also came with a wig), sleep eyes, open mouth nurser, and tear ducts. The doll is wearing its original romper. Marks: Pat. No. 2675644/Ame-Character. Circa 1957-1958. ($75-85).

20" Sweet Sue pictured in the 1956 catalog dressed in a costume called American Beauty. Her tag reads "Sweet Sue/Queen of Dolls." She is all original. ($275-350). *Doll from the collection of Jan Clanton. Photograph by Darek Clanton.*

This advertisement from the Sears Christmas catalog in 1957 pictures the Sweet Sue walking dolls that were then being made. The dolls were also sometimes called Sweet Sue Sophisticates. They had vinyl heads, hard vinyl bodies, Saran hair, turning waists, fashion bodies, jointed arms, and some had jointed ankles. They came in sizes of 14", 29", and 25'. They were priced from $11.27 to $19.95 each. *Catalog from the collection of Patty Cooper.*

This advertisement from the Sears Christmas catalog for 1958 pictures several American Character Tiny Tears dolls, their accessories, and furniture. These dolls had hard plastic heads and rubber bodies.

Right: A similar 13" Tiny Tears doll circa 1959 is pictured with her original suitcase and layette. The bonnet is missing from the coat and several accessories including soap, pipe, and booties were also originally included with the set. This doll has a hard plastic head and a rubber body. The rooted wig is in a skull cap. On the back of her head is: "American Character Doll/Pat. No. 2675644." $150 and up).

29

8" American Character hard plastic Betsy McCall doll first made in 1957. She has sleep eyes, rooted hair in a plastic skull cap, closed mouth, and knee joints. The doll was authorized by *McCall Magazine*. The undressed dolls sold in the Sears Christmas catalog in 1957 for $2.07. ($125-135). Also shown is a company brochure picturing various costumes and a Betsy McCall McCall's pattern #2239/c 1958 by McCall Corp. to be used to make clothes for the doll. ($20-25).

The Toodles line of dolls was a big seller for the American Character Doll Corp. during the latter half of the 1950s. Pictured is a catalog page from the Sears Christmas catalog in 1959 which shows several different styles of dolls. The large Toodles Toddler dolls came with either molded hair or rooted hair. These dolls were 23" tall. The dolls had "Follow Me Eyes" and long eyelashes. An infant doll is also pictured in her own car bed. She was 16" tall. The dolls were all made of vinyl. *Catalog from the collection of Betty Nichols.*

8" Betsy McCalls wearing Holiday outfits #1, 2, and 3 from 1957, 1958, and 1959. The costumes are complete. (Dressed dolls $165-175) each. *Dolls and photograph from the collection of Leslie Robinson.*

A full page was devoted to the 8" Betsy McCall doll and her clothes in the Sears 1958 Christmas catalog. The basic doll was priced at only $1.87.

8" Betsy McCall wearing the blue version of "Sweet Dreams" circa 1958. ($150 and up). *Doll and photograph from the collection of Leslie Robinson.*

8" Betsy dressed in the cowgirl outfit sold as part of the "At the Ranch" gift set in 1958. The costume is complete. The set with Betsy and three outfits sold for $5.67. (Dressed doll $250 and up). *Doll and photograph from the collection of Leslie Robinson.*

8" Betsy McCall dressed in her original lovely formal and hat. (Dressed doll $250 and up). *Doll and photograph from the collection of Leslie Robinson.*

Left: 8" Betsy McCall with an unusual side part from 1963 dressed in the complete Green ballerina outfit from 1959. (Dressed doll $200 and up). *Doll and photograph from the collection of Leslie Robinson.*

8" Besty McCall dolls dressed in black and white coats and dresses with two different patterns of checks. An identical outfit was also made for the 14" Betsy McCall doll in the large check in 1958. ($175-200 each). *Dolls*

In 1958 some of the regular wood Strombecker furniture designed for 8" dolls was also issued under the Betsy McCall label to be used with the new Betsy McCall dolls. The dolls and their furniture were promoted by *McCall Magazine* during this time period. Pictured is a set of Strombecker bunk beds changed to the Betsy McCall design by the addition of white paint and decals. The original box is also shown. ($200 and up). *Furniture and photograph from the collection of Leslie Robinson.*

The Betsy McCall wardrobe and chest of drawers are pictured along with an 8" Betsy McCall doll. These pieces were also based on regular Strombecker designs. (Wardrobe $100-125, chest $100 and up). *Furniture, doll, and photograph from the collection of Leslie Robinson.*

This bed with canopy is one of the most desirable of the Betsy McCall collectibles. This one includes all of its original bedding. The bed was also from one of the regular Strombecker designs. (Bed $150 and up). *Furniture, doll, and photograph from the collection of Leslie Robinson.*

Left: American Character also made 14" vinyl walking Betsy McCall dolls. They were advertised in the Sears Christmas catalog in 1958 and were pictured in two different outfits.

The Betsy McCall table and chairs set made by Strombecker is pictured along with a Betsy McCall doll. The furniture is marked on the bottom "c McCall/Made by Strombecker." ($75-100 set). *Furniture, doll, and photograph from the collection of Leslie Robinson.*

Below: 14" Betsy McCall in her original dress from 1958. The hat may have been replaced. The vinyl doll has rooted hair, sleep eyes, closed mouth and a jointed waist. She is identified with the McCall name on the back of her head. ($150-175). Also pictured is a Betsy and Sandy McCall's Everyday Calendar produced by Milton Bradley Co. ($30-35).

A dressed up 8" American Character Betsy McCall doll is pictured beside her rocker and bed which were the regular Strombecker designs from their 8" doll line of furniture. (Rocker $65-75, bed $100 and up). *Furniture, doll, and photograph from the collection of Leslie Robinson.*

Left: Three 14" Betsy McCall dolls circa 1958 wearing three of the many costumes made for the doll. ($225-275 each). *Dolls and photograph from the collection of Leslie Robinson.*

20" Betsy McCall Sugar and Spice doll from 1959. The vinyl doll has sleep eyes with long lashes, rooted hair, closed mouth, and is MIB. The doll sold for $11.89 in the Sears catalog in 1957. ($500 and up). *Doll and photograph from the collection of Leslie Robinson.*

This advertisement in the Montgomery Ward Christmas catalog for 1959 pictured both the 8" and 20" Betsy McCall dolls. The large 20" doll came in only one costume while a variety of outfits were available for the 8" doll. The 20" doll sold for $10.98. *Catalog from the collection of Marge Meisinger.*

Left: 36" Betsy McCall and 38" Sandy McCall dolls were manufactured by American Character circa 1959-1960. The dolls pictured are original except for shoes and are marked "McCall Corp." on the back of their necks. ($550 and up each). *Dolls from the collection of Edith Wise. Photograph by James Wise.*

This full page ad for three sizes of Betsy McCall dolls appeared in the Sears Christmas catalog for 1959. Pictured are the 8" dolls, the 14" Betsys, and the larger 20" size Betsy McCall dolls. *Catalog from the collection of Betty Nichols.*

Glamorous **Toni** Doll $2.82 10½ inch Doll only

[J] Full-figured vinyl doll with soft, bisque finish. Jointed arms, legs, turning head. Lashed moving eyes. Rooted Saran hair . . you can comb, brush, set it in fashionable undies, high-heel shoes, see below.
49 N 3912—Shipping weight 1 pound..$2.82
49 N 3913—Play Wave Kit (not shown). Includes solution, squeeze bottle, applicator, curlers, comb, brush and make-up cape. Shpg. wt. 8 oz..................89c

Clothing for 10½-inch Toni Doll. Exquisite detail. Shpg. wt. each 8 oz.
[K] 49 N 3958—Tea Time. Rayon taffeta dress, straw hat, long hose, shoes....$1.87
[L] 49 N 3959—Stewardess. Blue cotton tailored uniform, hat, Hand bag, shoes.. 1.87
[M] 49 N 3960—Coat and Hat. Felt coat, straw hat, kerchief, long hose, shoes.. 2.37
[N] 49 N 3961—High Society. Taffeta bell-shaped harem skirt dress, posy hair-band, long hose, high-heel shoes. High-style for Toni's partying..............2.37
[P] 49 N 3962—Bon Soir. Glamorous nylon ensemble: sheer nighty, lace-trimmed negligee, "jewelled" slippers......................................2.83
[R] 49 N 3963—Suburbanite. Plastic car-coat, corduroy hood, slack suit, shoes.. 2.83
[S] 49 N 3964—Romance. Satin formal dress in the new chemise style. Lined with taffeta. Genuine Ranch Mink stole. Rope of "pearls," long hose, shoes.....3.79

10.5" Toni dolls are pictured in two of the company costumes for 1958. On the left is Romance ($3.79) and on the right is High Society ($2.37). The vinyl dolls have rooted hair, sleep eyes, closed mouths, and fashion bodies with arched feet. They are marked "Amer. Char Doll Corp. 1958" in a circle on the back of the head and "American c Character" in a circle on the lower back. (Costumes only $30-40 each).

This ad appeared in the Sears Christmas catalog in 1958 to advertise American Character's new 10.5" Toni doll. Like Ideal's Little Miss Revlon, this was a fashion doll with lots of costume changes.

The Toni doll on the left wears a felt coat and straw hat which was still MIB and was pictured in the Sears catalog for 1958 selling for $2.37. The costume on the right is a Cheerleader outfit with Toni inscribed on the skirt. (MIB outfit $40-45, Cheerleader doll $125-150). *Cheerleader from the collection of Marge Meisinger.*

20" vinyl Toni doll with a fashion body, rooted hair, sleep eyes, closed mouth, pierced ears, arched feet, and jointed at the waist. Marked "American c Character" in a circle on the lower back. Also pictured is her box, tag, and Toni Play Wave Kit. Her dress is exactly like the one designed for the 10.5" Toni in 1958. ($225-300).

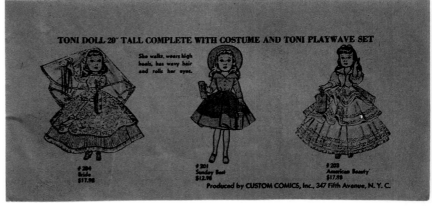

34

Arranbee (R & B)

The Arranbee Doll Company had been in business over thirty years in 1950 and the firm had produced some wonderful composition dolls during that time. Included were the composition Debuteen, Nancy, and Nanette girl dolls as well as smaller 9" tall boy and girl sets dressed in nursery rhyme costumes.

In 1947 the company began making their dolls of hard plastic. These dolls were even nicer than the composition dolls made earlier. Two of these new plastic dolls used names from the earlier dolls, **Nanette** and **Nancy Lee**. Nanette continued to be made until the late 1950s. She came in sizes of 15", 18", and 23". These basic dolls were also used for other named dolls so a wrist tag is the only true identification of a specific doll. Although the dolls were little girl models, many of them were dressed as brides or in fancy formal gowns.

Another popular Arranbee doll of the 1950s was the **Littlest Angel**. The all plastic little girl was 10.5" tall and was modeled as a chubby toddler. Many different outfits could be purchased for this doll in keeping with the 1950s tradition. By 1956 the doll was being made with a vinyl head.

Arranbee also produced several baby dolls during the period. Some had plastic heads and others, like the 1950 **Dream Baby,** were made of early vinyl. This doll had a vinyl head and limbs and a cloth body. The babies came in sizes of 16", 18", and 21" and sold for $4.98. In the larger size, Arranbee also produced a 24" tall **Nancy walking doll** in 1951. This doll had a vinyl head, arms, and legs, and a hard

plastic body. A smaller **Nancy Lee** was also issued with a stuffed vinyl head and a vinyl body. This doll was 15" tall and had very unusual heavy eyebrows. Her head was marked "Arranbee" so she is easy to identify.

In 1955 Arranbee made a 30" tall **Nanette** with a plastic body and vinyl head. She was a head turning walker. The same year a smaller 15" Nanette walker was produced with a vinyl head. This doll could also be purchased with a wardrobe.

One of the R&B tagged ballerina dolls with a vinyl head was marked **"17 VW"** on the back of her head. This mark is usually associated with the Valentine Company. Arranbee may have purchased dolls from other firms during the 1950s, dressed them, and then marketed the dolls under the Arranbee name.

The 10.5" **Coty Girl** doll is presently one of Arranbee's most collectible dolls. Like the ballerina, the doll itself was probably made by another firm and dressed and marketed by Arranbee. Like many of the 10.5" vinyl high heel type dolls (similar to Ideal's Little Miss Revlon) Coty Girl is marked with a circle containing a P on the back of her head. The only way a Coty Girl can be identified is by her clothing, box, or tag. The doll was used to promote Coty cosmetics (Coty Div. Pfizer). Additional outfits could be purchased for the doll.

Arranbee was sold to Vogue in 1958 and it became a part of Vogue. The popular Littlest Angel continued to be made by Vogue and was re-named Li'l Imp in 1959.

This Arranbee Doll Company advertisement appeared in the September 1950 edition of *Playthings* magazine. Featured are three styles of hard plastic Nanette dolls in sizes of 15", 18", and 23". The smaller dolls were priced at $7.98 each. The hard plastic dolls had either Dynel or Saran wigs. Also pictured is the Dream Baby with a vinyl head, arms, and legs, and a cloth body. This baby doll came in sizes of 16", 18", and 21" and sold for $4.98 in the small size.

Another later Arranbee ad circa 1957 featured a walking Nanette doll in sizes of 15", 18", and 23". The 23" doll sold for $19.98. The dolls came in fourteen different costumes. Also pictured is a vinylite Nancy Lee doll for $9.98, an Angel Face baby doll which was also made of vinylite priced at $7.98, and a boy doll with a latex body and vinyl head which sold for $2.98.

18" Arranbee tagged original hard plastic Nancy Lee Bride doll circa 1952. She has a closed mouth and sleep eyes. ($300-350). *Doll from the collection of Jan Clanton. Photograph by Darek Clanton.*

14" hard plastic Arranbee doll with mohair wig. Circa 1949-1950. Probably a Nanette. She has sleep eyes and closed mouth. She is wearing her original skating costume with replaced skates and hat. She is marked on her neck "R & B." ($135-150).

14" hard plastic Bride doll in her original costume. She has a closed mouth and sleep eyes. She is marked "R & B" on her neck and "Made in U.S.A. on her back." ($200-250).

18" Arranbee hard plastic walker, probably Nanette. She has sleep eyes, a closed mouth and is wearing her original dress. ($200-250). *Doll from the collection of Jan Clanton. Photograph by Darek Clanton.*

TC-4D LITTLEST ANGEL (4-9 years) makes any little girl's Christmas dreams come true! Toddler doll of washable plastic—she walks, sits, stands, sleeps. Her Saran hair can be washed, combed, curled. She comes with panties, socks, shoes—and see all the smart outfits you can buy for her! 10½" tall. $2.98
HER OUTFITS: TC-4E Overalls $1.98. TC-4F Formal $2.50. TC-4G 2-pc. knit sleeper $1.00. TC-4H Flocked organdy dress $1.98. TC-4J TV outfit $2.50. TC-4K Coat, dress, bonnet $2.98. TC-4L 3-pc. pajamas $1.50. TC-4M Bridal $2.50.

Advertisement from a catalog issued by the Emporium in San Francisco, California, in 1954 which pictured the hard plastic Littlest Angel doll and her outfits. The doll itself sold for $2.98. The clothes were priced from $1.00 to $2.98 for each costume. *Catalog from the collection of Marge Meisinger.*

Right: The back of the Littlest Angel clothing box pictures several of the costumes available for the doll in 1955. There were thirty-six costumes made for the doll that year. Pictured are the Drum Majorette Costume ($2.98), Roller Skating Set ($2.49), Tennis Ensemble ($1.49), Sailor ($1.49), Party Dress ($1.49), and Rain Outfit ($1.49).

11" hard plastic Littlest Angel dolls modeling the ballerina and nurse's outfits circa 1955. Nurse's hat is a replacement. (Costumes only $25-35 each).

Below: 11" Arranbee hard plastic Littlest Angel doll. She is a hip pin walker with jointed knees. She has sleep eyes, closed mouth, and an applied wig. The doll is marked "R & B" on her back and also on her neck. She is wearing her original Drum Major costume dating from 1955. The tag reads "R & B Littlest Angel/Kneels/Walks/Sits/Stands/Turns Her Head/Look! I Have Saran Hair/R & B Doll Co Inc. New York City." ($75-100). Also pictured is a "fur" coat, one of many costumes designed for the Littlest Angel Dolls. It also dates from 1955. ($35-45).

Right: Additional costumes for 1955 included this pink corduroy coat and hat and the Littlest Angel outfit. None of the clothing for the Littlest Angel appears to be tagged. (Costumes only $20-30 each).

This suitcase is marked Littlest Angel was advertised in the 1955 Littlest Angel brochure. Also pictured are a pajamas and robe set as well as the "fur" coat. (Trunk $20-30, pajamas and robe $10-15).

Two mint with box Littlest Angel dolls circa 1956-1957. These dolls have the rooted hair and vinyl heads. (MIB doll $75-100, doll only $50-75). *Dolls and photograph from the collection of Rhonda Schoenick.*

Rhodes of Seattle devoted a full page in its catalog in 1955 to the hard plastic Littlest Angel dolls and their clothing. *Catalog from the collection of Marge Meisinger.*

Page from the Arranbee sales brochure from 1958 which featured the new "Dutch Boy" hair style for the Littlest Angel dolls as well as the new fashions. *Catalog from the collection of Marge Meisinger.*

By 1956 the Littlest Angel dolls were being made with vinyl heads on hard plastic bodies. This advertisement appeared in the G.F. Fox & Co. catalog in Hartford, Connecticut. in that year. The dolls came with pony tail or bob hair styles. *Catalog from the collection of Marge Meisinger.*

10.5" Arranbee vinyl Coty Girl doll in her original dress (hat a replacement). Also pictured is another of the many dresses made for this doll. The Coty Girl is jointed at the waist and is marked with a P in a circle. These dolls are hard to identify because many "P" mold dolls were produced which are not Coty Girl dolls. (Clothes $25-35 each, played with doll $35-45). *Doll from the collection of Marge Meisinger.*

More Coty Girl costumes from the 1958 Arranbee 1958 brochure. *From the collection of Marge Meisinger.*

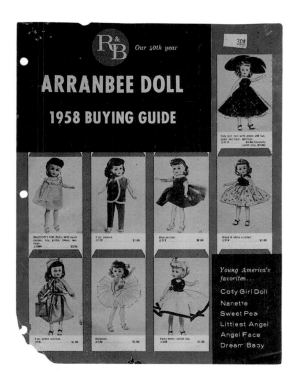

The Arranbee 1958 Buying Guide pictures many of the Coty Girl dolls in various outfits. The basic doll sold for only $2.98 dressed in a simple shortie nightie or for $3.98 in a fancy black dress and hat. The outfits were priced from $1.00 to $2.00 each. *Brochure from the collection of Marge Meisinger.*

Dolls called Nanette were still being marketed by Arranbee in 1958 but the dolls had undergone many changes from the earlier dolls of the 1950s. The new dolls were fully shaped fashion models with arched feet to compete with Ideal's Miss Revlon dolls. They came in both the 15" and 18" sizes and were dressed in high fashion clothing. *Brochure from the collection of Marge Meisinger.*

Artisan Novelty Co.

In 1950 Artisan Novelty Company of Gardena, California, began advertising their new all plastic Raving Beauty Walking doll. Unlike the new dolls that could walk with a key mechanism, these dolls walked because of the structure of the leg joints. According to an article in *Playthings* magazine in the June 1950 issue, more than a year had been spent by the company in designing and perfecting an aluminum walking mechanism. The doll was 20" tall and her wig was made of Ravon, a material that could be washed and set. The doll's costumes were designed by Michele. They could be purchased separately as well as on the dolls. Some of the outfits included negligees, party dresses, formals, cowgirl outfits, skating costumes, square dancing dresses, sun suits, and bridal dresses. Many of the dolls were packaged in an unusual tubular container. The suggested retail price for Raving Beauty was $13.95.

Since these hard plastic dolls were chunky in construction, it is likely they were not able to compete with the slim high heel type dolls on the market a few years later. The dolls remain quite popular with today's collector, however.

An additional page of the June 1950 ad in *Playthings* showed the unusual tubular box made for the dolls and the ad listed a suggested retail price of $13.95 for each doll. Costumes shown included a sun suit and four different dresses.

A Raving Beauty June 1950 ad from *Playthings* pictured several different outfits for the series of Raving Beauty Walking dolls. Included were a skating costume, square dance clothes, and cowgirl outfits. Also pictured on another page were negligees, dresses, and a wedding gown. The clothing designs were by Michele.

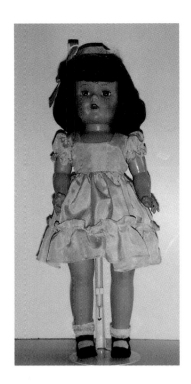

This hard plastic Raving Beauty is 20" tall and is shown with her original box. The doll includes a walking mechanism. She is wearing her original dress which is listed in the company advertisement as an afternoon costume #104. This dress was also made in white. The doll has an open mouth with teeth, sleep eyes, and a Ravon hair wig ($300-325). *From the collection of Jan Clanton. Photograph by Darek Clanton.*

This Raving Beauty doll is dressed in a party costume #101 from 1950. The dress is made of taffeta. Because of the walking mechanism, these dolls have legs that are more widely spaced than most hard plastic dolls of the period ($300-325). *From the collection of Jan Clanton. Photograph by Darek Clanton.*

Another original Artisan Raving Beauty with her box and tag. The tag reads "She Walks!/She Has Ravon Hair/Costume by Michele." Her dress dates from 1950 and is #103. It also came in blue and white check. All of the Raving Beauty dolls were 20" tall and were made from hard plastic ($300-325).

Although this 20" hard plastic doll came in her original box there was no writing on it for identification. She is dressed in a very fancy Southern Belle costume and was evidently a later Raving Beauty doll ($300-325). *From the collection of Jan Clanton. Photograph by Darek Clanton.*

Cosmopolitan Doll and Toy Corp.

The Cosmopolitan Doll and Toy Corporation was located in Jackson Heights, New York, during the 1950s. The company was quite active in producing several popular dolls of the era. Kathryn Kay, Inc. was involved with the company and was listed as the sole sales representative. This firm was run by Kathryn Kay Fassel who was also involved in the production of the "look alike" Terri Lee doll called Mary Jane.

The most famous doll marketed by the Cosmopolitan firm was the 8" **Ginger** hard plastic doll made to compete against Vogue's Ginny. Ginger also had an extensive wardrobe that could be purchased in addition to the doll. One catalog featured forty-eight designs of clothing. Several different styles of Ginger dolls were produced during the decade. The dolls were all approximately 8" in size. The earliest hard plastic dolls had painted eyelashes and straight legs. Later the eyelashes were molded, and still later the dolls came with jointed legs and elbows. Several different sizes of eyes were used on the various models of Ginger Dolls. The 1957 company catalog offered consumers a choice of either an all hard plastic walking Ginger doll or the same doll with a vinyl head and rooted hair. The hard plastic model was priced at $1.59 while the more modern doll with a vinyl head cost $1.98. Ginger dolls with "cha cha" heels were also available toward the end of production. Outfits for Ginger cost from $1.00 to $3.98 each. Accessories included trunks, glasses, shoes, skates, and wigs. The hairstyles included pigtails or curls in platinum honey, blonde, or brunette. Cosmopolitan also offered a unique selling plan for Ginger. A customer could enroll in the Doll Dress-of-the-Month Club and would receive a gift box including a doll and several outfits for $2.98. In addition the member would pay $26.95 to receive a different costume for the Ginger doll each month. These plans were advertised in catalogs, magazines, and by retail stores. Another advertising gimmick used by the company was the Disney licensing they secured for several of Ginger's outfits that depicted Disney related themes. In addition, many Ginger dolls were dressed in Terri Lee Girl Scout and Brownie Scout uniforms and sold by that firm.

Although the Ginger doll proved to be quite successful, new products were developed by Cosmopolitan in order to meet the competition. The 10.5" **Miss Ginger** doll was first marketed in 1957. The new vinyl doll had feet molded to fit high heel shoes and rooted hair. Many costumes were available in teen styles for this doll. Miss Ginger was priced at $3.98 for the doll dressed in a slip. Her clothing cost from $1.98 to $3.98 per outfit. Memberships were also offered for Dress-of-the-Month clubs for Miss Ginger. In 1958 a smaller **Little Miss Ginger** was marketed. The doll was approximately 8" tall made in a high heel style similar to the Little Miss Nancy Ann dolls sold by the Nancy Ann Storybook Company. Little Miss Ginger was also pro-

vided with many different costume changes. **Ginger Baby** was another Cosmopolitan product from the 1950s. This 8" vinyl doll competed in the market which Vogue dominated with their Ginnette dolls. The Ginger baby doll was also used as an advertising premium (see chapter on Advertising Dolls) so many of the dolls still survive. Many different outfits were made for this baby doll. They include dresses, snow suit, coats, bonnets, pajamas, coveralls, sunsuits, bunting, blanket, and other accessories. The clothing was priced from $1.00 to 2.98 for each costume.

Cosmopolitan also offered an unusual "doll" in its catalog for 1957. He was made in the image of **Zippy the Chimp**, a CBS Television star. The all vinyl figure was 8" tall and fully jointed. Several clothing changes for the chimp were also produced. These original dolls and clothing are hard to find when in mint condition.

Cosmopolitan also manufactured 8" hard plastic walking dolls for several other firms including Fortune Toys, Inc. Many of these dolls look very much like the Ginger dolls and when dressed in Ginger clothing many would pass as Ginger products.

7.5" hard plastic walking Ginger doll with straight legs made by the Cosmopolitan Doll and Toy Corporation. She has an applied wig, sleep eyes, and closed mouth. She is wearing the original School Dress featured in the "Doll Dress-of-the-Month" for September 1957. (Doll and dress $75-85). Also pictured is the book *Ginger Paper Doll* A Little Golden Activity Book published by Simon and Schuster in 1957. ($30-40).

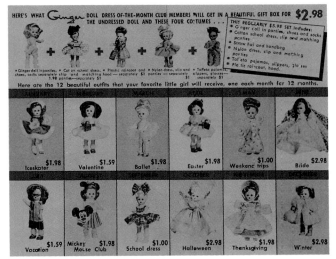

Advertisement for the Ginger Doll Dress-of-the-Month Club for 1957. A member paid a total of $26.95 to receive a different Ginger costume each month. Another set of clothes was marketed along with a Ginger with a vinyl head circa 1958. *From the collection of Marge Meisinger.*

Pictured are two of the Ginger ballerina outfits. The one on the left was the costume selection for March 1957 called "Ballet." The doll on the right is wearing the ballerina costume from a different year. She is standing on a Ginger stand. (Outfits only $35-40).

7.5" Ginger dolls model two more of the costumes available to members of the Doll Dress-of-the-Month Club. The Blue Fairy was the costume for October 1957 honoring Halloween. It is missing the wand with a star on top. The outfit was included in the regular Ginger brochure in 1957 as one of the Disneyland Fantasyland costumes. (Outfit only $45 and up). The Ice Skater clothing was sent to club members in January 1957. (Outfit only $35 and up).

The costume for June 1957 was the Bride outfit as pictured. It sold for $2.98. (Outfit only $50-55).

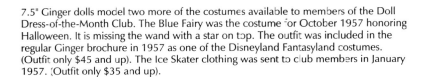

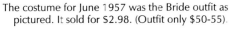

Other outfits offered in the Ginger club included this one on the left called Thanksgiving in November 1957. In the regular Ginger brochure it was part of the Disneyland Frontierland series called Frontier Girl. (Outfit $45-50). The Mickey Mouse Club costume was the club selection for August 1957. This one is missing the original Mickey Mouse mask. (Outfit $45-50).

43

A vacation outfit was the July selection for the Ginger club in 1957. It included jeans, shirt, hat, and sunglasses. (Outfit only $35-40). Original boxes from the club clothing are also pictured.

38C. PERT LITTLE GINGER, the first 8" walking doll with moving eyes, vinyl head and rooted hair that can be wet, set, combed and curled. She wears panties, shoes and socks —ready to be dressed in one of her many outfits. Choose her with a ponytail or long bobbed hair in platinum, honey blonde or brunette. 1.98 (All outfits shown come with panties, shoes and socks except 38E.)

38D. Flower print taffeta dress. 1.00
38E. Peignoir set and slippers. 1.59
38F. Plaid taffeta dress and slip. 1.98
38G. Gay roller skating outfit. 1.98
38H. Pierette costume. 1.98
38J. Traditional bridal outfit. 2.98
38K. Student nurse ensemble. 1.98
38L. Trim skirt, jersey top. 1.59

Catalog page from Heibst in Fargo, North Dakota, in 1957 features Ginger and several of her outfits. The doll pictured has a vinyl head, rooted hair, and a hard plastic body. She is a walker. *Catalog from the collection of Marge Meisinger.*

Left: This is the May club selection called "Weekend Trips" and it included a nightgown, peignoir, and slippers. (Outfit only $35-40).

Ginger outfits were also sold individually in stores. Pictured is #441 along with the box. The boxed clothing included underwear, shoes, and socks, and sometimes a hat and/or purse along with the main item of clothing. This costume was pictured in the 1957 brochure. This dress like all the clothing is tagged "Fashions for Ginger/Cosmopolitan Doll and Toy Corp./Jackson Heights, N.Y." (Clothing MIB $50-55).

Hard plastic Ginger modeling a skating outfit as pictured in the Heibst catalog. It sold for $1.98. (Outfit only $30-35).

Right: The Disneyland costumes are some of the most collectible of the Ginger outfits. Pictured are two pages from the Ginger brochure that show both Tomorrowland and Fantasyland clothing produced for the Ginger dolls with Disney authorization. Other styles were made to tie-in to Frontierland and Adventureland. *Catalog from the collection of Marge Meisinger.*

Later hard plastic Ginger dolls featured joints at the knees and elbows. This one is wearing her original dress. ($55-60). *From the collection of Carolyn Sharp. Photograph by Mark W. Carpenter.*

This page from the 1957 Cosmopolitan Doll and Toy Corporation brochure pictures six dresses with hats #441, #442. #443, #444, #445, and #446. In addition two skating outfits are shown #551 (ice skates), and #552 (roller skates). A nurse #553, two masked costumes #554, and #555, and a drum major #556, are also pictured. These dolls had vinyl heads with rooted hair.

This page from the Montgomery Ward Christmas catalog for 1957 features Ginger, Miss Ginger, and the Baby Ginger dolls, many of their costumes, and gift sets. Several matching outfits were made for both Ginger and Little Miss Ginger. The Gingers had vinyl heads. *Catalog from the collection of Marge Meisinger.*

10.4" vinyl Miss Ginger marketed by Cosmopolitan beginning in 1957. The doll has sleep eyes, closed mouth, pierced ears, arched feet, and a jointed waist. She is marked "Ginger" on the back of her head. She is wearing her original slip, panties, and shoes. ($100 and up in mint condition). Also shown is a jumper and blouse which was listed in the 1957 company brochure and which originally came with a hat and purse for $2.98. ($20-30).

Miss Ginger clothing was illustrated in the Cosmopolitan brochure for 1957. Some of the outfits were made for Ginger as well.

These simple Miss Ginger dresses are made alike except for the trim. They are tagged "Fashions for Ginger/Cosmopolitan Doll and Toy Corp./Jamaica New York." Most of the Ginger lines of clothing fasten with a small snap that has a simple design around the edge. (Outfits $20-30 each).

Other Miss Ginger clothing as pictured in the company brochure in 1957. Included were a formal, bridal gown, jeans, Fireside Ensemble, and several dress-up outfits.

Cosmopolitan also offered a Miss Ginger Dress-of-the-Month club. This advertisement is from Mandel Brothers in Chicago in 1957. The customer paid $4.98 for the Miss Ginger gift set which included the doll, her slip, taffeta dress, plaid dress, blue dress, and pink and white check dress. Then each month a new outfit for Miss Ginger was sent to the customer and the cost was charged to her account. *Advertisement from the collection of Marge Meisinger.*

8" vinyl Little Miss Ginger was first marketed in 1958. She has rooted hair, sleep eyes, closed mouth, and arched feet. She is marked "Ginger" on the back of her head and "Little Miss Ginger" on her back. Most of the clothing for this doll is very simple as are the two dresses pictured. The belt on the blue and white dress is not original. The dresses are tagged "Fashions for Little Miss Ginger/Metropolitan Doll and Toy Corp. Jamaica, New York." Her undergarments consist of a simple bra and panties. These dolls look very much like the Little Miss Nancy Ann dolls but the Nancy Ann dolls are not marked. (Dressed doll $75 and up, dress $20-25).

Brochure for the 8" Baby Ginger doll, another member of the Cosmopolitan family of dolls. The advertisement lists it as the first 8" all vinyl jointed drink and wet baby doll to come on the market. The doll was also used as an advertising premium (see Advertising Dolls chapter).

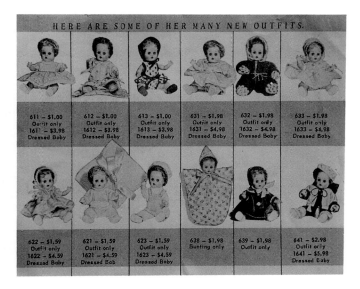

The inside of the brochure for Baby Ginger pictures twelve more outfits that could be purchased for the doll. The clothes cost from $1.00 to $2.98 each.

Cosmopolitan Zippy doll representing the Chimp who was a CBS television star. He is 8" tall and fully jointed. He is all original and pictured with his box and tag. ($175 and up). *From the collection of Marge Meisinger.*

8" Cosmopolitan Baby Ginger doll on the left is circa 1958-1959. Her dress is tagged "Fashions for Ginger/Cosmopolitan Doll and Toy Corp./Richmond Hill, N.Y." the doll has rooted hair, sleep eyes, open mouth, and five painted eyelashes under her eyes. The black doll probably dates from the early 1960s. It is marked "Ginger" on the back of the head. The doll has molded hair, sleep eyes, a nurser mouth, and is 7" tall. ($50-75 each).

Six different outfits were made for Zippy. Pictured are #4021 which sold for $1.98 and #4041 priced at $2.98. The doll also cost $2.98. (MIB outfits $50-75 each).

Effanbee Doll Corp.

The Effanbee Doll Corp. had been known as one of the best of the companies that produced composition dolls in the 1940s. In the 1950s, the firm again achieved excellence with their production of hard plastic dolls. Fine as these dolls were, it is amazing in looking back that this well known company did not market a small hard plastic 8" little girl doll or a 10.5" high heel doll. Nearly all of the other well-known doll manufacturers of the 1950s produced these types of dolls, along with their clothing and accessories. Perhaps Effanbee's failure to compete gave rise to its change of ownership during the decade.

The company had its beginning in 1910 when Bernard E. Fleischaker and Hugo Baum joined forces to sell toys. In 1912 the firm began to manufacture dolls. Their trademark became Effanbee in honor of the founders initials, F & B. The firm produced many famous composition dolls including Grumpy, Bubbles, the Patsy family line, Little Lady, American Children, Candy Kid, plus the successful Dy-Dee babies.

In 1947 Noma Electric purchased the company and was in control until 1953. Effanbee was slower than most of the other doll companies to begin using hard plastic to make their dolls. As late as 1950, some of the firm's dolls were still being made of composition but by 1951 hard plastic and vinyl had become Effanbee's doll material of choice. Baby dolls featured during the early 1950s included **Noma's Electronic Talking Doll**, **Dy-Dee** with a hard plastic head and rubber body (by 1956 the doll was being made with a hard plastic head, vinyl limbs and either molded hair or a wig), **Mommy's Baby** with a hard plastic head and latex body, **Lil 'Darlin** with a vinyl head and limbs and a cloth body, and **Sweetie Pie** with a hard plastic head, vinyl arms, and a cloth body. In the little girl line Effanbee offered their **Honey Walker** doll in all hard plastic. She came in sizes of 16", 18", 21", 24", and 28". Another hard plastic girl doll very much like Honey was called **Tintair Honey** because she came with hair color that could be used to change the color of her hair. She came in 14", 16", and 18" sizes. She was made in 1951.

Effanbee received widespread publicity in 1951 as a result of a contract made with famous designer Elsa Schiaparelli. She was to design a line of clothing for the famous Honey dolls. Many of these dolls had adult hair styles pulled back from the face. At least fourteen designer outfits were made. These dolls are especially desirable for collectors today.

Besides the baby and little girl dolls, Effanbee offered a character doll called **Howdy Doody** during this time period. The doll had a plastic head, sleep eyes, and a cloth body. It was based on the character from the popular kid's program broadcast by NBC. The doll was made through 1952.

In 1952 Effanbee issued the hard plastic Honey Girl dressed in beautiful costumes including those of Prince Charming and Cinderella. Smaller size dolls were also issued in a 12" size that were displayed in picture boxes. Costumes for these dolls included Bo Peep, Majorette, Gibson Girl, Bride and Groom, and Southern Belle.

In 1953 Noma sold the Effanbee company to several of the original members of the firm. These partners formed a corporation to manage the purchase. The quality of the dolls continued to be high even with new management.

In the mid-1950s, while still concentrating on baby dolls and little girl dolls much as they had done in the 1940s, Effanbee introduced a few newly designed dolls. One was **Melodie**, a 27" tall doll with jointed knees. The doll included a talking mechanism and the advertising stated that the doll could walk, talk, and sing. Melodie was made with a vinyl head and a hard plastic body. She was produced from 1953 to 1956. Also new, **Fluffy** was first issued in 1954 and she would remain in the company line for many years. Fluffy came in sizes of 8" and 12", was made of vinyl, and had rooted hair and sleep eyes. She was especially appealing in her role as a Girl Scout, Brownie, Camp Fire Girl, and Bluebird. Perhaps Fluffy was Effanbee's Ginny contender but she did not have the wardrobe to compete with Vogue's star.

Another interesting pair of dolls from 1954 was a vinyl set of **Candy Kid** dolls (boy and girl). The dolls had molded hair and sleep eyes. These dolls are seldom found by collectors and must not have been very successful.

The vinyl **Mickey** doll was another unusual doll made by Effanbee beginning in 1956. He varied in size but was usually about 11" tall. He came dressed in many outfits including a fireman, Boy Scout, Air Cadet, boxer, baseball player, jockey, hunter, Marine, cowboy, clown, and football player. The doll had painted eyes, molded hair, and usually featured a molded hat.

Although Effanbee never did jump on the 1950s band wagon and make small dolls with extensive wardrobes, the company did follow the trend when the larger "high heel" dolls became popular. One of these dolls was used to represent the **"Champagne Lady"** from the Lawrence Welk television show. There were two singers on the show who held the title at various times. Since the doll was marketed in 1957, Alice Lon probably carried the title at that time. Norma Zimmer was the later "lady." The doll was made with a vinyl head and a hard vinyl body, rooted hair, and sleep eyes. She had extra joints at both the knees and the ankles, and her feet were molded to fit high heeled shoes. The Champagne Lady was 20" tall.

Another similar doll was used as the mother in the set of dolls called **"Most Happy Family"** in 1957. This doll was 21" tall and did not have the jointed ankle although the other characteristics were the same as the Champagne Lady doll. Sold with the mother doll were a Brother 8" tall (Mickey mold), Sister 8" tall (Fluffy mold), and Baby 8" tall (**Baby Kin** mold). All of the dolls were vinyl. The family set of dolls was also sold in 1958 with different costumes. Both of the adult high heel dolls were also marketed in different outfits and sold as Honey Walkers.

Other notable Effanbee dolls from the late 1950s included a reissue of the **Patsy Ann** composition doll in vinyl. She was 15" tall with rooted hair and sleep eyes. The company also sold a 11" vinyl doll called Patsy but it did not look like the earlier composition Patsy dolls.

The Effanbee Doll Corporation again followed the leader when the large child size dolls became popular and issued a 32" tall doll called **Mary Jane**. The doll was a flirty eye walker made of plastic and vinyl and became a good seller for Effanbee in 1959.

Despite changes in management, Effanbee produced many excellent examples of collectible dolls during the decade of the 1950s. Perhaps most attractive to today's collector are the mint hard plastic Honey dolls when found with their original crisp clothing and excellent skin coloring. These dolls rank at the top of any hard plastic doll collection.

The company continued in business for many more decades, offering varieties of vinyl play dolls as well as limited editions of dolls for collectors. It is however, the quality of the hard plastic dolls of the 1950s, along with the fine composition dolls of earlier years, that make Effanbee's reputation secure as one of America's finest doll manufacturers.

20" Dy-Dee doll circa 1950. She has a hard plastic head, rubber body, sleep eyes, and open mouth. Her rubber ears are applied. She is marked on the back of her head "Effanbee." Her back is marked "EFF-An-Bee/DYDEE BABY/U.S. PAT.-1857-485." Other patent numbers are also given for several other countries. She is dressed in an older Dy-Dee dress circa 1940. She can drink and wet and blow bubbles. ($150-175).

27" Noma Electronic Talking Doll. Equipped with battery powered mechanism so the doll could sing, talk, laugh, and pray. Has vinyl arms and legs, soft body, hard plastic head with shoulder plate, sleep eyes, open mouth with teeth, and molded hair. All original. Marked on back of neck "Effanbee." The early vinyl has darkened with age. Sold for $23.89 in the Sears Christmas catalog in 1950. ($125 and up).

15" Effanbee hard plastic doll with an unusual hair style, sleep eyes, and closed mouth. Her original costume is unidentified. She may be one of the dolls designed by the designer Elsa Schiaparelli in 1951. Those dolls had more fashionable hair styles than the usual Honey dolls. She has large hands and is marked "Effanbee" on her back. ($200-250).

16" mint hard plastic Honey that looks very much like a "Tintair" doll although she is tagged "Honey." Curlers were attached to her original tag. ($350 and up in this condition). *From the collection of Jan Clanton. Photograph by Darek Clanton.*

14" Honey type hard plastic walker. Marked "Effanbee" on the back of the head and on her back. Wearing her original clothing. She has sleep eyes, a closed mouth, and a line at the corner of her eye to indicate longer lashes unlike most of the Honey dolls. ($200-225).

Right: 18" Effanbee hard plastic Honey Walker pictured in the G. Fox and Co. catalog from Hartford, Connecticut, in 1953. She is all original but came with a tag and curlers when new. She is marked "Effanbee" on her back. The doll was also made in the 15" size which sold for $7.98. The larger 18" size was priced at $9.98. A 15" Honey was also marketed with a complete wardrobe for $14.98 in the G. Fox catalog in 1953. ($200-250).

This 18" mint hard plastic Honey was featured in the company catalog in 1952. Her tag reads "Honey/All Plastic/An Effanbee Sweet Child." ($500 and up in this condition). *From the collection of Jan Clanton. Photograph by Darek Clanton.*

8" Fluffy doll first introduced in 1954. The vinyl doll has sleep eyes, rooted hair, and a closed mouth. She also came dressed as a Girl Scout, Brownie, and Blue Bird. Her outfit is original. ($40-50).

"Most Happy Family" from 1957. There were four dolls in the set. Missing is the 8" baby. The four dolls sold for $24.98 in 1957. The Mother is 19" tall and is marked "Effanbee" on the back of her head. She has sleep eyes, closed mouth, pierced ears, rooted hair, and a fashion styled body with arched vinyl feet shaped to wear high heels. The vinyl Fluffy is 10.5" tall with sleep eyes, rooted hair, and a closed mouth. Mickey is also 10.5" tall, made of vinyl, with molded hair, and painted features. He is marked "Mickey/Effanbee" on the back of his head. All three dolls are wearing their original clothing. ($225-250 for all three dolls).

11" vinyl Mickey doll first issued by Effanbee in 1956. He came in a variety of costumes. He has a molded hat and painted features. This outfit dates from 1959. Marked "c F&B." ($50-60).

An advertisement from the Sears Christmas catalog in 1958 features the Effanbee family of dolls wearing different clothing. The set was priced much cheaper during the second year selling for only $15.98 for the four dolls.

15" Patsy Ann Brownie Scout doll from 1959. The vinyl doll has sleep eyes, closed mouth, rooted hair, freckles, and a jointed waist. She is original except for her hat. She is marked on the back of her head "Patsy Ann/c 1959." The doll also came dressed as a Girl Scout and in a boxed set with a wardrobe. ($125-150).

11" Happy Boy first offered by Effanbee in 1959. The vinyl doll has molded hair and painted features. He is wearing his original clothing except for his house shoes. ($45-55).

20" Sweetie Pie circa late 1950s. The vinyl doll has sleep eyes, molded hair, and a crier in her tummy. The doll's original price was $10.35. *Doll and photograph from the collection of Carol J. Lindeman.* ($225-250).

E. I. Horsman Dolls, Inc.

E.I. Horsman Dolls, Inc. had been in business over seventy-five years, but by 1950 the quality of its doll product did not seem to be as high as it had been in the 1920s and 1930s. In earlier years the firm had produced many famous composition dolls including the Campbell Kids, Baby Bumps, and Dimples. In contrast, most of the Horsman dolls of the '50s were sold through hardware stores, lesser catalog companies, or dime stores instead of in fine department stores or Sears or Montgomery Ward catalogs.

The company was founded by Edward Iseman Horsman circa 1865 in New York City. The firm dealt in children's toys, games, tricycles, skates, and sleds.

Although the Horsman Company had imported doll heads and bodies earlier, around 1900 the firm began producing their own dolls. The first dolls in their line were cloth dolls called "Babyland." By 1911 the company was also marketing the popular Campbell Kid dolls and Baby Bumps dolls of composition.

In 1940 the E.I. Horsman Doll Co. was purchased by Regal Dolls and the name was changed to Horsman Dolls, Inc.

During 1950 Horsman doll offerings included **Bright Star** little girl dolls made of either composition or hard plastic. The composition models were 13" tall while the hard plastic dolls were 15" or 18" tall. Composition **Campbell Kid** dolls were also still in the company catalog in a 12.5" size. In addition, Horsman sold many dolls made partly of latex during 1950. Many of the baby dolls that year had latex arms and legs with hard plastic heads. Some toddler dolls were made entirely of latex. Other baby dolls came with vinyl arms and legs and a hard plastic head. Some of these dolls came in both black and white. One of the most popular dolls in the Horsman line was the **Tynie Baby**. These types of babies which looked like newborn children were made by many companies at the time. They were made of an early vinyl material which sometimes became sticky with age. The Tynie Baby came in sizes of 15" or 20". Another similar baby doll was produced in 1951 with closed eyes and its mouth opened in a yawn. This doll, called **Sleepy**, was dressed in Hanes sleepwear and had a vinyl head and arms and a cloth body and legs. The doll came in 17" and 21" sizes. The smaller doll sold for $5.89.

By 1952, the Campbell Kids, as well as all other dolls made by Horsman, were being made of vinyl or hard plastic. Tynie baby was offered in either black or white that year.

In 1953 Horsman joined other companies in offering a walking doll when they marketed **Cindy Strutter**. She was made of vinyl and plastic and was sold in sizes of 20", 23", and 26". A smaller 14" doll was sold complete with a wardrobe. The same year the company offered a **Shadow Wave** doll to compete with Ideal's Toni doll. The little girl doll came in sizes of 14", 16", 19", or 21" and came with wave hair setting lotion, and other hair accessories. She had a hard plastic body and a vinyl head.

All through the early 1950s, Horsman also marketed a line of dolls for younger children made of vinyl and latex. These dolls sometimes came with one-piece latex bodies, and some had rooted hair and others came with molded hair.

As American Character's Tiny Tears and Ideal's Betsy Wetsy dolls gained popularity, Horsman offered a drink and wet doll called the **Perma Nurser Bottle Baby** to compete in that market. The vinyl doll came in sizes of 13", 15", and 21" in 1955. It could be purchased with various accessories in a suitcase.

In 1956 the company entered the "high heel" market with their **Cindy** "Grown-Up" doll. She was a vinyl doll sized at 18" or 20", jointed at the elbows as well as the shoulders and hips. The doll was also sold as a ballerina. Also in 1956 Horsman began the production of an 8" little girl doll made of vinyl to compete against Vogue's Ginny doll. At least fourteen different outfits were made for the doll.

1956 also brought two of Horsman's most unusual dolls to market when they produced black vinyl twins called **Polly** and **Pete**. Although Horsman had always made more black dolls than other doll companies, the earlier dolls had always been copies of the regular white doll line made with black coloring. The new twins, however, were actually modeled with African features. The vinyl dolls were 13" tall with molded hair and painted eyes.

The smaller 10.5" **Traveling Cindy** joined the Horsman line in 1957. The doll was made of vinyl with an added jointed waist. Her feet were molded to fit the high heel shoes. Many additional clothing changes were made for Cindy. She was similar to the other dolls of the period like Little Miss Revlon (made by Ideal) but was of lesser quality. The larger Cindy was also sold with many additional outfits.

Although Horsman again followed the last trend of other doll makers of the 1950s by producing a child size doll, the **Princess Peggy** doll did not appear on the market until 1960. She was 36" tall, made of vinyl and plastic, and came in both black and white models.

Although Horsman made some notable dolls in the 1950s including Tynie Baby, the Campbell Kids, Bright Star, Cindy, and Pete and Polly, most of the company's dolls were issued to follow the trends set by other companies. Many of the Horsman dolls were not quality dolls but they did offer a cheaper alternative to the more expensive Vogue, Ideal, American Character, and Alexander lines of popular dolls of the period.

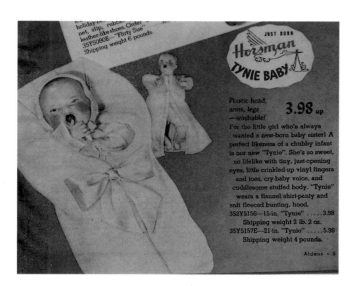

Advertisement for the Horsman Tynie Baby which appeared in the Alden Christmas catalog in 1950. The dolls came in sizes of 15" and 21" and were priced at $3.98 and $5.98. The doll had the look of a newborn baby with an open mouth and painted eyes. The head, arms, and legs were vinyl and it had a cotton stuffed body.

20" Fairy Skin mint doll with original clothing, tag, and box. Circa 1953. Made of a soft vinyl plastic "Fairy Skin." Tag reads "Horsman Fairy Skin Doll." Curlers were included on the tag. The box has a price tag of $9.95 and says "Another Fine Horsman Doll/Manufactured in Trenton, New Jersey." ($125 and up).

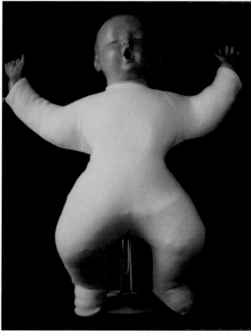

15" hard plastic Horsman Bright Star with a fur wig. The doll has sleep eyes and an open mouth. It was marketed by Horsman in 1951. She is all original. ($200 and up).

15" hard plastic Horsman Bright Star in a different model. She is marked "Horsman" on the back of her head. She has her original tag reading "Bright Star/Horsman/All Plastic." She also has her original curlers on a tag that says "This Horsman Doll Has Saran Hair." ($200 and up).

17" Sleepy doll dating from 1951. The doll had a soft vinyl head and arms with the body and legs stuffed with cotton. The eyes were molded shut in the earlier models and the mouth was open in a yawn. It was dressed in "Hanes"-like baby pajamas. ($75-85)

13" Horsman Polly doll dating from 1956. Polly was one of a pair of black dolls called Polly and Pete. The company used faces that were modeled to look like real black children instead of just painting a white doll with a darker color. The dolls were made of vinyl with molded hair and painted eyes. The mouth was molded open with teeth. Her dress and shoes and socks have been replaced. ($125 and up).

20" Cindy Mardi Gras doll from 1957. The vinyl doll has sleep eyes, rooted hair, closed mouth, and pierced ears. She has a full figure body with arched feet for high heels. Some of the Cindy dolls were jointed at the waist but this one is not. The later dolls were jointed at the elbows as this one is. They were all made of vinyl. This doll is all original with her box. Her tag reads "Horsman's Cindy Mardi Gras." On the box is printed "Horsman's Cindy/ Horsman Dolls, Inc./Trenton, New Jersey." She sold for $11.95 when new. Cindy came in both the 18" and 20" sizes. ($150 and up).

14" ballerina doll circa 1956-57. The doll has a vinyl head, hard plastic body, sleep eyes, and a closed mouth. She is jointed at the ankles. She is marked "Horsman/81" on her head and "Made in USA/Patent Pending" on her body. She wears her original clothing except the straps on her dress have been replaced. ($50-60).

10.5" Cindy dolls model extra clothes made for the doll which included this short formal and three-piece sports outfit. ($15-20 for each outfit).

10.5" Horsman Cindy from 1957. She has a soft vinyl head, hard vinyl body, arched feet, pierced ears, and bends at the waist and knees. She is marked "Horsman" on the back of her head. Pictured in her ballerina outfit with her original box. ($100 and up).

Several other costumes were marketed for the small Cindy doll. Included were a negligee, dress, nightgown, slip, and toreador pants and top.

Ideal

Ideal Toy Co. had its beginning when Morris Michtom and his wife began producing stuffed bears above their candy store in Brooklyn, New York, in 1903. The couple called the bears "Teddy Bears" after President Theodore Roosevelt. Michtom went into partnership with Aaron Cone in 1907 and the Ideal Novelty Co. was born. In 1912 this partnership ended and Michtom changed the name of the company to the Ideal Novelty and Toy Co.

In 1950 Ideal had already been in business nearly fifty years and had produced many popular composition dolls during the 1920s and 1930s. Some of these successful dolls included Tickletoes, Judy Garland, Deanna Durbin, Mortermer Snerd, Fannie Brice and, of course, the Shirley Temple dolls.

Beginning in 1947 the Ideal firm began scoring hit after hit in their new lines of dolls. This success continued throughout the decade of the 1950s. Perhaps Ideal was the most successful company in the doll industry during this time period.

The successes began with the introduction of the **Sparkle Plenty** doll in 1947. This doll, based on a character in the Dick Tracy comic strip, remained a best seller through 1951. She was joined by **Bonnie Braids**, another Dick Tracy comic strip character, in 1951. Three more of these comic dolls appeared in Ideal's doll lines by 1953. They included **Joan Palooka**, **L'l Honest Abe**, and **Little Wingy**. (See chapter on Comic Dolls for more information.)

Besides comic strip babies, Ideal also produced a line of **Baby Coos** dolls from 1948 to 1952. These dolls had hard plastic heads and stuffed magic skin bodies. Later the limbs were made of vinyl and the bodies of cloth. These dolls came in sizes of 14", 16", 18", 20", 27", and 30". Some of the dolls were dressed as boys and others as girls. By the late fifties the Baby Coo dolls were produced entirely of vinyl.

The **Blessed Event** was a new Ideal baby doll marketed in 1950. The doll came in 19" and 21" sizes and looked like a newborn infant. The baby had a vinyl head and limbs and a cloth body. When a plunger was pushed in the back, the doll's expression changed to look as if the doll was crying or pouting.

The same year a key wind talking baby doll called **Talking Tot** was also marketed. This 22" baby came with a hard plastic head, cloth body, and vinyl limbs.

The **Betsy Wetsy** baby doll also continued to be a good seller for Ideal. The doll had first been introduced by Ideal in the late 1930s. By 1954 the doll was no longer made with a rubber body, instead the doll had a vinyl body and limbs with a hard plastic head. By 1956 the doll was made of all vinyl including the head. These dolls were always of the drink and wet style.

Ideal made another unique doll in 1955 when they issued **"Magic Lips."** The doll was 23" tall with a vinyl head and limbs and a cloth body. She had sleep eyes and rooted hair. When her back was pressed, she closed her mouth and when her back was released, she opened her mouth and cooed. This doll attracted a lot of attention but she was not made for very long.

One of the most profitable dolls ever made by Ideal was the hard plastic **Toni** doll first produced in 1949. The doll came in sizes of 14", 16", 19", and 21". Ideal used a tie-in to the popular Toni Home permanent from the Gillette Co. to give the doll more selling power. The dolls came with Toni doll products and Toni received royalties in return. By 1954 the Toni dolls were being made as walkers and these dolls continued to be manufactured until 1956.

The basic Toni Bodies were also used for several other little girl hard plastic dolls in the Ideal Line. The **Sara Ann** doll which sold in 1951 came with Saran hair and was basically a Toni doll except there were no royalties paid for this product. The **Betsy McCall** dolls which joined the line in 1952 also used the Toni hard plastic bodies. The McCall dolls were modeled on the paper dolls then included in each *McCall* monthly magazine beginning in May 1951. Seven different outfits were sold for the dolls. Unlike Ideal's other little girl dolls, these dolls had vinyl heads and rooted hair.

Collectible **Mary Hartline** dolls also used the Toni mold. These dolls were dressed in copies of the costumes worn by Mary Hartline on the ABC television show, "Super Circus." (See Personality chapter.)

Two other dolls which used the Toni bodies were the **Miss Curity** dolls which debuted in 1953 and the **Princess Mary** dolls from 1955. The Miss Curity dolls used a tie-in to the Bauer and Black Co. and the doll came with their first aid kit and a book. The Princess Mary doll was made with a stuffed vinyl head mounted on the Toni hard plastic body. She came in sizes of 16", 19", and 21".

Another type of little girl doll that became a big hit for Ideal in the early 1950s was the **Saucy Walker** doll. These dolls were chunky in style and were equipped with a walking mechanism. Saucy was introduced in 1951. By 1952 there was also a boy Saucy Walker. In 1953 a Toddler Saucy Walker was produced and in 1954 a Big Sister Saucy Walker was made. In 1955 Saucy was produced with a vinyl head and in 1960 a new 28" vinyl version was made.

Ideal must have found dolls that tied to other companies profitable because they continued to produce this type of doll throughout the decade. In 1953 the **Harriet Hubbard Ayer** dolls appeared on the market. The doll had a vinyl head with light coloring. The owner was supposed to apply make-up to the doll by using the eight-piece Harriet Hubbard Ayer cosmetic kit that accompanied the doll. A beauty table and booklet was also part of the doll package. The Ayer head was vinyl stuffed with cotton and the wig was glued onto the head. The doll came in 14", 16", 19", and 21" sizes.

In 1956 Ideal's famous **Miss Revlon** doll was introduced. She also tied into the Revlon Cosmetic Company. The doll came in sizes of 15", 18", 20", and 22.5". She was all vinyl with extra joints at the waist and knees and had feet molded to wear high heeled shoes.. The doll continued to be made through 1959. A smaller vinyl **Little Miss Revlon** was added to the line in 1957. She was produced until 1960. The 1957 brochure for the doll pictured forty-six outfits that could be purchased.

Other memorable dolls made by Ideal during the decade included the vinyl **Saralee** doll from 1951. This baby doll was 17" tall with a vinyl head and limbs and a stuffed body. She was a "Negro" doll designed by Sara Lee Creech and was not just a white baby painted brown. Another popular doll was **Posie** from 1954. This doll was advertised that she could pose in various positions because she had jointed knees. Posie was a walker with flirty eyes, rooted hair, a vinyl head, and a hard plastic body. **Baby Big Eyes** was also a good seller in 1954. This baby came with a vinyl head, soft body, and vinyl arms and legs. The **Trilby** doll was one of Ideal's most unusual dolls of the 1950s. This three-faced doll was marketed in 1951. Her vinyl faces turned through the use of a knob on the top of her head. Trilby's body was cloth and her limbs were vinyl. Besides all of these successful dolls, Ideal also made several other personality dolls during the decade including **Hopalong Cassidy**, and another edition of the **Shirley Temple** dolls. (See chapter on Personality and Shirley Temple Dolls for more information).

By 1959 the larger high heeled fashion dolls had lost their selling power and the hard plastic Toni dolls were no longer in style, so a new type of doll was needed to try to capture lost sales. Ideal came up with the large child sized doll and began the manufacture of these vinyl dolls in the **Patty Play Pal** line. The original Patty doll was modeled after a three-year-old child. She was 35" tall and was marked "Ideal Toy Corp. G 35" on the back of her head. Her vinyl arms featured jointed wrists. **Penny Play Pal** was modeled after a two-year-old child and stood 32" tall. She was made only one year. She was marked "Ideal Doll 32 E-L" on the back of her head. **Suzy Play Pal** was only 28" tall and was supposed to be the size of a one-year-old child. She was marked "Ideal Doll O.E.B. 28-5" on the back of her head. **Johnny Play Pal** was 24" tall and was the size of a three month old baby. **Bonnie Play Pal** was the little girl version. These dolls were marked "Ideal Doll BB-24-3" on the backs of the heads. **Peter Play Pal** was added to the line in 1960 and he was 38" tall.

The Ideal company was run by family members through the early 1980s. According to Judith Izen in her book *Collectors Guide to Ideal Dolls* the firm was sold to the Columbia Broadcasting System in 1983 for $58 million. The line then merged with CBS's Gabriel Toy Co. and it was called Ideal-Gabriel. Viewmaster then bought the Ideal trade mark but after a short time they sold out to Tyco Industries, Inc. in 1989.

The toys made by the original Ideal company are still remembered fondly by today's collectors. The hard plastic dolls from the 1950s remain some of the finest dolls ever made.

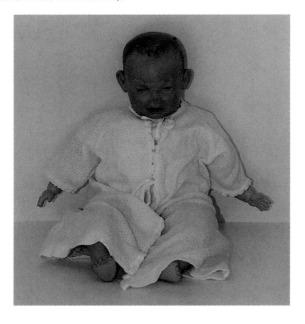

19" Blessed Event doll from 1950. The doll had a vinyl head and limbs and a cotton stuffed body. When her body was pressed, her mouth opened and she cried. The doll was made to compete with other newborn baby dolls then on the market. It came dressed in a kimono and a blanket. This doll's clothing has been replaced. Marked "Ideal Doll/Patent Pending." ($80-100).

Another newborn baby doll was "snoozie" which came in sizes of 11.5", 15", and 21". The doll had a vinyl head and a one-piece latex rubber body. It was featured in this ad from Aldens Christmas catalog in 1950.

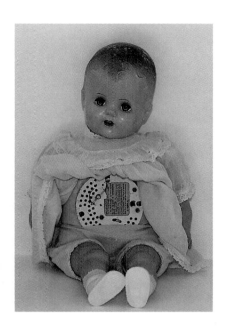

22" Talking Tot baby doll from 1950. The doll has a hard plastic head, sleep eyes, closed mouth, molded hair, vinyl arms and legs, and a cloth body. A key wind talking mechanism is included in the body. Her dress is original. ($85-125).

Saralee "colored doll" as pictured in the Sears Christmas catalog in 1951. The doll was priced at $5.99. The 18" doll had a vinyl head and limbs, a cotton stuffed body, and molded hair. She was designed by Sara Lee Creech.

24' Talky Tot doll labeled "Ideal's Talking Doll." The doll is all cloth except for a plastic face. Her tag reads "It's A Wonderful Toy It's Ideal." When a handle is turned, the doll talks. She is all original with her box. ($50-60).

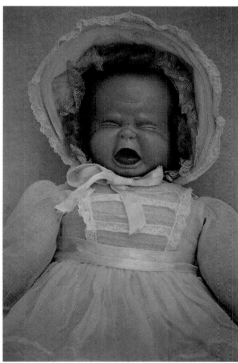

18" Triby doll marketed by Ideal in 1951. She is a three-faced doll with a vinyl head, arms, and legs, and a cloth body. A knob on the top of her head can be turned to display the different faces. Her hair is attached to her bonnet. She is wearing her original clothing. ($75-100).

Advertisement for the Ideal hard plastic Toni doll from Aldens Christmas Book in 1950. The 14" size doll sold for $9.49. Toni also came in sizes of 15.5", 19", and 21" in this ad. The Toni Playwave set, curlers, and other accessories also came with the doll.

14" hard plastic Toni doll all original in her box. She has a nylon wig, sleep eyes, and a closed mouth. Her plastic shoes date her a little later than 1950. She is marked "P-90/Ideal Doll/Made in U.S.A." on the back of her head. On her back is marked "Ideal Doll/P-90." ($300-350). *Doll and photograph from the collection of Carol J. Lindeman.*

15.5" Ideal hard plastic Toni all original with her box. This doll dates from 1949. She is marked "P-91/Ideal Doll" on her head and "Ideal Doll/P-91" on her back. ($550 and up). *Doll and photograph from the collection of Carol J. Lindeman.*

15.5" Toni in near mint condition with her tag, box, and accessories. She is marked "P-91/Ideal Doll" on the back of her head and "Ideal Doll/P-91" on her back. ($550 and up). *Doll and photograph from the collection of Carol J. Lindeman.*

Left: 21" Toni doll in her original clothing with replaced shoes and socks. This doll is marked "P-93/Ideal Doll." Toni's 22.5" tall were also made which were marked "P-94." Toni Walkers were produced from 1954-1956. ($400-450). *Doll and photograph from the collection of Carol J. Lindeman.*

Right: Several different outfits were made for the McCall dolls. Pictured are two from the 1952-1953 era. The doll on the left is all original while the one on the right has replaced shoes. ($100 and up each). *Dolls from the collection of Marge Meisinger.*

16" beautiful Mary Hartline doll circa 1953. She is in mint condition all original with box, tag, pin, and oversized baton. The doll was originally priced at $11.98. She is marked "P-91/Ideal Doll/Made in U.S.A." on her head and "Ideal Doll/P-91 on her body." (In this condition $650-700). *Doll and photograph from the collection of Carol J. Lindeman.*

14" Betsy McCall doll circa 1952 with a vinyl head, rooted hair, hard plastic body, closed mouth, and sleep eyes. The doll was designed by Bernard Lipfert in the image of the *McCall Magazine* Betsy McCall paper doll. She is marked on the back of her head "McCall Corp" and on her back, "Ideal Doll/P-90." She is all original. ($250 and up). *Doll and photograph from the collection of Leslie Robinson.*

Box for Ideal's 16" Mary Hartline doll. Label reads "The Pretty Princess of TV/Ideal Toy Corp." Mary appeared in the ABC television show "Super Circus." The doll was also made in a 23" size. *Box and photograph from the collection of Carol J. Lindeman.*

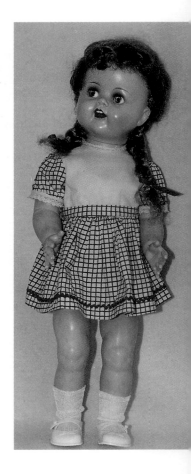

A catalog page from Herpolsheimer's in Grand Rapids, Michigan, in 1953 pictures six Ideal dolls popular at the time. The 14" hard plastic Miss Curity doll was dressed in a nurse's uniform and came with a variety of accessories in her first aid kit. She was priced at $11.95. Other dolls shown are the Harriet Hubbard Ayer makeup doll at $11.95, Magic Flesh Baby Doll at $7.98, Betsy McCall at $7.98, Toni Doll at $11.95, and Saucy Walker in the 24" size for $15.95. *Catalog from the collection of Marge Meisinger.*

14" hard plastic Miss Curity doll circa 1953. She has sleep eyes, closed mouth, and an applied wig. She is marked on the back of the head "Ideal Doll/Made in U.S.A." On the back of her body is "Ideal Doll/P-90." The body is the same as that used for the Toni Dolls. The doll is all original with her cape, hat, dress, and curlers. She is missing her first aid accessories. ($500 and up). *Doll and photograph from the collection of Peggy Millhouse.*

22" Saucy Walker first made in 1951. The doll is all hard plastic with an open mouth, flirty sleep eyes, a crier, and an applied wig. She is all original except her hair ribbons. She is marked "Ideal Doll" on the neck and back. The doll also came in a 16" size. She walks, and moves her head from side to side when her arms are held. ($125-150).

14" Harriet Hubbard Ayer doll marketed by Ideal in 1953. The doll was a tie-in to the cosmetic company of the same name. She has a vinyl head, plastic body, closed mouth, sleep eyes, and rooted hair. She came with a cardboard beauty table, curlers, and various cosmetics. On the back of her head is marked "MK-14/Ideal Doll." Little girls were to use the makeup on the doll and then wash it off so the doll could be made up again. She has long fingernails so they could be painted. ($300 and up). *Doll from the collection of Jan Clanton. Photograph by Darek Clanton.*

13" Betsy Wetsy doll circa 1954 in her original suitcase and dress. Other items originally came with the doll including a bottle, diaper, and soap. The doll has a hard plastic head, vinyl body, sleep eyes, and open mouth. She is a drink and wet doll. She is marked "Ideal Doll/Made in U.S.A." on her neck. ($85-125).

25" Magic Lips doll circa 1955. The doll has a vinyl head, arms, and legs, soft body, open mouth, sleep eyes, and rooted hair. When her back is pressed, she closes her lips and when released she opens her lips and makes a sound. The doll originally sold for $14.98. She is marked on the back "Ideal Doll/T-25." She is all original. ($75-85).

20" Miss Revlon in original condition. She is marked "Ideal Doll/VT-20" on the back of her head. Her dress tag reads "Revlon Doll by Ideal." She has a closed mouth, sleep eyes, swivel waist, no pierced ears, and rooted hair. Her nylon dress is decorated with hearts and she wears a rickrack trimmed slip, matching panties, hose and high heel shoes. The bottom of her original box is also shown. The Miss Revlon dolls were tied into the Revlon Cosmetic Company. ($250 and up).

16" Princess Mary doll circa 1955-1956. She has a stuffed vinyl head, hard plastic Toni Walker body, rooted hair, closed mouth, and sleep eyes. She is marked "Ideal Doll/V-87" on her head and "Ideal Doll/16" on her back. She is all original. ($85-125).

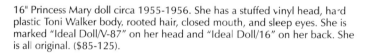

20" MIB Miss Revlon wearing "Cherries a la Mode" dress. This doll has pierced ears with pearl earrings. Her original price was $15.95. She is marked "VT20/Ideal Doll." ($300 and up). *Doll from the collection of Jan Clanton. Photograph by Darek Clanton.*

Left: 22.5" Miss Revlon circa 1956-1957. Made of vinyl with fashion body and arched feet. She is wearing a "Queen of Diamonds" outfit with rhinestone earrings. She is missing the fur stole. She is jointed at the waist. She is marked "VT-22/Ideal Doll." ($75-100 not completely original).

Right: 10.5" Little Miss Revlon dressed in Debutante Gown #9159 which originally sold for $4.50. (MIB dress only $45-55). *From the collection of Marge Meisinger.*

Advertisement in the Sears Christmas catalog for 1958 which features several of the Miss Revlon dolls. The dolls came in sizes of 15", 18", and 20". The doll wearing the outfit called "5th Avenue" has jointed knees and came only in the 20" size.

10.5" Little Miss Revlon dressed in nurse outfit #9256. Originally sold for $3.00. (Outfit $30-35). *From the collection of Marge Meisinger.*

Left: Little Miss Revlon Gift package contained a 10.5" vinyl doll plus four outfits. The doll had a jointed waist, arched feet, rooted hair, sleep eyes, and pierced ears. Marked on the head: "VT-10 1/2". This set originally sold for $10. ($225 and up). *From the collection of Marge Meisinger.*

Left: Two more Little Miss Revlon dresses are modeled here. The dress on the left is Pinafore #9127 and sold for $3.00. The School Dress on the right is #9114 and sold for $1.50 in the original brochure. The dresses are tagged "Ideal Toy Corp./ Hollis, N.Y." Forty-six outfits were pictured in this brochure. ($30-35 each dress). *From the collection of Marge Meisinger.*

Advertisement from the Sears Christmas catalog in 1958 which pictured the Little Miss Revlon doll and several of her costumes. The clothes were priced from 88 cents to $1.79 each.

21" vinyl Baby Coos all original with box. The doll has sleep eyes and molded hair. It was pictured in the Sears Christmas catalog in 1957 and was priced at $6.97. It also came in sizes of 19" and 24". ($100-125).

Little Miss Revlon's Formal Series as featured in the company brochure. The gowns were priced from $4.00 to $4.50 each.

35" Ideal Patti Play Pals first sold in 1959. The vinyl dolls are the size of a three-year-old child. They are marked "Ideal Doll/ G 35." The dolls have sleep eyes, rooted hair, closed mouths and are all original. ($300 and up). *From the collection of Edith M. Wise. Photograph by James Wise.*

Sears Christmas catalog for 1959 featured several of the Ideal big dolls including Patty Play Pals, Penny Play Pal, and Suzy Play Pal. A doll the size of a three-month-old baby girl was also available but was not pictured. The large dolls sold for $23.75 while the 29" size was priced at $16.95, and the baby was $12.97. *Catalog from the collection of Betty Nichols.*

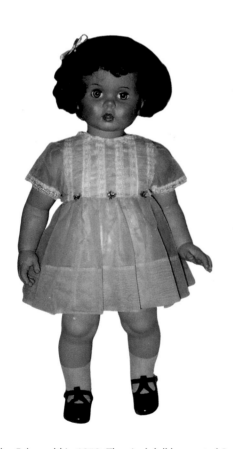

32" Penny Play Pal as sold in 1959. The vinyl doll has rooted Saran hair and sleep eyes. She was advertised as being the size of a two-year-old child. She is marked "Ideal Doll/32-E-L" on her head. She also has "Ideal" in an oval on her back. She is wearing her original dress but her shoes have been replaced. ($250 and up). *From the collection of Edith M. Wise. Photograph by James Wise.*

Mary Hoyer Doll Manufacturing Co.

Mary Hoyer began her career designing children's fashions that were to be knitted or crocheted by consumers. Soon the company, located in Reading, Pennsylvania, began selling undressed dolls along with patterns for clothing to be made at home. According to Mary Hoyer in her book *Mary Hoyer and Her Dolls*, the first dolls marketed in 1935 were composition body twist models which had been produced by Ideal Novelty and Toy Co. These dolls were to be discontinued by Ideal so Mary Hoyer bought the remaining stock to begin her doll enterprise. When these dolls sold well, Hoyer contacted famous doll designer Bernard Lipfert and hired him to design a doll for the Hoyer Company. The doll was a 14" tall slim girl model with a closed mouth. It was produced by the Fiberoid Doll Co. The doll was sold either undressed or with clothes made by the Mary Hoyer Co.

When hard plastic dolls became fashionable in 1946 the **Mary Hoyer** dolls were then produced of this new material. These dolls were also 14" tall with sleep eyes, a closed mouth, and an applied wig. On the back of each doll was the Mary Hoyer trademark inside a circle. The dolls were sold mainly through mail order and the company's advertising appeared in many of the popular ladies' magazines of the time.

As styles in dolls changed during the 1950s, the Hoyer company marketed new dolls to meet the competition from other firms. Some of the designs were sold only for a short time while others proved successful and were kept in the Hoyer line for years.

One of the most desirable Hoyer dolls for today's collector is the **Gigi** doll dating from 1954. The doll was 18" tall, made of hard plastic, and featured a glued on wig, closed mouth, and sleep eyes. She sold for $6.96 undressed when new. The doll was produced by the Frisch Doll Co. and according to the Hoyer Company, only 2,000 were made. The doll is clearly marked as a Hoyer doll exactly in the same manner as the 14" dolls. Although the variety of costumes was not as plentiful as those made for the 14" dolls, there were several outfits for Gigi that were produced by the Hoyer firm. Included were several designs of evening gowns (one was the popular Dolly Madi-

son number), a bridal gown, ballerina costume, pajamas, pleated skirt, sweater, shorts, slacks, shirt, halter top, cotton dress, bathing suit, fur cape, and many accessories. The doll was not kept in the Hoyer line for long and it is extremely scarce today.

According to information included in the Hoyer book, other dolls were also added to the Hoyer line during the mid-1950s. Included was a **20" doll** that was produced by Ideal for the Hoyer Co. This doll had a vinyl head with rooted hair styled in a pony tail, bending knees, and arched feet to wear high heel shoes. The doll sold for $6.95. This doll was also soon dropped from the Hoyer line.

The **Vicky** doll was introduced in 1957 and was also made by Ideal. At first the doll came in three sizes, 10.5", 12", and 14". Soon the two larger sizes were dropped and only the 10.5" doll was continued. The dolls were made of vinyl with rooted hair, arched feet, and could bend from the waist.

By 1958 a 10" all vinyl **Margie** toddler doll joined the line. She, too, had rooted hair and sleep eyes. In 1960 an infant vinyl doll called **Cathy** was offered. She was 10" tall with molded hair and sleep eyes. An 8" **Jamie** baby doll was also sold during this time.

In the early 1960s, the Hoyer Company discontinued the 14" hard plastic doll. The new doll used to replace the popular 14" child doll was a vinyl doll called **Becky**.

Although the dolls were a big part of the Mary Hoyer business, most of the profits came from the sale of the clothing and patterns designed for the dolls. The firm sold finished costumes, kits that included materials to make the clothing for the dolls, and booklets called "Mary's Dollies" that included patterns to make outfits for the various dolls. The company also marketed many accessories for their dolls including trunks, shoes, socks, glasses, skis, skates, wigs, and much more.

The Hoyers retired in 1972 but they were not forgotten by the doll world. In 1992 Mary Hoyer was honored with a Lifetime Achievement Award presented by the International Doll Academy and the *Doll Reader* magazine.

Right: The cover of an undated catalog from the Mary Hoyer Doll Mfg. Co. in Reading, Pennsylvania, pictures the fancy Dolly Madison dress along with its matching parasol. The company also sold wardrobe trunks to hold the many outfits designed for the dolls.

14" hard plastic Mary Hoyer walking doll with unusual pigtail hair style along with several of her original outfits made from the patterns offered by the Hoyer company. These dolls are marked in a circle "Original Mary Hoyer Doll." The dolls have sleep eyes, closed mouths, and applied wigs. (Dressed doll $400-425, each outfit made from original pattern $35-45). *Doll and clothing from the collection of Carol J. Lindeman.*

Besides sewing kits, the Hoyer company also marketed crochet kits that offered materials and instructions to produce the clothing shown in their catalogs. Pictured are a skating costume for Olga, a majorette outfit for Maybelle, and a coat and hat called "short and sweet" for Connie.

The last style of clothing kits offered for the 14" hard plastic dolls were those that were to be knitted. Pictured are a bathing ensemble for Arlene, a riding habit for Billie, a skiing costume for Anita, a Red Cross Nurse for Nadine, a roller skating outfit for Lucille, and cowboy and cowgirl costumes for Nancy and Dick.

The Hoyer company offered kits that contained all the materials needed to complete their various costume designs. The outfits were already cut out and ready to be sewed. Pictured are the Bride's Kit, Bride's Maid Kit, and the Ballerina Kit. In another Hoyer publication from the period, the Ballerina Kit was priced at $1.25.

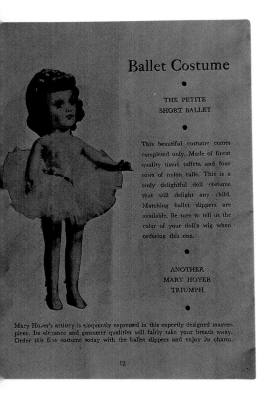

In addition to the other offerings, the Hoyer firm sold some costumes already made. Pictured is the short Ballet Costume sold only this way. It was made of taffeta and nylon tulle. In addition to clothing the firm also sold accessories which included all kinds of footwear (from boots to ballet slippers), hats (even rubber bathing caps), underwear, latex bathing suits, girdles, and wigs.

14' matching groom also all original with his box. The boy dolls were the same basic Hoyer doll with male clothing and a short haircut added. ($600 and up). *Doll from the collection of Jan Clanton. Photograph by Darek Clanton.*

14" hard plastic Mary Hoyer doll dressed in another style crocheted skating costume that also includes a small purse and fancy stockings. (Dressed doll $400 and up). *Doll and photograph from the collection of Marge Meisinger.*

14' Mary Hoyer doll dressed in a three-piece crocheted costume made from one of the Hoyer patterns. The copy from the company publication called "Mary's Dollies" Volume No. 5 says that the doll is on her way to the race track at Santa Anita but the costume really appears to be more appropriate for skating. Skates not original. (Costume only $35-40).

14" hard plastic strung Mary Hoyer Bride all original with her box. A so pictured is a paper signed by the maker, Mary Hoyer. ($500 and up). *Doll and photograph from the collection of Carol J. Lindeman.*

14" hard plastic Mary Hoyer doll modeling two pieces of the Bonnie Lassie ensemble by Mary Hoyer. The kit sold for $1.95. The completed costume was priced at $3.95 and included a handbag. The handbag could also be purchased separately for 59 cents. (Costume $35-45).

18" Gigi hard plastic doll marketed by Hoyer in 1954. The doll has sleep eyes, closed mouth, and an applied wig. She is marked "Original/Mary Hoyer/Doll" in a circle on her back. She is dressed in an original Hoyer pattern dress. ($700 and up). *Doll from the collection of Sidney Jeffrey. Photograph by Peggy Millhouse.*

Right: 14" vinyl fashion doll that came in the pictured original box along with the Mary Hoyer Vicky Doll pamphlet. The doll pictured in the pamphlet was only 10.5" tall. It is known that originally the Vicky doll was sold in three sizes including 12" and 14". Ideal made these dolls for the Hoyer company. The pictured doll is made of a heavy vinyl like the Ideal Miss Revlon dolls. She has rooted hair, sleep eyes, pierced ears, and a closed mouth. She bends at the waist. She is dressed in her original clothing. (Boxed original doll $200-225).

14" hard plastic Mary Hoyer doll dressed in fancy summer formal trimmed with lace and flowers. She also wears a matching slip. She carries the Mary Hoyer mark in a circle on her back. ($350-400).

Nancy Ann Storybook Dolls, Inc.

Nancy Ann Storybook Dolls, Inc. was incorporated in 1945. It had earlier been founded by Nancy Ann Abbott (real name Rowena Haskins) as the Nancy Ann Dressed Dolls Co. in 1936. Her partner, Les Rowland, joined her in the business in 1937.

The early dolls of the firm were beautifully dressed figures of painted bisque. The dolls were produced at potteries in California, then they were completed and dressed at the company's plant in San Francisco. Nancy Ann Abbott headed the design end of the business while Rowland handled the business side.

In 1948, the company followed the lead of other doll manufacturers and began producing the dolls in hard plastic. At first the dolls had painted eyes but around 1950 the doll designs were modified to include sleeping eyes. The dolls ranged in size from 3.5" to 7". They were jointed at the shoulders and hips and the larger dolls were also jointed at the neck.

Perhaps the most collectible of all the Nancy Ann Dolls are those called **Nancy Ann Style Show Dolls**. These dolls came on the market in the fashion of all the early hard plastic dolls, with the bodies of young girls. In spite of that, the clothing designs for the dolls were quite grown up. The elaborate dresses included ball gowns and fancy designs based on the clothes of the last century. The dolls were 18" tall and featured saran wigs and sleep eyes. The Style Show dolls were probably only produced from 1952 until 1955. The first dolls were non-walkers while the dolls from 1954 feature a walking mechanism. In 1955 a few vinyl head dolls were made. These are very rare. Style show dolls were quite expensive and some models sold for $24.95 at FAO Schwarz in 1953. None of the style show dolls are featured in brochures of the late 1950s so it is probable that production ceased in 1955.

As the doll market changed in the 1950s to focus on dolls with extensive wardrobes, the Nancy Ann Corporation followed the trend by expanding their market to include this type of doll. Since the company had always been known for its lovely doll clothing, it was to be expected that Nancy Ann Abbott would enter the competition by making beautiful costumes to accompany the new dolls.

The first doll of this type to be marketed by the firm was the hard plastic **Muffie** doll first produced in 1953. The doll was 8" tall and the first models were produced in a straight leg strung design. Most of the dolls were sold dressed in only panties, shoes, and socks. The customer was expected to purchase the clothing from the many Nancy Ann designs that were available each year.

In 1954 Muffie became a "Walker" and also acquired molded eye lashes. By 1956 Nancy Ann followed the trend of other doll manufacturers and gave Muffie bending knees. In order to meet the competition from other manufacturers of 8" dolls, in 1956 customers were given a choice of four differently constructed Muffie dolls. The dolls were produced as all hard plastic models with either straight legs or bending knees; or they could be purchased with vinyl heads which included either the straight leg or the bending knee model bodies.

By 1957 an all vinyl Muffie walker doll was being advertised by the company. The doll featured the new rooted hair. Since the Muffy dolls were not marked and tags are sometimes missing from the original clothing, collectors may need help in identifying their dolls. A self-published book called *The Muffie Puzzle* by Lillian Roth and Heather Browning Maciak may help. This book contains lots of Nancy Ann original advertising and colored photographs of many original Muffie dolls with clothing identification.

By the late 1950s (circa 1958) an 8" doll called **Lori Ann** was featured in the company brochure along with the new Miss Nancy Ann doll.

Both the Lori Ann vinyl dolls and the vinyl Muffie dolls look alike and only the original boxes can identify the different dolls. Some hard plastic dolls have also been found in original boxes which identify them as Lori Ann models. Since these later dolls were produced after the onset of illnesses to both of the company founders, it may be that dolls were produced with a "mix and match" method in order to use up spare parts that were on hand.

Although Nancy Ann Abbott had been diagnosed with cancer in 1956, new dolls from the organization continued to make their appearance on the doll market for the next several years.

These dolls, for the most part, followed the leader (Vogue Dolls, Inc.) as styles of dolls were copied by one manufacturer from another.

The Nancy Ann Corporation's strong suit had always been in the dressing of dolls so many of the later dolls used by the company were blanks produced by other manufacturers to be dressed by the Nancy Ann firm.

By 1955, besides the popular Muffie doll, the Nancy Ann company was also offering the new 10 1/2" hard plastic **Debbie** walker doll. Most of the new costumes made by the company were produced in both Debbie and Muffie sizes. The Debbie doll did not prove to be as popular as the earlier Muffie and was only retained in the firm's line for a few years. The Debbie doll was also produced with a vinyl head before it was dropped.

The company next introduced a small 9" tall baby doll called **Sue Sue**. The all vinyl doll had sleep eyes and molded hair. This doll (circa 1956) was modified later with the addition of rooted hair.

As the popularity of dolls like Ideal's Little Miss Revlon continued to grow, the Nancy Ann Company again added dolls to its line in order to compete in the teen-aged glamour girl market. Their first doll of this type (circa 1958) was called **Miss Nancy Ann**. The all vinyl doll was 10.5" tall, jointed at neck, shoulders, and hips with feet molded in the "high heel" style. Another similar doll was added circa 1959 that was only 8" tall. She was called **Little Miss Nancy Ann** and was also an all vinyl model with feet made to accommodate high heel shoes.

A brochure from the period features Miss Nancy Ann, Little Miss Nancy Ann, Muffie, and Sue Sue. Many of the clothing items could be purchased in the same styles for all the dolls except Sue Sue. The baby doll was shown with hair and was no longer pictured with molded hair at this time.

As the decade of the 1950s drew to a close, so did the success of the Nancy Ann Storybook Company. According to Marjorie A. Miller writing in her book *Nancy Ann Storybook Dolls* the business moved to smaller quarters in San Francisco in 1961 as its owners' health problems continued to escalate. Nancy Ann died in 1965 and Lee moved the company into bankruptcy in 1965, after a search to find a buyer was unsuccessful. Eventually the assets were purchased by Albert M. Bourla and he brought out a new "Muffie Around the World" series in 1967. There were twelve dolls in the series.

Despite the hardships endured by Nancy Ann Abbott during the last years of her life, collectors will continue to remember her because of the beautiful doll clothing she designed. The products of Nancy Ann Storybook Dolls, Inc. remain near the top in popularity with today's collectors of 1950s dolls and accessories.

Around 1950 the Nancy Ann Storybook dolls began featuring sleeping eyes. At first the eyes had no pupils but later dolls were modified to include a pupil. Pictured is a Nancy Ann Storybook hard plastic Christening baby #70. The jointed doll is 3.5" tall, has sleep eyes with no pupils (circa 1950), and is all original. The doll is marked "Storybook//Dolls//U.S.A.//Trademark//Reg//" as are all these later dolls. ($75-85).

The first plastic Nancy Ann Storybook dolls were made in 1948. These dolls had painted eyes. Pictured is a black Topsy doll from the Fairytale Series (#26) that dates from this time period. Her arms, legs, and neck are jointed. She stands 5.5" tall and is completely original with her wrist tag. She also has her box and brochure. ($125-135).

Two different all original Nancy Ann hard plastic First Birthday dolls #71. Both dolls have sleep eyes and wear diapers to make them appear to be toddlers. The dolls are 4.5" tall. ($100-125 each). *Dolls and photograph from the collection of Jackie Robertson.*

Nancy Ann hard plastic all original First Day of School doll, #72. The doll is 5.5" tall and has sleep eyes. ($85 and up). *Doll and photograph from the collection of Jackie Robertson.*

Nancy Ann hard plastic all original First Communion doll, #73. The doll is 5.5" tall and has sleep eyes. ($145 and up). *Doll and photograph from the collection of Jackie Robertson.*

Nancy Ann hard plastic all original Graduation doll, #74. The doll is 6.5" tall and has sleep eyes. ($125 and up). *Doll and photograph from the collection of Jackie Robertson.*

Nancy Ann Style Show strung doll from 1952. These beautiful dolls were sold by Nancy Ann for only a few years. They were made of all hard plastic with sleep eyes, closed mouths, and beautiful clothing. The dolls are 18" tall and have little girl bodies with flat feet as opposed to feet shaped for high heel shoes. Pictured is the doll named Gay Evening #2902. She originally sold for $29.95. She is all original with her tag. ($650 and up). *Doll and photograph from the collection of Jackie Robertson.*

Nancy Ann hard plastic all original Debut doll, #75. The doll is 6.5" tall and has sleep eyes. ($125 and up). *Doll and photograph from the collection of Jackie Robertson.*

Another Style Show doll pictured in the brochure from 1952. This one is #1902 Heavenly Blue. She is all original with her tag and first sold for $19.95. These were blank dolls purchased by the Nancy Ann Company to be dressed and marketed by Nancy Ann. ($650 and up). *Doll and photograph from the collection of Jackie Robertson.*

Below: Nancy Ann hard plastic all original wedding party. Group includes bride, groom, bridesmaids, flower girl, and ring bearer. All have sleeping eyes. (Set $550 and up). *Dolls and photograph from the collection of Jackie Robertson.*

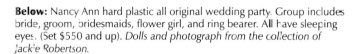

Pictured is Style Show Doll #1901 Afternoon Tea. This original strung doll is also circa 1952. She sold for $19.95 in the company brochure. ($500 and up). *Doll and photograph from the collection of Jan Clanton. Photograph by Darek Clanton.*

The Style Show dolls are not marked and the dolls, themselves, were probably used by other companies as well. This early model is #1904 and is called Garden Party. She is circa 1952 and is all original. She originally sold for $19.95. ($500 and up). *Doll and photograph from the collection of Carol J. Lindeman.*

This original doll is also one of the strung dolls circa 1952 and she is #1903 Demure Miss. She cost $19.95 when new. ($500 and up).

This early Style Show doll circa 1952 is called Lilac Time #1504 and she is all original. She was priced at $15.95. ($500 and up). *Doll and photograph from the collection of Carol J. Lindeman.*

These Style Show dolls were pictured in the company brochure which came with "Demure Miss." It is circa 1952. Included were #1501 Summery Day, #1502 Breath of Spring, #1504 Lilac Time, and #1901 Afternoon Tea.

Other Style Show dolls pictured in the brochure include #1902 Heavenly Blue, #1903 Demure Miss, #1904 Garden Party, #2401 Moonlight Mist, #2402 Dinner Date, and #2403 Sweet and Lovely.

In the same brochure are pictured #2404 Sophistication, #2901 Grand Bal, #2902 Gay Evening, #2903 Opera Night, #2904 Wedding Day, #3401 Her Royal Majesty Wedding, and #1503 Enchantment. The dolls were priced from $15.95 to $34.95.

Style Show #1503 Summer Resort also is a strung doll circa 1953. She is all original. ($600 and up). *Doll and photograph from the collection of Jackie Robertson.*

Another original strung Style Show doll circa 1953. It is #2903 and is called Roses in Bloom. She also includes her tag. ($600 and up). *Doll and photograph from the collection of Carol J. Lindeman.*

Tea Roses is another of the strung Style Show dolls circa 1953. ($500 and up). *Doll from the collection of Jan Clanton. Photograph by Darek Clanton.*

Another style show doll from this same time period is #1904 Lawn Party. Many of the dolls pictured here still have their original name tags as does this doll. ($650 and up). *Doll and photograph from the collection of Jackie Robertson.*

In 1954 the design of the Style Show dolls was changed to include a walking mechanism. This #2401 Gaiety doll from that year was labeled a walker in the company brochure. She is all original with her tag. ($650 and up). *Doll and photograph from the collection of Jackie Robertson.*

The brochure for the Style Show dolls circa 1954 included #1501 Miss Checker Board, #1502 Pinkie, #1503 White Lilacs, and #1504 Strawberry Festival.

Other Style Show dolls circa 1954 included #1901 Miss Pinafore, #1902 Golden Gleam, #1903 Summer Afternoon, #1904 Sweet Miss, #2401 Gaiety, and #2402 Pink Pearl.

The rest of the Style Show dolls pictured in the brochure circa 1954 were #2403 Senior Prom, #2404 Lace Butterflies, #2901 Beautiful Lady, #2902 Forget-me-not, #2903 Dinner Dance, and #2904 Bride. All of these hard plastic dolls were walkers.

Before the Nancy Ann Corporation deleted the beautiful style show dolls from their line, they included some dolls with vinyl heads. Pictured is one of those dolls circa 1955. This is a strung doll, not a walker. (Not enough examples to determine a price). *Doll and photograph from the collection of Carol J. Lindeman.*

Strung 8" hard plastic Margie made by the Nancy Ann Storybook Co. in 1953. In this first year, the dolls were given three names: Margie, Muffie, or Missie. This doll is pictured with her original Margie box and brochure and is wearing a dress from the Dress-Up Styles series #603. The dolls were advertised as Playtime Dolls and were usually sold in panties, shoes, and socks. There were fifty-three costumes made for the dolls in 1953. The dolls had painted lashes and no eyebrows. (MIB $250). *Doll and photograph from the collection of Carol J. Lindeman.*

In 1954 the Nancy Ann 8" dolls were all issued as walkers and each of the dolls was identified as "Muffie." Many more new costumes were designed for the new line. Shown is #607 on the left. This design was the one chosen by the company to use on its business card as pictured. The doll on the right is wearing dress #608 but she is missing her blue straw hat. Molded eyelashes were also added to the dolls in 1954. ($150-175 each). *Dolls and photograph from the collection of Jackie Robertson.*

Also from 1953 is this Muffie doll wearing costume #512 from the Nursery Styles series. These early costumes are fastened with plain brass snaps. The dolls are marked "Storybook//Dolls//California." ($150-175). *Doll and photograph from the collection of Jackie Robertson.*

Another original Muffie doll is pictured wearing costume #603 from the 1954 brochure. ($150-175). *Doll and photograph from the collection of Jackie Robertson.*

Muffie bride and groom. The bride dates from 1954 while the Bridegroom has painted eyebrows which were first used in 1955. The veil is a replacement. (Bride $150, Groom $175).

This lovely blonde strung Muffie was also featured in the 1953 brochure. She wears costume #903. ($175-200). *Doll and photograph from the collection of Jackie Robertson.*

muffie's favorite fashions

THEY WALK!

601   602   603   604   605   606   607   608

muffie's dress-up styles

THEY WALK!

701   702   703   704   705   706   707   708

muffie's special occasion styles

THEY WALK!

801   802   803   804   805   806   807   808

Muffies as pictured in the 1954 brochure. Costumes included a ski outfit, ballerina, nightwear, play time, school and party dresses.

The 1954 brochure also pictured a trunk and wardrobe for Muffie. The trunk included a circus motif on the inside. ($200). *Trunk and photograph from the collection of Jackie Robertson.*

This wardrobe circa 1954 is furnished with items representing what originally came in it it, but they are not original to this case. A wardrobe which includes the original contents is rare. *Wardrobe and photograph from the collection of Jackie Robertson.*

3—"Muffie," Nancy Ann Story Book
l. Dynel hair you wash, comb,
l. Sits, stands, walks. 1.59
y "Muffie" undressed and dress her
the many costumes shown here:

B83—Daytime costume, pants, hair
ribbon, shoes, socks, etc. 1.50
C83—Organdy costume. Dress with
all accessories: straw hat, shoes,
socks, etc. 1.98

D83—Robe and nightgown costume
with pompon slippers. 2.50
E83—Ballet costume, silver shoes. 2.50
F83—Raincoat costume with dress,
overshoes, other accessories. 2.98

A   B   C   D   E   F

G. Fox and Co. featured Muffie dolls and costumes in their 1955 catalog. The undressed doll sold for $1.59 and her clothes were priced from $1.50 to $2.98. Included were school and party dresses, nightwear, ballerina costume, and a raincoat. *Catalog from the collection of Marge Meisinger.*

she'll adore "Muffie" and her night-and-day wardrobe

Hours of fun for little busybodies with 8" tall "Muffie", from Nancy Ann's story book, and her own doll-size furniture by Strombecker. She's a washable, plastic charmer who sits, stands, walks—has blonde, brunette or honey color Saran hair that washes, combs, curls.
A83—Buy basic "Muffie" with undies, socks and shoes. **1.59**
There's no limit to the fun of dressing "Muffie" in one of these fashions: (Following prices for outfits only)
B83—Crisp, puffy confection in yellow striped taffeta, lavished with lace. **1.98**
C83—Frothy lace negligee and gown. **2.50**
D83—Real nurse's uniform. **1.98**
E83—Picture-pretty pink party coat and hat, soft, furry angora trim. **2.98**
F83—Bridal outfit, all the trimmings. **3.50**
Furniture for "Muffie"
G83—Wardrobe, finished hardwood, clothes rod, shelf, 10" high. **2.98**
H83—Bunk beds, finished hardwood, use as separate beds. 10½" high. **2.98**
J83—Bedding for bunk beds, pillows, mattresses, coverlets. Set. **2.98**
K83—Rocker, hardwood, 6" high. **1.89**

her "Littlest Angel" changes moods with each new mode

G. Fox and Co. from Hartford, Connecticut, also featured the Muffy dolls in their 1956 catalog. A nurse's outfit and a bridal dress were also part of the line in that year. The pictured furniture was made by Strombecker. *Catalog from the collection of Marge Meisinger.*

Hard plastic Debbie is marked "Nancy Ann" on the back of her head. She is wearing a costume from 1956 #654. The boxed outfit pictured with her is a Debbie lounging pajamas set #805. (Dressed doll $90-110, clothes $40-50). *Boxed set from the collection of Marge Meisinger.*

In 1955 a 10.5" tall hard plastic toddler doll was introduced by the Nancy Ann company. The sleeping eyed walking doll was called Debbie. Most of the clothes designed for this doll were also made in a smaller Muffie size as well. Pictured are Muffie and Debbie dolls dressed in matching outfits #802 from 1955. ($350 pair). *Dolls and photograph from the collection of Jackie Robertson.*

The Nancy Ann Debbie groom was the same doll without a wig and dressed as a male. The same practice was followed in making the Muffie grooms also. ($350). *Doll and photograph from the collection of Jackie Robertson.*

Two mint-in-box Debbie costumes from 1955 are shown. The two coats, hats, and dresses are #810 and #812 (royal blue coat). ($40-50 each costume). *Clothes from the collection of Marge Meisinger.*

Hard plastic Muffie and Debbie wearing identical #907 nurse outfits from 1956. (Debbie $200, Muffie $175-200). *Dolls and photographs from the collection of Jackie Robertson.*

Another mint Debbie with vinyl head pictured with Muffie. Both are wearing bridesmaids dresses #902 dating from 1956. ($450 a pair). *Dolls and photograph from the collection of Jackie Robertson.*

Later Debbie (circa 1956) with vinyl head, hard plastic body with bending knees, rooted hair, and sleep eyes. She is marked "Nancy Ann" on the back of her head. She is pictured with her original box and an outfit #3705 dating from 1955. (Doll $75-100, outfit $40-50). *Clothes from the collection of Marge Meisinger.*

This Muffie circa 1956 featured a vinyl head with a hard plastic body and bending knees. The back of the head is marked "Nancy Ann." The printing on the body says "Storybook//Dolls//California//Muffie." The original box is also shown. Her dress is pictured in the Lori Ann section of the Nancy Ann brochure circa 1958 and is #9504. ($100 and up).

Three hard plastic Muffie dolls circa 1958. These dolls were all sold in starter sets. The boxes were marked "Muffie Starter Set/1 Muffie Walking Doll, 1 Muffie Dress/Both for $1.98." The dolls feature saran wigs. The dresses are snapped with large gripper snaps. ($150 and up each). *Dolls and photograph from the collection of Jackie Robertson.*

A different style Muffie Trunk was also offered by the Nancy Ann Company. It used the famous dot motif for the inside decoration. ($135 and up). *Trunk and photograph from the collection of Jackie Robertson.*

The Lori-Ann dolls came with three hair-dos, "Dutch Cut, Top Tie and Long Locks." The company brochure pictures thirty different costumes for the doll including those shown.

MIB Lori Ann doll made by Nancy Ann circa 1958. The 8" doll is all vinyl. She is marked "Nancy Ann" on the back of her head and also "Nancy Ann" on the back of her body. Her dress (not original to the doll as she was sold in panties, shoes, and socks) tag reads "Styled by//Nancy Ann//San Francisco, Calif." The later large gripper snap is used to fasten the dress. Her box retains the original price tag of $2. ($150 and up).

This vinyl Lori Ann doll is wearing an original bridal gown with a replaced veil. The dolls all have rooted hair and sleep eyes. ($50-75).

Right: Miss Nancy Ann, an all vinyl teenage fashion doll was marketed by the Nancy Ann Company beginning around 1958. The 10.5" tall doll was jointed at the waist, shoulders, and hips. She wore earrings, had rooted hair, sleep eyes, and feet molded to fit the high heel shoes then so popular for fashion dolls. Also pictured is her box, and a sundress with its original box. The dress is circa 1958 and is #930. The doll is marked "Nancy Ann" on the back of her head. The dress tag reads "Styled by Nancy Ann/Nancy Ann Storybook Dolls Inc./San Francisco, California." (Doll $100 and up, MIB dress $40-50).

The 1959 Sears Christmas catalog featured the Miss Nancy Ann doll with a complete wardrobe. The package sold for $7.87. Included were a sundress, party dress, pajamas, coat and hat, and accessories. *Catalog from the collection of Betty Nichols.*

In keeping with the styles of the day, Miss Nancy Ann was also costumed as a ballerina. This outfit also circa 1958-59 is #347. ($135 and up). *Doll and photograph from the collection of Jackie Robertson.*

The Nancy Ann Company continued to produce the clothing in styles that could be adapted to several dolls in their line. Pictured are Muffie and Miss Nancy Ann wearing dresses circa 1959 probably #502. ($125 and up each). *Dolls and photograph from the collection of Jackie Robertson*

Pictured is a MIB Miss Nancy Ann (#319) dating from the late 1950s. ($185 and up). *Doll and photograph from the collection of Jackie Robertson.*

Another beautiful mint Miss Nancy Ann is pictured as a bride wearing #342 circa 1958-1959. ($225). *Doll and photograph from the collection of Jackie Robertson.*

This company brochure pictured forty-five different costumes for the Miss Nancy Ann doll. Included were outfits for skiing, skating, shopping, and parties.

With the addition of the Little Miss Nancy Ann doll, clothes continued to be made in various sizes to fit the different dolls. Pictured are both the Little Miss and the Miss Nancy Ann dolls in identical nurse outfits #346 circa 1959. ($135 large, $150 small). *Dolls and photograph from the collection of Jackie Robertson.*

Left: With the success shown by sales of the Miss Nancy Ann doll, the company marketed a smaller similar doll circa 1959. The 8" doll was called Little Miss Nancy Ann. She wore no earrings and did not feature a bending waist. Pictured is a MIB doll as well as a MIB outfit. (MIB doll $125 and up, outfit $40-50).

Another beautiful Little Miss Nancy Ann wearing her original costume circa 1959 #322. ($135-145). *Doll and photograph from the collection of Jackie Robertson.*

Little Miss Nancy Ann and Miss Nancy Ann again pictured in identical red and white dresses #305 circa 1959. The hats have been added. Both of these dolls were made in two different styles of vinyl. Some had very hard vinyl arms while others featured soft vinyl arms. The 8" dolls were not marked so unless they are wearing tagged clothing, it is difficult to identify them.($125 each).

Two more Little Miss Nancy Ann 8" dolls in original clothing with added hats. Most of the dresses for these dolls were made very simply. ($100-125 each). *Dolls and photograph from the collection of Jackie Robertson.*

Nancy Ann Baby Sue Sue circa 1957. Marked "Nancy Ann" on neck. Wearing outfit #905. The doll has molded hair and sleep eyes and is jointed at shoulders and hips. ($200 and up). *Doll and photograph from the collection of Jackie Robertson.*

Little Miss Nancy Ann wearing outfit #408X which was MIB. She also has her purse. (MIB outfit only $45-50).

Baby Sue Sue wearing original clothing. The doll is 9" tall and has molded hair and sleep eyes. ($150-200). *Doll and photograph from the collection of Jackie Robertson.*

Later Sue Sue doll which features rooted hair. There is no mark on the doll but she wears an original dress. The Sue Sue doll with hair is circa 1959. ($125-135). *Doll and photograph from the collection of Jackie Robertson.*

Richwood Toy Co.

8" hard plastic Sandra Sue doll marketed by the Richwood Toy Co. circa 1953. In 1954 forty different costumes were sold for the dolls. This doll is all original with her tag. The dolls had sleep eyes, closed mouths, and applied wigs. Sandra Sue was a much slimmer doll than the Vogue Ginny dolls. ($150 and up). *Doll and photograph from the collection of Peggy Millhouse.*

Richwood Toy Co. was a small family operation which started in the late 1940s when Ida Wood began dressing and selling small dolls from her home in Larchmont, New York.

In 1948 the operation was moved to Highland, Maryland, where business improved when FAO Schwarz became a customer.

According to Marian Schmuhl in her article "The Richmond Toy Co." in the October 1991 issue of *Doll Reader*, Hungarian sculptor Agop Agopoff built the molds for the 8" **Sandra Sue** dolls in 1952. At first the hard plastic dolls had flat feet and were non-walkers. Later the dolls were changed to walking models. By 1956 the small dolls were being made with arched feet to wear high heels. Ida Wood continued to design the clothes for the new dolls.

Ida Wood's son, Jerry, began designing the popular wood furniture to accompany the dolls in 1952. According to Schmuhl, the furniture pieces included a tester bed, wardrobe, dining room table and chairs, bureau, high boy, twin beds, vanity, sand box, slide, and swing.

After moving to larger quarters in 1953, the firm began marketing more products. Although Richwood did not produce any more original doll designs, the company did market two more dolls. The firm purchased blank dolls at wholesale prices and then finished the dolls themselves. The Richwood dolls had hand painted eyebrows, eyelashes, and lips. The firm also made their own saran wigs as well as clothing for the dolls. The 14" **Cindy Lou** dolls were made in this way. The hard plastic dolls were not marked by the company and many seem to be made from the same mold as the Mary Hoyer dolls except the Cindy Lou dolls were pin jointed walkers. Other dolls dressed in Cindy Lou clothing have been found that are marked R&B so it is possible that Richwood purchased dolls from that company as well. Cindy Lou furniture included only a bed.

An 8" **Tina Sue** baby doll was also issued by Richwood in the late 1950s. The doll was made of vinyl and a cradle was sold to accompany it.

The Richwood Company was always a family operation with Ida Wood designing the doll's clothing and son Jerry working as the sales representative. The small firm had difficulty competing with the larger toy companies and it closed its doll operation, then located in Annapolis, Maryland, in late 1958. Ida Wood died in 1991.

The clothes for the Sandra Sue dolls were packaged in dress bags as pictured. This jeans outfit came in the bag and originally sold for 59 cents. The shoes for the Sandra Sue dolls were quite unusual and are hard to find. (MIP outfit only $30-40).

Al original "Heidi" Sandra Sue. The dolls are unmarked. ($175 and up). *Doll and photograph from the collection of Marge Meisinger.*

8" Sandra Sue in her original clothing and shoes. ($150 and up). *Doll and photograph from the collection of Marge Meisinger.*

Right: Sandra Sue wearing an original summer print dress with her original tag. ($150 and up). *Doll and photograph from the collection of Peggy Millhouse.*

Richwood Toys marketed this wardrobe as part of its Sandra Sue furniture line. The doll pictured is the Sandra Sue doll with flat feet instead of the high heel model. (Wardrobe $100 and up).

Advertisement in the Strawbridge and Clothier catalog from Philadelphia in 1956. The undressed doll with arched feet for high heel shoes sold for $1.98. Her costume was priced at $2.50. The skier outfit was $2.50. The 8" baby Tina Sue doll made of vinyl was priced at $2.98. Her sleeper cost $1.00. Richwood furniture was also shown. Included was the canopy bed for $5.98 and the cradle for $4.98. *Catalog from the collection of Marge Meisinger.*

This Sandra Sue dining room chair was made by Richwood to accompany their Duncan Phyfe table. ($50 and up with box). See Alexander chapter for another picture of Richwood furniture. *Chair and photograph from the collection of Marian Schmuhl.*

Richwood Toys, Inc. produced mahogany furniture to be used by their 8" Sandra Sue dolls. This tester bed with canopy is one of their products. ($100 and up). *Bed and photograph from the collection of Marian Schmuhl.*

This unusual slide and sand box was also produced in the 1950s by Richwood Toys to accompany their line of dolls. Pictured with the slide is a hard plastic Sandra Sue doll. ($125 and up each). *Doll, playset, and photograph from the collection of Marian Schmuhl.*

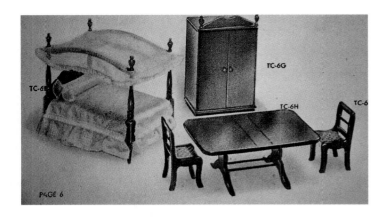

The Emporium catalog from San Francisco, California, in 1954 featured several pieces of Richwood furniture. Included are the canopy bed priced at $4.98, the wardrobe which cost $3.98, and the table and two chairs for $5.98. Extra chairs were available for $1.50 each. *Catalog from the collection of Marge Meisinger.*

Right: Some of the Richwood clothing was designed in sizes to fit both the Cindy Lou and the Sandra Sue dolls. Pictured are two walkers with their original tags dressed in identical outfits. The 8" Sandra Sue is the high heel style doll. (Cindy Lou $250-300, Sandra Sue $150 and up). *Dolls and photograph from the collection of Peggy Millhouse.*

During the mid-1950s Richwood also marketed a 14" hard plastic doll called Cindy Lou. The company purchased flat feet, unwigged, slender body dolls from a supplier and finished the dolls themselves. They made their own wigs. The dolls are usually marked "Made in USA." Most of the dolls look very much like Mary Hoyer dolls except they have pin joints. This walker doll is original except for her shoes. ($175-250). *Doll and photograph from the collection of Peggy Millhouse.*

14" hard plastic Cindy Lou and 8" Sandra Sue wearing similar outfits circa 1954-1955. Both dolls are walkers and this Sandra Sue is the flat feet model. Since the dolls are unmarked, the 14" dolls are hard to identify unless they have their original tags. (Cindy Lou $250 and up, Sandra Sue $150 and up). *Dolls and photograph from the collection of Peggy Millhouse.*

Two Cindy Lou dolls model Richwood clothing made for them. The dolls are circa 1955. Both dolls appear to have been made from the Hoyer molds. (Tagged $250 and up, untagged $175 and up). *Dolls and photograph from the collection of Peggy Millhouse.*

This Cindy Lou brochure was issued by Richwood Enterprises from their location in Highland, Maryland, circa 1954-1955. It pictures many of the outfits being marketed for their 14" hard plastic Cindy Lou doll. *Brochure from the collection of Marge Meisinger.*

Left: 14" Cindy Lou hard plastic walker wearing her original clothing. ($175 and up). *Dolls and photograph from the collection of Peggy Millhouse.*

Two more pages of the Cindy Lou brochure feature various dresses plus an evening dress. *Brochure from the collection of Marge Meisinger.*

Right: These two pages of clothing for Cindy Lou picture a ski suit, formal evening dress, skating costume, coats, and sleepwear. Cindy Lou dressed in slip, panties, shoes, and socks sold for $5.95. If the doll was dressed, she cost from $7.50 to $11.95 depending on the outfit. The clothes alone were priced from $1.50 for pajamas to $5.95 for a formal and fur jacket. The ski suit cost $3.95 and a coat, hat, and dress costume was priced at $5.95. *Brochure from the collection of Marge Meisinger.*

Terri Lee

The Terri Lee dolls were first made in 1946. The dolls were marketed by Violet Gradwohl although they had been designed by her niece, Maxine Sunderman. The dolls were modeled after Maxine's daughter, Drienne, and were named after Violet's daughter Terri Lee.

The first Terri Lee company was located in Lincoln, Nebraska, with ten employees working in one room. After Violet was lucky enough to have her dolls featured in the Montgomery Ward Christmas catalog in 1946, the dolls were given national exposure. By 1951 the company had expanded to a two floor factory that employed 190 people.

At first the dolls were made of composition but by 1947 the Terri Lees were being made of painted plastic. These dolls were marked "Terri Lee/Pat. Pending."

In the beginning, Violet designed all the clothing for the dolls and there were dozens of different Terri Lee outfits made each year. As the business grew, Violet's daughter took over the designing of the clothing.

For a short time in 1950 vinyl dolls were produced. This material had a sticky feeling to it so the material for making Terri Lee dolls was changed to hard plastic (not painted plastic) by 1952. In 1951 3,000 dolls were being sold each week.

As the company grew, new dolls were added to the line. According to Peggy Wiedman Casper writing in her book *Fashionable Terri Lee Dolls*, Jackie Ormes, a cartoonist whose cartoon appeared in the *Pittsburg Courier*, designed a black doll named **Patty Jo**. This doll was carried by the company from 1947 until 1951.

Black Terri Lees called **Benjie** and **Bonnie Lou** were also part of the company's line during most of the 1950s. These dolls were simply given a different paint job to represent black children, but were really the same as the white Terri dolls.

A Terri Lee matching boy doll called **Jerri Lee** was also included as part of the regular line of dolls from approximately 1948 until the end of production in 1958.

In 1949 this doll was given a different look when it was marketed as a **Gene Autry** doll. The doll was endorsed by the famous cowboy star but it was not a best seller. The clothes for the doll were tagged "Gene Autry." At $10.95, the doll was quite expensive for the time. This doll is the most sought after Terri Lee product for today's collectors and therefore the most expensive. See Personality chapter for more information.

Up to this time all the Terri Lee dolls had been just alike with different wigs and facial paint to distinguish the male and female dolls.

In 1951 an entirely new doll was designed for the company by Brenda Putnam. The all vinyl baby doll was named Linda Lee, but soon after she was made her name was changed to **Linda Baby**. This doll had molded hair and several different costumes.

In December 1951 a fire destroyed the Terri Lee factory in Lincoln, Nebraska. A local newspaper article estimated the loss at $75,000. The company then relocated to Apple Valley, California, in 1952. The Terri Lee Fashion, Inc. part of the company remained in Lincoln. In the early days much of the Terri Lee clothing was made by fifty people sewing in their own homes. The proper pattern, materials, and trim were sent to home workers who completed the clothing and returned the finished product to the company.

The new doll factory opened in California in 1952 with a building which covered 10,000 square feet. By 1953 the company was selling 100,000 dolls a year. By 1954 3,000 dolls a day were being made. During the peak of the season 500-600 people were employed making the Terri line of dolls. Three hundred more worked in Lincoln sewing clothes for the dolls. There were also two doll hospitals to repair the earlier dolls. One was located in Apple Valley and one was in Lincoln. Since the dolls carried a life-time guarantee, many were returned to the hospitals for repair.

More new dolls were added to the line after the move to California. In 1955 the **Tiny Terri** doll was marketed with the innovation of sleep eyes. The new doll also followed the trend of the time and was produced as a walker. In 1956 the **Tiny Jerri** was introduced in the line.

Also in 1955 a larger baby doll was produced. She was named **Connie Lynn** after Violet's granddaughter. This doll also had sleep eyes.

In 1957 the Linda Baby doll was also manufactured as a **"So Sleepy"** model with closed eyes. This doll had a soft body.

The first boxes used for the Terri Lee dolls featured a cut-out circle so the doll could be seen inside. By 1951 the design of the boxes had been changed to yellow and by 1956 the doll boxes were being produced with a red design.

According to Peggy Wiedman Casper, the first of several law suits involving the Terri Lee Co. was filed against A.H. & E. Freydberg, Inc. and Kathryn Kay Fassel in 1954. The action concerned a "look alike" doll called **Mary Jane** then being produced by the defendants. The Terri Lee firm was successful in court and the competing dolls were ordered to be discontinued or changed. Even some of the clothing provided for the Mary Jane dolls seemed to be based on the Terri Lee designs. The hard plastic Mary Jane dolls had sleep eyes and were made as walkers. See Miscellaneous chapter.

At least four different catalogs were produced by the Terri Lee firm which pictured the Terri Lee clothing. Other brochures featured Tiny Terry and Connie Lynn clothing. The company also produced monthly bulletins, beginning in December 1951, which featured the new clothing and dolls offered by the Terri Lee Co.

Besides dolls and clothing, the company sold several pieces of doll furniture to be used with the dolls. Included were different designs of trunks and wardrobes, as well as a bed, bassinet, play pen, walker, and clothes rack.

Perhaps the Terri Lee Co. took on too much debt with the move to California. The new factory had been expensive and even with continued success in doll sales the firm was having financial problems by 1958.

Another company fire, this time in the California plant in November 1958, was found to be arson. Although Violet Gradwohl was not charged in the criminal action, one of her advisers was convicted of the crime.

The Terri Lee plant was auctioned in 1960 and law suits continued to hamper the return of the Terri Lee dolls to the market place.

A brief enterprise by Mar-Fan Inc. of Glendale, California resulted in some **talking Terri Lee** dolls being marketed for a short time before another law suit ended the effort.

Violet died in 1972 without realizing her dream of again marketing her famous Terri Lee dolls. Hundreds of thousands of the dolls were made during the glory years and today's collectors still enjoy the search for the elusive Terri Lee dolls like the "Queen of Dolls" or "Silver-Blu Mink." Most collectors, however, are satisfied to settle for something a little less extravagant because the workmanship on even the school dresses can compete quite well with the best doll clothing made during the 1950s.

Family members still have many letters that were sent to the Terri Lee company by children of the period. If any current collectors could be one of those early correspondents, the family would like to hear from you. Address your letter to Schiffer Publishing.

16" painted plastic black Benjie circa 1949. He is marked "Terri Lee Patent Pending" on his back. He is wearing his original costume and has a caracul wig. ($800-900). *Doll and photograph courtesy of the Denver Doll Emporium.*

16" Jerri Lee Cowboy doll made by Terri Lee, Inc. circa 1950-1951. He is made of painted plastic and is marked "Terri Lee Patent Pending" on the back. He is wearing his original tagged clothing. ($350-400). *Doll and photograph from the collection of Carol J. Lindeman.*

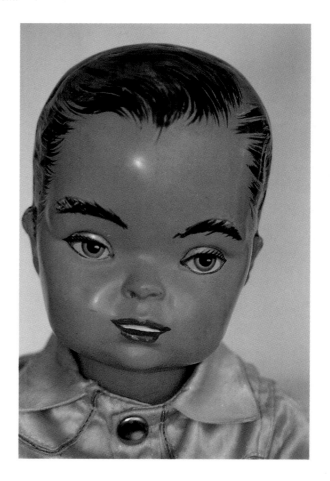

16" Gene Autry doll made by Terri Lee, Inc. in 1949. The doll is made of painted plastic and is marked "Terri Lee/Patent Pending" on the back. He is wearing his original tagged ("Gene Autry") shirt and pants but his boots and belt are replaced. He is missing his hat and tie. See also chapter on personalities. ($1300 and up).

This advertisement for the new Gene Autry doll appeared in *Playthings* magazine in July 1950. He is wearing the same clothing as the doll pictured.

Terri Lee with unusual very dark hair circa early 1950s. She is wearing a tagged blue formal of taffeta and netting and a silver lame coat. She is all original. ($550-650). *Doll and photograph from the collection of Carol J. Lindeman.*

Pair of Jerri Lee and Terri Lee dolls dressed in cowboy and cowgirl outfits circa early 1950s. These dolls are all original and in mint condition. ($450-500 each). *Dolls and photograph courtesy of the Denver Doll Emporium.*

Here's "Terri Lee"... the best-dressed doll in America

34A—Terri Lee is 17" tall, made of unbreakable Tenite plastic. Little girls can comb and curl her hair, and dress Terri Lee in the hand-made clothes, designed especially for her. Specify blonde, brunette or auburn hair-do; in shoes, socks, chemise____10.95

84B—Velveteen coat, bonnet, muff, mittens, galoshes _____ 9.95
84C—Brownie uniform _____ 2.50
84D—3-pc. Nite outfit _____ 4.50

84E—6-pc. Cowgirl outfit____6.95
84F—Pique dress, straw hat. 2.95*
84G—3-pc. Knit ensemble. 2.95*
84H—Belted jeans, shirt__2.50*
*prices do not include doll

The G.F. Fox Co. located in Hartford, Connecticut, featured Terri Lee dolls in their catalog in 1952. The basic doll sold for $10.95 while the Cowgirl outfit was priced at $6.95. *Catalog from the collection of Marge Meisinger.*

This mint Terri Lee is dressed in the Garden Party Dress and is #560D in the company brochure for 1952. Terri Lee dolls beginning in 1952 are marked "Terri Lee" only on the back. ($550-650). *Doll and photograph courtesy of the Denver Doll Emporium.*

Brunette Terri Lee dressed in the Southern Belle costume #570A in the 1952 company brochure. The doll is mint and all original. ($550-650). *Doll and photograph courtesy of the Denver Doll Emporium.*

This pair of Terri Lee and Jerri Lee dolls also dates from 1952. They are Sailor girl #540F and Sailor Boy #1540G. ($650-850 pair). *Dolls and photograph courtesy of the Denver Doll Emporium.*

Bonnie Lou Terri Lee doll in original cotton play dress circa 1952. ($650 and up). *Doll and photograph courtesy of the Denver Doll Emporium.*

Another mint Terri from 1952 #570C has auburn hair and is dressed in the Irish Colleen dress. ($550-650). *Doll and photograph courtesy of the Denver Doll Emporium.*

Terri Lee Majorette #3560H 1952. The doll is all original. ($400-450). *Doll and photograph courtesy of the Denver Doll Emporium.*

Another mint Bonnie Lou doll in her original tagged cotton dress. ($650 and up). *Doll and photograph from the collection of Leslie Robinson.*

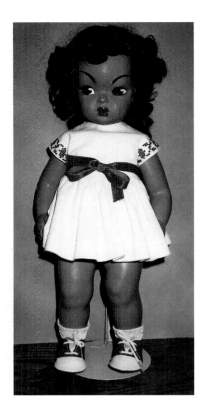

Patty Jo Terri Lee designed by cartoonist Jackie Ormes. The doll was carried by the company beginning in the late 1940s. This doll is dressed in a playtime outfit from the 1952 catalog. The dress is pictured on a regular Terri in the brochure (#3520F). ($700 and up). *Doll and photograph courtesy of the Denver Doll Emporium.*

A very collectible original Terri Lee with braids dressed in the "Heart Fund" dress from 1953. Each year the company issued a different doll for this cause and part of the profits were donated to the fund. ($400-450). *Doll and photograph courtesy of the Denver Doll Emporium.*

Brunette Terri wearing her original leopard fur sport coat and hat #630H circa 1954. ($550-650). *Doll and photograph courtesy of the Denver Doll Emporium.*

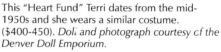

This "Heart Fund" Terri dates from the mid-1950s and she wears a similar costume. ($400-450). *Doll and photograph courtesy of the Denver Doll Emporium.*

Another Patti Jo is dressed in the Calypso costume #3540K which is also from 1952. ($700 and up). *Doll and photograph courtesy of the Denver Doll Emporium.*

Mint Terri Lee Irish Colleen #560S pictured in the catalog for 1954. This doll wears Terri Lee shoes in black. ($550-650). *Doll and photograph courtesy of the Denver Doll Emporium.*

Terri Lee Square Dance #540NN in the catalog for 1954. She is all original and mint. ($400-450). *Doll and photograph courtesy of the Denver Doll Emporium.*

Terri Lee wearing Garden Party Formal circa 1954. She is mint and all original. ($550-650). *Doll and photograph courtesy of the Denver Doll Emporium.*

Pair of Jerri and Terri dolls dressed in matching knit suits. The dolls are #1560M (Jerri) and #560M (Terri) in the 1954 company brochure. ($750-800 pair). *Dolls and photograph courtesy of the Denver Doll Emporium.*

Terri Lee #3570G dressed in a formal ballerina tagged costume with original marked box. She is near mint and all original. ($550-650). *Doll and photograph from the collection of Carol J. Linderman.*

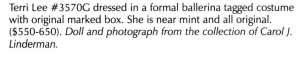

This pair of Jerri Lee and Terri Lee Dutch dolls was featured in the company brochure in 1954. They were #540U (Girl) and #1540U (Boy). The dolls were priced at $14.95 each in 1954. The girl in this pair has replaced wooden shoes. ($400-500 each). *Dolls and photograph from the collection of Carol J. Lindeman.*

Rare Terri and Jerri Lee Hispanic dolls dressed in their original clothing. ($1800 a pair and up). *Dolls and photograph from a private collection.*

Terri Lee in nylon raincoat and ponytail hat circa mid-1950s. ($400-450). *Doll and photograph courtesy of the Denver Doll Emporium.*

Jerri Lee dressed in wool coat and hat circa mid-1950s. ($275-300). *Doll and photograph courtesy of the Denver Doll Emporium.*

Terri Lee Davy Crockett doll circa 1955 in all original condition. ($800-900). *Doll and photograph from the collection of Marge Meisinger.*

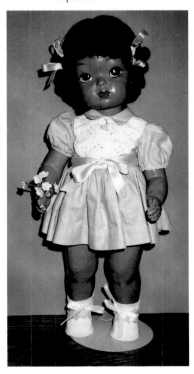

Bonnie Lou made by Terri Lee dressed in a pink party dress from 1955. She is all original. ($700-750). *Doll and photograph courtesy of the Denver Doll Emporium.*

Jerri and Terri Lee dressed in matching nautical print outfits. Circa 1955. ($650-750 pair). *Dolls and photograph courtesy of the Denver Doll Emporium.*

Original Terri Lee dressed in the Southern Belle costume from 1955. ($550-650). *Doll and photograph courtesy of the Denver Doll Emporium.*

Terri Lee dolls model two of the many sports outfits available for the Terri dolls. Almost all of the Terri company costumes could be purchased individually without a doll. These date from the mid-1950s. All of the Terri company clothing was tagged. (Outfits only $35-45 each). *Blond doll from the collection of Carolyn Sharp.*

Left: Jerri Lee tagged #2858 Cowboy all original with felt hat. ($400 and up). *Doll and photograph from the collection of Carol J. Lindeman.*

Terri Lee wearing the costume pictured on the front of the Terri Lee booklet for April 1955. Her hair bows and shoe laces have been replaced. ($200-250).

Many dresses, coats, formals, and sleepwear were also provided by the Terri Lee company for their dolls. Pictured are a coat and hat with play dress #3510F from 1954 underneath. Also shown is the Chambray School Dress #3530A from the same year. It was priced at $1.75 in the company brochure. (Dresses $40-50, coat and hat $50-60). *Blond doll from the collection of Carolyn Sharp.*

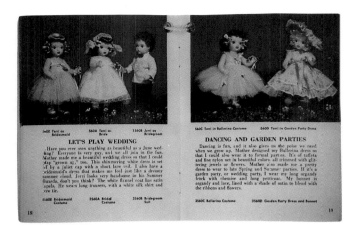

A Terri Lee brochure was issued in color in 1952-1953. Shown are several of the more expensive Terri Lee dolls and costumes including a Terri Bride (#560A) and Jerri Lee groom (#15608). Also pictured is a Bridesmaid (#560E), Ballerina (#560C), and Garden Party Dress (#560D). *Brochure from the collection of Leslie Robinson.*

Many extra clothes were also made for the 16" Jerri Lee dolls. Pictured are the pants and shirt #4530D from 1954-1955. The belt has been replaced. Also shown is a denim shirt and jeans tagged with the Jerri Lee tag. ($45-50 each piece).

The wood Terri Lee Fashion Rack is pictured with Terri Lee clothing. The rack is marked "Terri Lee" on the bottom. Shown is the robe ($40-50) and lounging pajamas ($30-40), a bathing suit ($30-35), Brownie dress (missing cap $45-55), shorts set ($30-40), and wedding dress (missing veil $75-100). All of the clothing is marked with the "Terri Lee" tag. (Rack $125-150).

Right: Terri Lee is wearing the school girl dress pictured on the front of the September 1955 Terri Lee bulletin. ($325 and up). Also shown is a small wood wardrobe which was marketed by the company. The 1954 brochure offers the wardrobe for $8.95 or complete with clothing for $24.95. A larger wardrobe was also sold. ($250 and up). *Doll, wardrobe, and photograph from the collection of Leslie Robinson.*

A canopy bed was also shown in the brochure from 1954. It was priced at $24.95 complete with canopy and spread.

Two Tiny Terri Lee dolls model other clothes made for these dolls. Both dresses are tagged "Terri Lee." The one on the right is one of the many versions of Play dress #3306. These dresses came in assorted colors and sold for only 79 cents each. ($20-25 each dress).

Tiny Terry wearing the Cotton Suit and hat #3356 as pictured in the company brochure. She is tagged and all original. ($165-185). *Doll and photograph from the collection of Carol L. Lindeman.*

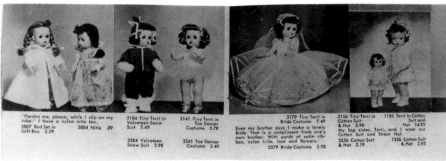

10" Tiny Terri Lee which was first marketed in 1955. The hard plastic doll has sleep eyes (which don't work very well), closed mouth, and an attached wig. She is marked c on her back. She is shown in the Nurse Uniform (#3137) along with a Tiny Terri Lee box. Similar outfits were also made for Tiny Jerri Lee as well as the larger Terri and Jerri Lee dolls. (Outfit only $50-60, box $20-30).

These pages are from the Tiny Terri brochure which was used from 1956-1958. Pictured are several of the costumes designed for the small Terri. Included are a #3807 Bed Set in Gift Box for $2.59; #3804 Nitie for 89 cents; #3184 Velveteen Snow Suit for $3.98; #3341 Toe Dancer Costume for $2.49; #3379 Bride Costume for $3.98; and matching Cotton Suits for both Tiny Terri (#3356) and regular Terri Lee (#1356). *Brochure from the collection of Leslie Robinson.*

Two more of the Tiny Terri dresses are #3324, a Taffeta Sunday Dress, and #3332, an Organdy Party Dress, both pictured in the company brochure. They each sold for $1.49 when new. ($20-30 each dress).

10" Tiny Jerri Lee doll introduced in 1956. He is marked with a "c" on his back. He is wearing his original tagged Terri Lee clothing. Variations of this costume were made for each of the dolls in the Terri Line. This doll also has sleeping eyes, closed mouth, and a caracul attached wig. ($150 and up).

Most of the Tiny Jerri Lee clothing was made as a matching outfit to one produced for Tiny Terri Lee. Included were the #4340 Drum Major Costume; #4330 Cheerleader Outfit; #4331 School Suit; #4312 Doctor Uniform; #4310 Sport Suit; #4121 Summer Suit; #4322 Sailor Boy; #4323 Masquerade; and #2320 Engineer outfit, which matched one made for the large Jerri Lee. *Brochure from the collection of Leslie Robinson.*

10" Linda Baby vinyl baby doll first known as Linda Lee in 1951. The doll has molded hair and painted features ($150 and up). The clothing pictured includes a kimono, a creeper set (#6115 from 1957), dress and slip, and taffeta coat and hat (L-7 from 1954). Other outfits also made for the doll included a Christening Dress (6365 in 1956), and a corduroy snowsuit (6340 from 1958), creeper set (LF62) in 1954, hand crocheted jacket and bonnet with dress (LF59) in 1954, a Bunting (LF-74 in 1955), and Pajamas (LF-66 also from 1955). The tag for the clothing says "Linda Baby." (Clothing $30-60 each outfit).

Accessories were also made for the Linda Baby dolls. Linda's Play Pen was featured in the company brochure for 1954-55. It sold for $3.95 when new. ($200 and up). The Linda Baby also pictured wears the taffeta coat and hat (L-7) from 1954 ($175-185). Her picture brochure can also be seen. *Doll, playpen, and photograph from the collection of Leslie Robinson.*

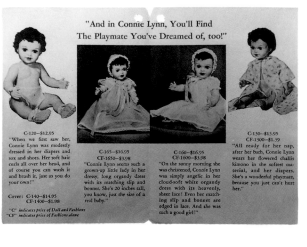

Other articles of clothing were also produced for the Connie Lynn doll. Pictured are a long organdy dress, matching slip and bonnet (CF-1650). Christening dress of white organdy with slip and bonnet (CF-1600), and kimono (CF-1300). Other clothes included pajamas (CF-1450), short dress with matching bonnet (CF5322), bunny suit (5335), corduroy snowsuit (CF2000), flannel bunting (CF1950), and family suit (5315F), velveteen coat and bonnet (5355), and windjammer costume (5352).

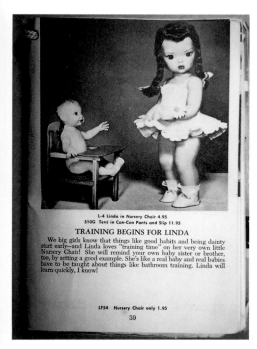

Linda's Nursery Chair was also pictured in the 1954-1955 brochure. It sold for $1.95. Also offered in the same brochure was a Musical bassinet and Tree for the Linda Baby doll (#LF60) and a Rocking Cradle on metal stand with or without a skirt (L-14).

Talking Terri Lee doll circa early 1960s. It was made by Fischer Plastics for Mar-Fan, Inc. The box, however, is labeled I & S Industries, Doll and Toy Division, 2134 West Rosecrans, Gardena, California. Soon lawsuits involved Violet Gradwahl, Mar-Fan, Inc. and Fischer Plastics, Inc. and the dolls were discontinued. The doll came with a record and a cord which was to be hooked from the back of the doll to a record player. The record was to be played on the player and the sound was to come from the doll. This original mint Terri is wearing a tagged "Connie Lynn" family outfit which appears to have been her original clothing.

Left: 10" So Sleepy doll first manufactured by Terri Lee in 1957 ($200 and up). The doll was the Linda Baby made with closed eyes and a soft body. She is all original. Also pictured with her is the Connie Lynn doll from 1955. She is wearing her original tagged clothing CF1400 Dimity Creeper. The 20" doll is made of hard plastic, has sleep eyes, closed mouth, and a caracul wig ($350 and up). *Dolls and photograph from the collection of Leslie Robinson.*

Right: MIB Connie Lynn. She is wearing a satin coat and bonnet (CF-1900), a dress and slip (CF-1500), booties, plastic diaper, and a daisy on her wrist. All the clothing is tagged "Connie Lynn." The doll originally sold for $19.95. ($550 and up in this condition). *Doll and photograph from the collection of Carol J. Lindeman.*

Vogue Dolls, Inc.

Perhaps more than any other company, Vogue Dolls changed the way dolls were marketed in the decade of the 1950s. This marketing strategy was based on selling an inexpensive undressed doll and then providing various outfits that the consumer could purchase separately. Other companies soon followed Vogue's lead and the foundation for the phenomenon that was to become "Barbie™'s World" (made by Mattel Inc.) was begun. The practice continues to this day.

The Vogue Doll Company was involved with the production of fine doll clothing from its beginning in the 1920s. Its founder, Jennie Graves, began the business by selling doll clothes for dolls made by other manufacturers under the name Ye Olde Vogue Dolle Shoppe. By 1932 the name had changed to the Vogue Doll Shoppe located in Somerville, Massachusetts. Jennie began buying nude dolls, making the clothes for the dolls and selling dressed dolls. The German bisque "Just Me" doll was a popular model.

Jennie's husband died in 1939 and she relocated to Medford, Massachusetts, where Jennie continued to dress dolls made by other manufacturers. These dolls included those made of cloth, rubber, and composition.

Because Jennie's speciality was doll clothing, she came up with the idea of producing a basic doll that could be dressed in many different costumes. Bernard Lipfert designed an 8" doll for Vogue Dolls, Inc. It was first made of composition under the name Toddles. Boy and girl sets dressed in matching costumes were especially appealing.

Ginny

In 1948, Vogue Dolls joined other doll companies in issuing their dolls in hard plastic. Vogue continued the marketing of the boy and girl dolls and also marketed a baby doll called "Crib Crowd." Commonwealth Plastics molded the dolls and later made the plastic shoes. At first the plastic dolls had mohair wigs and painted eyes. These dolls were marked "Vogue" on the head and "Vogue Doll" on the body. There were two types of tags issued for their clothing. One used white letters ("Vogue Dolls, Inc. Medford, Mass.") on a blue background. The other used blue letters ("Vogue Dolls") on a white tag.

Originally the 8" dolls were given various little girls' names including Carol and Becky, but in 1951 the doll was officially named Cinny after Jennie's daughter Virginia Graves Carlson. Virginia was also active in the firm as a designer of clothing for the small dolls.

Other changes had been made in the plastic dolls by 1951. Sleep eyes were added along with synthetic wigs that could be washed and set, an improvement over the earlier hard to manage mohair.

In 1952 many of the new Ginny dolls had wigs made of lambskin styled in a short poodle hair cut. The Crib Crowd babies also had wigs of this type. The dolls continued to be made with sleep eyes and painted eyelashes. The clothing tags for the period were white with blue lettering which read either "Vogue" or "Original Vogue Dolls, Inc." These tags were used through 1953.

During these early years of Ginny production, clothes were designed which were called "Twin Sets." These outfits were worn by dolls made to represent both a boy and a girl as twins. The dolls were actually the same models but the "boys" hair was cut shorter and his costume also indicated he was a male. These sets are very popular with today's collectors but didn't sell well for the company and were discontinued.

The next change in the construction of the plastic Ginny dolls came in 1954 with the addition of a walking mechanism. When the doll was "walked" her head turned from side to side. Plastic shoes replaced the leatherette snap shoes of the earlier dolls at this time. The shoes were marked "Ginny" on the bottom. The dolls still had painted eyelashes. The doll clothing tags were white with black print which read "Vogue Dolls, Inc., Medford, Mass. U.S.A., Reg. U.S. Pat Off."

Many accessories were listed in the catalog for 1954. Included were the E-Z-Do Wardrobe, shoe bag, sunglasses, Ginny's Pup (made by Steiff), miniature suitcase with overnight supplies, hat box with five hats, and Ginny's tripmates with several pieces of luggage.

The Ginny doll changed in appearance in 1955 when molded plastic eyelashes replaced the earlier painted ones. The body of the doll was marked with the patent number 2687594.

More new accessories were added to the Ginny line in 1955. Included were the very popular gym set, heart shape chair, metal wardrobe trunk, trousseau tree, wardrobe with sliding doors, and bed.

Although there were no changes made in the basic dolls for 1956, more interesting accessories were added to the line. Included were a new style wardrobe with opening doors, a rocker, pink wood trunk, a cardboard dollhouse (very rare), doghouse, and an oblong table and chairs.

The next substantial change for the Ginny doll occurred in 1957 when the legs were given bending knees. A new clothing tag was also used. "Vogue Dolls, Inc." was written in script in blue on a white tag. This tag was used until 1965. More accessories were added to the line with the addition of a chest of drawers and a redesign of several earlier items including a new bed, round table and chairs, and a new wardrobe.

The end of the 1950s was also the end of the "glory years" for Ginny. By 1963 Ginny dolls featured vinyl heads with rooted hair and only fifteen new outfits were advertised compared to the sixty plus from the popular years of the 1950s. By 1965 Ginny was an all vinyl doll and 1969 was the last year of production for the American Ginnys. In the early 1970s the vinyl Ginnys were made in Hong Kong but these dolls did not compare favorably in quality with the earlier dolls. Jennie Graves had already retired and she died in 1971. In 1973 the Vogue name was sold to the Tonka Corporation.

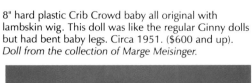

8" hard plastic Crib Crowd baby all original with lambskin wig. This doll was like the regular Ginny dolls but had bent baby legs. Circa 1951. ($600 and up). *Doll from the collection of Marge Meisinger.*

8" hard plastic Ginny Easter doll with painted eyes and mohair wig circa 1950 #8-12K. She is marked on the back "Vogue Doll." She is all original and in near mint condition. ($300-400). *Doll and photograph courtesy of the Denver Doll Emporium.*

8" strung Ginny with a poodle hair cut. She dates from 1952 and is all original wearing the Kindergarten Series #24. She has sleep eyes and painted lashes. ($400 and up). *Doll and photograph courtesy of Denver Doll Emporium.*

Another painted eye Ginny also circa 1950 with mohair wig. These early dolls wore the middle snap shoes. She is also marked "Vogue Doll." Her clothing tag is white rayon with blue lettering which says "Vogue." This tag dates the outfit to be from 1952. ($250 and up).

On the left is a mint strung Ginny from 1952 with sleep eyes wearing Kindergarten Series #30 and on the right is a mint Western Girl from Frolicking Fables Series wearing a black and silver outfit. She is also a strung doll with sleep eyes and is from 1951. Both dolls have painted lashes. ($300-350 each). *Dolls and photograph courtesy of Denver Doll Emporium.*

Three mint Ginny dolls from 1952 are shown. On the left is Angela from the Debutante Series #65, in the middle is Square Dance #52, and on the right is Kindergarten Series #30. The dolls are all strung with sleep eyes and painted lashes. The clothing tags for 1952 (and on some 1953 outfits) were white rayon with blue printing saying "Vogue." ($300-350 each). *Dolls and photograph courtesy of the Denver Doll Emporium.*

Black Ginny dating from 1952 in her original dress. This doll is very rare. ($1500 and up). *Doll and photograph from the collection of Marge Meisinger.*

Ginny strung bride from 1953 #55. She has sleep eyes and painted lashes. She still carries her original tag. The clothing label for 1953 was a white rayon tag with blue print reading "Original/ Vogue/Dolls, Inc." ($300 and up). *Doll and photograph courtesy of the Denver Doll Emporium.*

Ginny in a poodle-cut from 1952. She is a strung doll with painted lashes. The doll was called "Pixie" and she is the namesake of Mrs. Grave's grand-daughter. She is mint and all original. ($400 and up). *Doll and photograph courtesy of the Denver Doll Emporium.*

Right: The Dayton Company from Minneapolis, Minnesota, featured Ginny dolls and clothing in their catalog in 1953. Pictured are a basic Ginny doll for $1.98, a jeans outfit (Talon Zipper Series #70) for $1.98, Tiny Miss #43 costume for $1.98, a Debutante outfit #60 for $2.98, and a bridal costume #55 for $2.50. *Catalog from the collection of Marge Meisinger.*

This Brother and Sister pair #35 and #36 also date from 1952. The dolls are all original. They are strung with sleep eyes and painted lashes. ($700 and up for the pair). *Dolls and photograph from the collection of Marge Meisinger.*

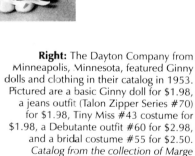

This knit sweater set was featured for several years in the Ginny catalogs including 1954. It was made in different colors. In 1954 the set was #130. The jeans clothing was also carried in several company catalogs. In 1954 it was #670. The clothing tags for the Ginny clothing from 1954-1956 was made of white rayon with black printing reading "Vogue Doll, Inc./Medford, Mass. U.S.A./Reg. U.S. Pat. Off." (clothing only $25-40, MIB outfits $60-75).

Two Ginny dolls wearing costumes from 1954. The Ballerina is #45 (head ornament a replacement), and Nurse #31. These dolls have sleep eyes, painted lashes, and have the new 1954 walking mechanism. The dolls are marked on the back "Ginny/Vogue Dolls, Inc. Pat. Pending/Made in U.S.A." (Dressed dolls $200 and up). Also pictured is a box and brochure from that year. ($30 each).

In 1954 Loveman's in Birmingham, Alabama, featured a page of Ginny dolls and accessories in their catalog. The dolls came with either braids or bobbed hair for $1.98. The clothing ranged in price from $1.00 for a nightie and bathrobe to $2.98 for a bridal outfit. Ginny clothes also included Beach Set #48, Knit Set #30, suitcase with nightie, robe, and accessories, Kindercrowd #21, Bride #64, Cowgirl #48, Fur coat #484, Tiny Miss #49, Whiz Kids #73, For Rain or Shine #32, and Whiz Kids #70. *Catalog from the collection of Marge Meisinger.*

Two pages from the 1954 Vogue Ginny brochure picture "My Twin Sets" of dolls plus the new "Tiny Miss" costumes.

Original Ginny #990 Davy Crockett doll with sleep eyes and painted lashes circa 1955. This doll is very hard to find, especially in this condition. ($450 and up). *Doll and photograph from the collection of Marge Meisinger.*

By 1955 the hard plastic Ginny dolls had molded lashes instead of painted ones. Pictured is a 1955 Ginny wearing Bridal Trousseau #464 from that year. The dolls from 1955 were also walkers. (Outfit only $50 and up).

These beautifully dressed Ginny dolls are pictured in the Ginny brochure from 1955. Included are dolls dressed to dance, skate, swim, and ski as well as Ginnys in bridal and bridesmaid attire. *Catalog from the collection of Marge Meisinger.*

This lovely Ginny with auburn hair and painted lashes dates from 1954. Her dress is Tiny Miss #244 from 1955. Although the doll is wearing a Ginny hat circa 1955, it is not the hat that came with the dress. (Dressed doll with replaced hat $175 and up). Also pictured is "Ginny's Pup" offered by Vogue as a Ginny accessory for several years beginning in 1954. He is #831 in the 1955 catalog. The dog was made by Steiff and had his own "blanket" with "Ginny's Pup" printed on it. ($150 and up).

These two Ginny walker dolls are modeling outfits from 1955. On the left is #182 Yellow Zippered Rain Slicker, Sou'wester Hat and boots. The other coat is #180 and the company text says it is "My Navy Blue coat with white collar and cuffs and my Straw Hat is my Sunday best coat. (Outfits only $40 and up).

This pink and white case was made of paper over wood with Ginny's name on the front. It was offered for several years and was #860 in the catalog in 1955 along with a Ginny doll, party dress, school dress and hat. (Trunk only $55 and up). Also pictured is a molded lash walker wearing Kinder Crowd dress #121 shown in the catalog for 1955. The outfit originally came with yellow socks. ($35 and up).

Ginny walker with molded lashes models a dress whose design was used several times through the years but this one has the tag from 1955-1956. Her hat goes with the Tiny Miss outfit #244 from 1955. Also pictured is a clothes rack offered for Ginny by Vogue as #915 in their catalog in 1955. This rack is hard to find in original condition. (Outfit $30 and up, rack $150 and up).

This Ginny walker with molded lashes models a 1955 swimming suit set. Although it is pictured in the catalog, it is not described nor numbered. It came with the suit, towel, wood pail, and plastic carrier. (Set only complete $40 and up). The wood heart chair was also pictured in the 1955 catalog as #920. ($65 and up).

There were many accessories offered for Ginny each year. Pictured are purses, sunglasses, jewelry, slip, Vogue tag from 1955, shoe bag from 1954, and suitcase. (Shoebag and suitcase $35 and up, other items $5-10).

Ginny's Gym Set was first offered in the catalog in 1955 as #925. It has a slide, swing, and glider and is marked "Ginny's Gym" on the unit. ($300 and up). *Set and photograph from the collection of Rhonda Schoenick.*

Also pictured in the 1955 catalog was this Ginny bed #910 made of hardwood ($50 and up), and the pink and white wardrobe #922 ($50 and up). On the bed is part of the Dream Cozy Bed Set #912. Missing is the bedspread. The molded lash walker Ginny is dressed in Ginny pajamas from 1958 #1301. (Pajamas $15-20).

Ginny's Rocking chair was also featured in the 1956 catalog as #6914. The chair sold for $2.00. ($40 and up). Sitting in the chair is a molded lash Ginny walker dressed in Kinder Crowd outfit #6125 complete with her Ginny hairband. (Outfit only $40 and up).

Ginny table and chairs from the 1956 catalog #6921. ($55 and up). Also pictured are two outfits from the same year. The blue dress on the left is Kinder Crowd #6126 which is missing the hairband ($20-25) and the Play Time costume on the right is #6154 ($25-35).

The 1956 catalog issued by Pomeroy's in Reading, Pennsylvania, featured Ginny dolls and accessories. The basic doll sold for only $1.98 while her costumes were priced from $1.49 to $2.98. Ginny's Pup cost $1.98 and the Party Package was $5.00. The outfits pictured are H-#6032, J-#6045, K-#6022, M-#6144, N-#6186, P-#6033, Q-#6050. *Catalog from the collection of Marge Meisinger.*

Left: This Tiny Miss outfit #6144 was pictured in the Pomeroy catalog and sold for $1.98. (Costume only $40 and up).

Vogue offered a special plan similar to the one Cosmopolitan used to promote its Ginger dolls. A member who was enrolled in "Ginny's 12 Star Plan" received a special Ginny outfit every month for one year. Pictured are the twelve costumes the customer received in 1956. *From the collection of Marge Meisinger.*

These two pages from the 1956 Ginny Brochure picture the new Play Time costumes as well as the Ginny Formals for the year. The formals sold as outfits for $3.00 each.

Left: Hard plastic walking Ginny with molded lashes and bending knees (new for 1957). She is dressed in her original skating costume and is #7050. (Dressed doll $125-150). Also pictured is the Ginny family booklet for 1957. ($25-30).

Right: This catalog page from Kilpatrick's in Omaha, Nebraska, in 1957 featured several of the Ginny family dolls. Included were the basic Ginny doll for $1.50, many costumes priced from $2.00 to $3.00, the Party Package for $5.00, and the new Ginny Wardrobe for $3.00. The Jill costume pictured is her bridal dress which sold for $4.00 while the basic Jill doll was priced at $3.00. The Ginnette dolls shown include a basic doll for $3.00 and various outfits priced from $1.25 to $2.50 each. The Shoo-Fly Rocker cost $2.00. *Catalog from the collection of Marge Meisinger.*

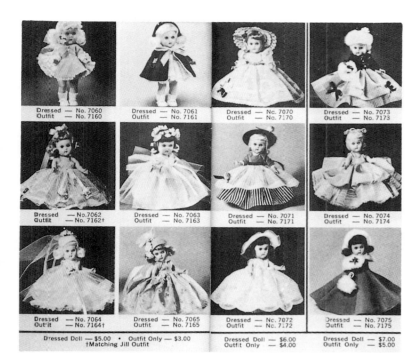

Dressed — No. 7060	Dressed — No. 7061	Dressed — No. 7070	Dressed — No. 7073
Outfit — No. 7160	Outfit — No. 7161	Outfit — No. 7170	Outfit — No. 7173
Dressed — No.7062	Dressed — No. 7063	Dressed — No. 7071	Dressed — No. 7074
Outfit — No. 7162†	Outfit — No. 7163	Outfit — No. 7171	Outfit — No. 7174
Dressed — No. 7064	Dressed — No. 7065	Dressed — No. 7072	Dressed — No. 7075
Outfit — No. 7164†	Outfit — No. 7165	Outfit — No. 7172	Outfit — No. 7175

Dressed Doll — $5.00 • Outfit Only — $3.00
†Matching Jill Outfit

Dressed Doll — $6.00
Outfit Only — $4.00

Dressed Doll — $7.00
Outfit Only — $5.00

Two pages from the 1957 Vogue brochure picture several of the many Ginny outfits for the year. The long gowns were particularly attractive although they were not very appropriate clothing for a child doll.

This metal Ginny trunk was offered by Vogue for several years complete with doll and clothing or by itself in 1957 for $4.00. ($50 and up). Pictured with the trunk are a bent knee Ginny dressed in an unidentified dress from the period along with two more dresses hanging in the trunk tagged with the white label with blue printing reading "Vogue Dolls, Inc." ($25 and up each dress). This label was used from 1957-1962. Also shown is a MIB Car Coat #7187 from 1957. ($35 and up).

Left: Ginny bending knee walker from 1957 models outfit #7038. the dress is black velvet with an organdy apron and white straw hat. Also shown is Simplicity Pattern #1809 which was to be used to make clothes for the 8" Ginny and other similar dolls.

Right: A newly designed Ginny bed was offered in the company catalog in 1957. It was called Ginny's Youth Bed and was #7910. It sold for $2.00. The bedding pictured is from the earlier bed in 1955. Ginny's nightgown is also earlier, circa 1955. It probably came in the miniature suitcase. (Bed $50 and up, nightie $10-15).

In 1959 Vogue offered the Ginny dolls in "Far-Away Lands" fashions. Included were British Islander, Israelian, Hollander, Scandinavian, Alaskan, Oriental, and Hawaiian. The dolls were the same bending leg models offered since 1957. These Ginnys are all original. Also offered was a U.S. Cowgirl. *Dolls and photograph from the collection of Marge Meisinger.*

The May Co. in Los Angeles, California, advertised both Ginny and Ginnette dolls in their 1957 catalog. A Ginnette with painted eyes with a layette sold for $5.00. The basic Ginnette had sleep eyes and sold for $3.00 compared with the hard plastic basic Ginny which was priced at only $2.00. *Catalog from the collection of Marge Meisinger.*

In 1958 Hutzler's of Baltimore, Maryland, issued this catalog featuring a full page of Ginny, Jill, and Ginnette dolls. The basic Jill was priced at $3.00 while her costumes ranged in price from $2.00 to $3.00. Ginny's bridal outfit cost $3.00. Included for Ginny were #1151, #1137, #1141, #1164, #1326, and #1114. Jill's clothing included a red and white dress #3138, pants and top #3139, coat and hat #3375 and a fancy dress #3170. Ginnette outfits included overalls #2131, coat and hat #2337, and pink dress and hat #2132. *Catalog from the collection of Marge Meisinger.*

Jill

Following the popularity of the Ginny doll, Vogue marketed the Jill doll in 1957. Using the same concept of producing a basic doll with lots of costume changes, the Jill doll also met with instant success. The doll was made of hard plastic and was 10.5" tall. She was marked "Jill/Vogue Dolls/Made in U.S.A./c 1957". Jill was made with sleep eyes, a synthetic wig, and bending knees. This walking doll was meant to be a teen-age big sister to Ginny. Jills were produced with two different hair styles either a short hairdo called an Angel Cut or a longer pony tail style. The wigs came in blonde, auburn, or brunette. The Jill doll's ears were pierced and her feet were molded to fit high heeled shoes.

The basic Jill doll came dressed in black leotards. Many other outfits were sold by Vogue to provide owners with a variety of play experiences. The basic doll sold for $3.00 and the outfits varied in price from $1.00 to $5.00 each. Included were coats, dresses, sleepwear, skiing costumes, skating outfits, formals, and bridal attire. In 1958 Vogue began marketing furniture for Jill just as they did for Ginny. The pieces were painted mint green and included a desk and chair, bed, dressing table, and wardrobe.

Jill was carried by the Vogue company through 1960 in the hard plastic model. In 1962 and 1963 Jill was re-issued in vinyl. Mattel's Barbie™ had already taken over Jill's market and the dolls were discontinued.

Jan

The Vogue Jan doll was introduced in 1958. This doll was the same size as Jill and the dolls could wear the same clothing. Jan was a vinyl doll with a soft vinyl head, rooted hair, and sleep eyes. She was marked "Vogue" on the back of her head. Jan also had a swivel waist as did many of the other small "high heel" vinyl dolls of the period. She came with two different hair styles, a bubble cut or a pony tail. Jan was discontinued after 1960. A new vinyl Jan was made in 1963 and 1964 in a larger 12" size.

The clothes for both Jan and Jill were tagged with white tags with blue printing reading "Vogue Dolls, Inc." Besides clothing, the dolls were provided with lots of different accessories. Included were shoes, hose, jewelry, handbags, hair ornaments, and sunglasses.

During the late 1950s, many matching outfits were designed in sizes to fit Ginny, Jill, or Ginnette. These clothes are especially popular with collectors who collect all these dolls.

Two hard plastic Jill dolls with sleep eyes, attached wigs, closed mouths, pierced ears, arched feet, and bending knees model two of the Jill outfits for 1957. On the left is #7516 which sold for $4.00 in the company catalog ($40 and up clothes only), and on the right is #7505 which was priced at $2.00 ($25 and up clothes only). Both pairs of shoes are circa 1958.

Several of the Ginny "Far-Away Lands" dolls are pictured in a May Company catalog from 1959. Basic Ginny, Ginnette, Jill, and Jan dolls could be purchased from this advertisement as well as the various costumes pictured for each doll. The vinyl Jan doll sold for $3.00 and the foreign Ginny outfits were priced at $2.50 each. Jill costumes include: yellow dress and hat #3263, coat and hat #3445, aqua dress #3235, and checked skirt and top #3211. *Catalog from the collection of Marge Meisinger.*

Some of the many outfits made for the new Jill doll in 1957 are pictured. The company brochure offered twenty-six different costumes for the new hard plastic 10.5" fashion doll. *Brochure from the collection of Marge Meisinger.*

Mint original Vogue Jill dressed in the bridal dress from 1957 #7415. The Jill dolls are marked on the back "Vogue Dolls/ Made in USA/c 1957." (In this mint condition in this outfit $200 and up). *Doll from the collection of Marge Meisinger.*

Two hard plastic Jill dolls dressed in clothes from different years. The Jill doll on the right wears a record skirt from 1957. Although the knit top is a marked Jill item, the original one which came with the skirt was red. The outfit also came with a pony tail type hat. The dress on the left is #3131 from 1960. (Clothes only $25-35 each).

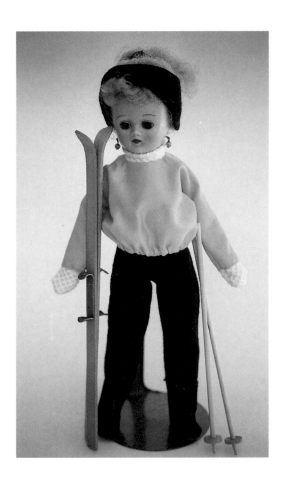

This 1958 catalog page from Stewarts in Baltimore, Maryland pictures outfits for Jill, Jeff, and Ginnette. Jill's short formal was priced at $2.00, Jeff's suit at $4.00, and Ginnette's playtime overalls at $2.00. Jeff was a new doll that year and the basic doll cost $3.00. Jill and Jeff clothes include clockwise: flowered dress #3168, strapless dress #3140, Jeff suit #6180, slacks #3312, raincoat #3345, skating #3164, pajamas and robe #3304, ballerina #3314, slacks #3139, Jeff pants and shirt #6130, jacket and skirt #3169, yellow dress #3134, and red coat #3385. Ginnette clothes include: snowsuit #2151, pink dress #2132, coat and hat #2337, yellow dress #2161, and overalls #2131. *Catalog from the collection of Marge Meisinger.*

This Jill is wearing a mint ski outfit #3367 from 1958. The costume included skis and ski poles. (Outfit only MIB $85 and up). *Clothes from the collection of Marge Meisinger.*

Jill models a MIB sundress #3130 from 1958. A matching outfit was also made for Ginny. (MIB outfit $65-$75).

Although a light green wardrobe was made to match the other pieces of Jill-Jan furniture, this marked Vogue pink wood wardrobe was also produced which could be used for any of the Vogue family dolls. ($50 and up). The Jill-Jan wardrobe had sliding doors and two drawers and was marked with their names. The Jill doll on the left is wearing a pajama set #3304 from 1958 while Jill on the right is wearing pajama #3961 and robe #3962 from 1959. (Clothing only $12-15 each item).

Two hard plastic Jills and a vinyl Jan model several sports clothes made for them. Jan first came on the market in 1958. She is marked "Vogue" on her head. She also has sleep eyes, a closed mouth, and arched feet. She is all vinyl and has rooted hair. On the left, Jill is wearing jeans and a white shirt circa 1958. Jan is wearing a later two-piece sundress #3110 from 1960. (Dressed doll $50-60). Jill on the right is wearing a swim suit set from 1958 #3304. The complete set also included a towel. (Clothes only swim suit set $35 and up, others $15-20 each).

This mint Jill is wearing a strapless formal, perhaps as a bridesmaid dress. Jills, like all dolls, are priced according to condition, popularity, and rarity. ($175 and up in this condition, the same doll in played with condition $65 and up). *Doll from the collection of Marge Meisinger.*

Pictured is part of the Vogue Jill brochure for 1959. The clothes continued to be of high quality and costumes varied from school dresses to skating outfits to bridal attire.

Several pieces of furniture were made for the Jill and Jan dolls. The furniture was all painted light green. Shown is the Jill vanity #3860 circa 1959. It was priced at $3.00. The Jill seated at the vanity is wearing outfit #7503 from 1957. (Vanity $100 and up, clothes $25 and up). *Vanity, doll, and photograph from the collection of Judith Izen.*

Left: The Jill dolls also had many accessories made for them. These included sunglasses, shoes and hose, purses, belts, and jewelry of all kinds. Pictured is a necklace with a profile of Jill and a charm bracelet, both on their original cards. (Necklace $100 and up, bracelet $50 and up, other items $15-25). *From the collection of Marge Meisinger.*

The Jill and Jan bed was also made of wood and painted light green. The original spread is shown on the bed. ($75 and up). The doll is wearing #3134 from 1960. The complete costume included a white apron and cook's hat. *Bed, doll, and photograph from the collection of Judy Izen.*

Jeff

Vogue introduced the Jeff doll in 1958 as a boyfriend for Jill and Jan. He was 11.5" tall, made of vinyl, with molded hair and sleep eyes. Jeff was marked "Vogue" on the back of his head. Like other dolls in the Vogue line, the basic doll was sold undressed and clothing could be purchased separately. Although this male doll was not provided with as many outfits as his female counterparts, he did have a varied wardrobe. Included were the following: pajamas, robe, shorts set, football uniform, ski outfit, suit, slacks and shirt, jeans and shirt, cowboy outfit, skating clothes, tuxedo, underwear, shoes, and socks.

A desk was also made for Jill and Jan. This one has been repainted. It was originally light green. Pictured with the desk are two Jills modeling sundresses and Jill jewelry. The pink and black dress dates from 1959 and is #3216. The pink checked dress is #3112 from 1960. ($25 and up each dress).

Pictured is the basic Jeff doll dressed in his underwear along with his box and brochure. The doll was first marketed in 1958. He is made of vinyl and is marked on the head "Vogue." He has sleep eyes, closed mouth, and molded hair. ($75 and up).

I'm Jeff

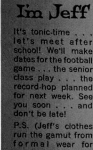

It's tonic-time . . . let's meet after school! We'll make dates for the football game . . . the senior class play . . . the record-hop planned for next week. See you soon . . . and don't be late!

P.S. (Jeff's clothes run the gamut from formal wear for evening, to the most rugged for fun and sports. Look for them at your favorite Vogue Doll dealer.)

Dressed 6130 $5.00   Outfit 6330 $2.00
For school Jeff wears tan chino pants and a brown leather belt. His Ivy League striped shirt has three white snap buttons.

Outfit 6310 $1.50
And so to bed . . . and Jeff wears his two piece pajamas of beige Broadcloth.

Outfit 6311 $1.50
This is Jeff's colorful plaid bathrobe with tuxedo collar and sash belt.

The brochure that came with the Jeff doll pictured clothing which could be purchased separately. The outfits included school clothes (#6330) and sleepwear (#6310 and #6311). *Brochure from the collection of Marge Meisinger.*

Dressed 6131 $5.00   Outfit 6331 $2.00
Jeff's Cabana Suit has colorful swim trunks and matching shirt lined with yellow terry cloth. He wears scuffs.

Dressed 6132 $5.00   Outfit 6332 $2.00
For after school Jeff wears rugged blue jeans with a black belt and long sleeve black jersey sweater.

Dressed 6133 $5.00   Outfit 6333 $2.00
Summertime finds Jeff in grey Bermudas, black belt and bright red checked shirt. His knee length socks are black jersey.

Outfit 6334 $2.00
This smart Tweed Sport Jacket can be worn with any of Jeff's slacks.

Dressed 6160 $6.00   Outfit 6360 $3.00
For skiing Jeff wears black felt ski pants, aqua sateen zipper jacket. Skiis and poles included.

Outfit 6361 $3.00
Jeff's car coat is made of water repellent beige mylon and fully lined. Has real button holes and toggle closings. Tweed Ivy League cap.

Dressed 6180 $7.00   Outfit 6380 $4.00
Jeff's dress-suit is navy wool felt. With it he wears an oxford cloth shirt and bow tie.

Dressed 6181 $7.00   Outfit 6381 $4.00
Jeff's tuxedo suit has black pants with satin stripe, white dress shirt, white wool jacket, plaid cummerbund and tie. Corsage is for his date.

Other Jeff costumes included swim suit (#6331), jeans and shirt (#6332), shorts set (#6333), sports jacket set (#6334), ski outfit (#6360), coat (#6361), suit (#6380), and tux (#6381). *Brochure from the collection of Marge Meisinger.*

Jeff dolls are shown wearing a tuxedo #6381 on the left (missing the corsage) and a navy blue dress suit on the right #6380 (missing his tie). (Dressed dolls $75 and up).

Other clothes for Jeff included pajamas #6310 and jeans set #6332 All of Jeff's clothing carries the Vogue label. (Outfits only $25 and up).

Ginnette

Ginnette was added to the Vogue line in 1955. Although she was advertised as Ginny's little sister, she was too large to really fit that description. She was designed as a baby and had curved legs but she is 8" tall. Ginnette was first made in vinyl with painted eyes and molded hair. The early advertising stresses that she could drink from her bottle and was a drink and wet doll.

In 1956 the painted eyes of the Ginnette doll were changed to sleep eyes. She was marked on her lower back "Vogue Dolls Inc."

The Vogue pamphlet for 1957 pictured twenty-one outfits for Ginnette plus several pieces of furniture including a baby tender, baby bath, crib, shoo-fly, baby toter, and swim set. In 1958 a Ginnette wood chest of drawers was also added.

A new doll called Ginny Baby was introduced in 1958. She was just like the Ginnette but she had rooted hair. These small versions of the Ginnette baby continued to be produced by Vogue under different names in one form or another until 1967. Black versions of the small babies were made in 1964. The dolls were manufactured with either molded or rooted hair.

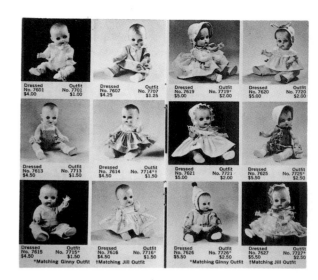

Two pages of the Vogue brochure from 1957 which picture clothing for the Ginnette dolls.

The 8" vinyl Ginnette doll was introduced by Vogue in 1955. The early doll had painted eyes. In 1956 sleep eyes were added. She is marked on her lower back "Vogue dolls Inc." She is wearing her mint #7619 blue dress from 1957. (Outfit only MIB $40 and up). Also shown are her blue and white checked set from 1958 ($40 and up), a pink corduroy coat probably from 1957 ($35 and up), and a boxed pair of shoes and socks ($12 and up).

Sleep eye Ginnette in outfit #7732 from 1957. (Dressed doll $85 and up). *Doll and photograph from the collection of Rhonda Schoenick.*

Many accessories were made for the Ginnette doll during the late 1950s. Pictured are several of these mint sets including bedding, shoes, diapers, a bath set, and a Baby Toter #7770 from the 1957 catalog. (Shoe sets $12 and up, others $35 and up, except for Baby Toter $50 and up). *All items and photograph from the collection of Rhonda Schoenich.*

Jimmy

The 8" vinyl Jimmy doll made his appearance in the Vogue family of dolls in 1958. The doll was actually a reissue of the original painted eye Ginnette from 1955 but dressed in different clothing to indicate his male status. Several of the Vogue outfits were designed as matching sets for both Ginnette and Jimmy. Some of the little boy clothing included a cowboy set, overalls, and a clown costume.

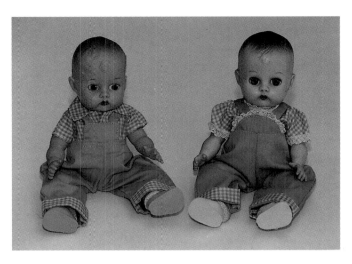

The vinyl Jimmy was introduced in 1958. He was really the earlier Ginnette with painted eyes. Jimmy and Ginnette are pictured in matching outfits from that year. (Clothes only not boxed: Girl, #2131 $35, Boy, #4131 $55).

Ginnette in her tagged flannel zipped sack (#711 from 1955) and Jimmy in pajamas (#7760 from 1957) are pictured beside their Ginnette wood crib with a drop side also dating from 1957 (#7787). (Clothes $10-12 each, crib with wear $35).

Vogue Jimmy from 1958 dressed in costume #4152. (Dressed doll $85 and up). *Doll and photograph from the collection of Rhonda Schoenick.*

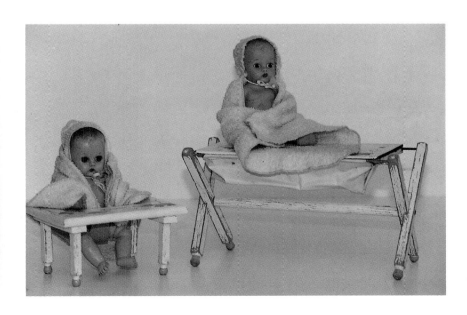

Ginnette and Jimmy are wrapped in their hooded towels from the bath set while they wait to be bathed. Both the Baby Bath (#7790) and the Tender (#7785) were featured in the company catalog for 1957. (Furniture $25 and up each in this condition).

Advertising Dolls

Although dolls have been tied to advertising all through this century, commercial tie-ins were especially prevalent during the 1950s. There were two types of advertising dolls during this time. One type was the doll that was obtained by the consumer as a premium. The customer had to send in proof of purchase seals or box tops along with a coupon plus a small amount of money to obtain the doll. Another example of the advertising doll was sold in retail stores as a regular toy. Doll companies received permission from corporations to name dolls after various products and tied-in the doll to the product. Both the corporations and the doll companies profited from this arrangement. Most popular were the dolls that promoted beauty and hair products like the Toni and Revlon dolls made by Ideal.

The advertising dolls in this chapter will be divided into two parts, beginning with many of the premium dolls produced during the 1950s.

Aunt Jemima Pancake Flour

Aunt Jemima Pancake Flour was first made in St. Joseph, Missouri, by the R.T. Davis Milling Co. In the early days, the company used an African-American woman named Nancy Green as Aunt Jemima to publicize the company. In 1925 the company was purchased by the Quaker Oats Company of Chicago. Cloth dolls representing Aunt Jemima were used as premiums for the company beginning in 1905. A new Aunt Jemima doll was offered in 1948 which was again carried in the 1950s. These dolls were made of a plastic oilcloth-like material. The 1948 offer included only one doll, the Aunt Jemima. The doll could be obtained by sending 25 cents and a package or sack top from Aunt Jemima Ready-Mix for pancakes or Buckwheats. By the 1950s a consumer could purchase the 12" Aunt Jemima doll, plus a similar 12" Uncle Mose doll, a 9" Wade doll, and a 9" Diana doll from the company.

12" Aunt Jemima doll first offered in 1948 and again into the 1950s by Aunt Jemima pancake mix. The stuffed doll was made of a plastic oilcloth type material. During the 1950s other dolls representing Uncle Mose, Wade, and Diana were also available. ($50-75).

Advertisement for the Aunt Jemima doll from 1948. The consumer had to send 25 cents plus the top from a package or sack of Aunt Jemima Ready-Mix for Pancakes or Buckwheats in order to obtain the doll.

Birds Eye Frozen Foods

According to Joleen Ashman Robison and Kay Sellers in their book *Advertising Dolls*, the General Foods Corp. offered three promotional dolls to advertise their Birds Eye frozen orange juice in 1953. The dolls were made of cloth and were to be cut out, sewn, and stuffed by the consumer. The dolls were 11" tall and were named Merry, Mike, and Minx.

Campbell Soup Company

The Campbell Soup Company used dolls to promote their products beginning in 1910. The early Campbell Kids dolls were made of composition and were sold in retail stores but by the 1950s the commercial Campbell dolls were made of "magic skin" and/or vinyl. In 1953 the Ideal Toy Company was licensed to produce Campbell Kids dolls. These dolls were sold through retail outlets and were 17.5" tall. The dolls from 1955 had magic skin bodies and they did not hold up well. In 1956 Campbell Soup offered its first premium Campbell Kid doll. It sold for $1.00 and a Campbell Soup label. The Campbell Cheerleader doll, another Campbell Kids model, was offered as a premium from 1957 until 1961. This premium also sold for $1.00 plus one soup label. Extra clothes could be obtained for the dolls for more soup labels and $1.00 for each outfit.

Pair of 8.5" Campbell Soup "Cheerleader" dolls made of vinyl. The dolls were offered from 1957 to 1961 by the Campbell Soup Co. The hair and features are painted and the shoes and socks are molded. They are marked on the back "Campbell Kid/Made by/Ideal Toy Corp." Each doll cost $1.00 plus one soup label. ($40-50 each).

Coca-Cola Company

The Coca-Cola Company offered a Santa Claus doll in 1958 to be used for that year's Christmas season. The doll was made by the Ruston Company of Atlanta. The doll was 15" tall with a vinyl face, hands, and boots. His body was red plush and Santa held a miniature bottle of Coca-Cola. This doll was made for several years with minor variations in color of boots and belt designs.

15" Coca-Cola Co. Santa Claus advertising doll circa late 1950s. The doll was made by the Ruston Co. of Atlanta, Georgia. He has a vinyl face with molded features and a beard. Santa holds a miniature bottle of coke. His hands are also vinyl. The doll was used to promote Coke products during the Christmas season and was also sold to the public. ($65-85).

Coco Wheat

Little Crow Foods used a Gretchen cloth doll to promote their Coco Wheat cereal from 1949 until 1966. The cloth doll came flat and was to be cut out, sewn, and stuffed by the consumer. The premium cost only 25 cents plus cereal proofs of purchase.

13" Coco Wheat Gretchen cloth doll used as a premium from 1949-1966. She was advertised on boxes of Coco Wheat cereal for a price of 25 cents in 1950. Coco Wheat was made by Little Crow Foods. ($10-15).

Fab

The Colgate-Palmolive Company offered several different dolls to promote their Fab laundry detergent during the 1950s. In 1954 the firm advertised an Americana Doll and Album. The doll was like most of the other inexpensive hard plastic 7" dolls of the period. Many similar dolls were sold by retail stores to be dressed by the consumer. The Fab dolls were costumed in different outfits to depict famous women of history including Martha Washington, Dolly Madison, Betsy Ross, Mary Todd Lincoln, Clara Barton, Barbara Fritchie, and Molly Pitcher. The dolls cost only $1 each. In 1956 the advertised Fab doll was a hard plastic walking doll. This 9" doll cost only $1.00 plus two box tops from the large size detergent. The dolls were manufactured for the company by Plastic Molded Arts Corp. In 1957 a different doll only 8" tall was offered by the company. She was also a walking doll and was dressed in a pink dress trimmed in blue. By 1958 the company was again offering the larger 9" tall doll.

Advertisement for the Fab 9" walking doll used by the Colgate-Palmolive Co. in 1956 to promote their Fab laundry soap. The doll cost $1.00 plus two box tops from a large size detergent box. Plastic Molded Arts Corp. manufactured the dolls. The dolls were made of hard plastic and had sleep eyes.

8" Fab hard plastic walking doll used as a premium to promote the laundry soap in 1957. This is the Fab doll most often found by collectors. Additional costumes could also be purchased for the doll. She is all hard plastic with sleep eyes and a walking mechanism. She is original except for her hat which has been replaced. ($40-50).

In 1958 Fab again offered a larger 9" hard plastic walker doll as a premium. This doll is wearing a replaced hat and shoes and socks. She came in a box with a label from Plastic Molded Arts Corp., so it is likely that company made all three of the hard plastic walking dolls used by Fab as premiums in the late 1950s. ($25-30).

Gerber Baby Foods

Gerber Baby Food of Fremont, Michigan, has immortalized its famous Gerber Baby trademark with numerous dolls since 1936. This trademark is a drawing of a baby by Dorothy Hope Smith in 1928. Although most of the dolls have been premiums issued by the company, several dolls have also been made as a tie-in product for the retail market.

The vinyl and rubber premium Gerber baby offered in the 1950s was very successful and continues to be sought by collectors today. The doll was 12" tall and was manufactured by the Sun Rubber Company. The doll was designed by famous doll designer Bernard Lipfert. In 1957 the Gerber baby was offered for $2.25 plus six Gerber labels or cereal box tops. The doll had a vinyl head and a rubber body. It was advertised to drink, wet, and cry. It came with a diaper, bib, bottle, and oatmeal playbox. The expiration date on the advertisement was June 30, 1957.

12" rubber and vinyl Gerber Baby used for a premium in 1957. The doll has a vinyl head and a rubber body. It cost $2.25 and six Gerber cereal box tops. The 1957 ad stated that the doll came with a bib, diaper, bottle, and oatmeal play box. It could drink and wet. The doll is marked "Gerber Baby/c Gerber Products Co." on the head. On its back is "Mfd. by/The Sun Rubber Co. Barbertson, O. U.S.A./Pat. 21188882/Pat 2160739." Also pictured is a Gerber orange juice advertising bank used to promote Gerber products. ($50-75).

Green Giant Peas

A "Country Girl" Doll was offered by Green Giant Peas with an expiration date of January 10, 1957. The doll had rooted saran hair and was 18" tall. The vinyl doll was dressed in a white taffeta dress with polka dots, a bonnet, and white shoes. Her outfit also included an apron decorated with the Green Giant trademark of the company. The doll cost $2.50 plus two labels from Green Giant peas. The offer was tied in to the coming Christmas season so the doll could be used as a gift.

Joy (Procter and Gamble Co.)

A walking doll was offered by Joy dishwashing soap in 1957. The 8" plastic doll appears to be one of the inexpensive dolls used for sewing projects during the decade. The consumer could order the doll by sending 50 cents and the top from a carton of any size bottle of Joy. The offer ended May 31, 1957. The doll's head was supposed to move as she "walked."

Advertisement from the Proctor and Gamble Co. promoting their 8" walking doll which was used as a premium for Joy dishwashing soap. The doll cost only 50 cents along with a number from the bottom of the Joy container. The doll appears to be the same type of inexpensive doll used by other companies for promotional purposes.

Green Giant Peas advertisement from 1957 promoting their 18" Country Girl doll. It could be purchased for $2.50 plus two labels from Green Giant Brand Peas. The vinyl doll had rooted Saran hair and sleep eyes. Her apron featured the Green Giant.

Kellogg Company

The Kellogg company offered an assortment of premium dolls beginning in 1925. All of their dolls were made of cloth to be sewn and stuffed at home until the company offered the Sweetheart Doll in 1954. The doll was made of vinyl and was 16" tall. She had rooted hair and sleep eyes. The doll was dressed in a red jumper, red tights, and white shoes and white blouse. She was marked "ACE 393" on the back of her neck.

Kellogg continued to offer some cloth dolls during the decade. These included Howdy Doody in 1952 and Snap, Crackle, and Pop in 1954.

In addition to these dolls, several additional plastic and vinyl dolls were available. These dolls were cheaper versions made to compete with Vogue's Ginny, Jill, and Ginnette dolls. In 1957 a hard plastic 8" tall walking doll was offered for $2.00 with several outfits of clothing also available. In 1958 a vinyl 10.5" doll with arched feet to wear high heel shoes was used as a premium for Rice Krispies or Raisin Bran. Other outfits were also available for this doll as well. In 1959 a Baby Ginger doll was offered. This 8" vinyl doll was a nursing doll with rooted hair and closing eyes. The doll could be purchased for $1.00 plus a box top from Rice Krispies or Raisin Bran cereal. For another dollar and an additional box top, a bunting, blanket, crib sheet, pillow case, peach dress, and pajamas could be purchased for the baby doll.

8" all original vinyl Baby Ginger doll offered by Kelloggs' as a premium in 1959. The doll cost $1.00 plus a box top from Rice Krispies or Raisin Bran cereal. For another dollar and an additional box top, a bunting, blanket, crib sheet, pillow case, peach dress, and pajamas could be purchased for the baby doll. ($40-50).

This 16" Sweetheart doll was offered as a premium by the Kellogg Co. in 1954. The vinyl doll has rooted hair, sleep eyes, and is marked "ACE 394" on the back of her neck. She is wearing her original clothing but the felt figures used as trim on her skirt are missing. ($35-40).

Nabisco Company

The National Biscuit Company has been in business for 100 years and they approved their first retail doll in 1914 when the Uneeda Kid was made in doll form by Ideal Toy and Novelty Co. Several more Nabisco tie-in composition dolls were produced by Ideal in the period before World War I. No other dolls of this type appear to have been used by Nabisco to promote their products until the 1950s.

During the later part of the 1950s, Nabisco offered a set of dolls from around the world that could be obtained by sending in two box tops from Wheat Honey and Rice Honey cereal plus $1.25 for each doll. There were twelve couples in the set of dolls but each doll was sold individually. Some of the countries represented by dolls in the set were Portugal, Greece, Italy, Israel, and Korea. Many of the dolls came with surprises including stamps or coins from the country they represented.

Dolls from the "Around the World" series of dolls offered as premiums by Nabisco during the late 1950s. Each doll cost $1.25 plus two box tops from Wheat Honey or Rice Honey Cereal. There were twelve couples in the set. Pictured is a man from Greece, a women from Portugal (missing large wooden utensil she originally held in her arms) and a woman from Italy. The dolls range in size from 7.5" to 8.5". ($10-15 each).

Star-Kist Foods, Inc.

Star-Kist Foods, Inc. offered a 16" tall vinyl doll dressed in a yellow slicker, sou'wester hat, and boots in 1959. The doll was used to promote the new label on the company's Chunk Light Tuna can that featured a fisherman with an earring dressed in a yellow hat and slicker. The doll had poodle-cut hair with sleeping eyes. She also wore a checked dress and panties. The doll cost just $2.50 plus two labels from Star-Kist Tuna. The offer ended December 31, 1959.

Star-Kist Foods advertisement for a 16" doll offered as a premium in 1959. The vinyl doll was dressed in a yellow hat and slicker to promote the new fisherman label on the can of tuna. He also wore a yellow hat. The doll cost $2.50 plus two labels from Star-Kist tuna.

Sunbeam Bread

Sunbeam Bread, a product of Quality Bakers of America Cooperative, Inc., used a picture of a little girl on their bread wrappers. In 1959 a doll was produced in that image to be used as a premium for the company. The Miss Sunbeam doll was 17" tall, with a vinyl head and arms and a harder vinyl body and legs. She had yellow rooted hair and sleep eyes.

17" Miss Sunbeam doll used in 1959 for a premium for Sunbeam bread, a product of Quality Bakers of America Cooperatives, Inc. The vinyl doll has yellow rooted hair, sleep eyes, and a molded open mouth with teeth. She is marked on the back of her head "Eegee" and "A" on her body. The doll represented the little girl used on the Sunbeam bread wrappers. On her apron is printed "Miss Sunbeam." ($35-45).

Tastee-Freez

Tastee-Freez offered an unusual premium at their "soft ice cream" stores in 1956. The stores issued punch cards that the customer could complete with the purchase of $2.00 worth of Tastee-Freez products. A "Personality Doll" could be bought for 99 cents and the completed card. The plastic doll appears to be similar to other 8" inexpensive dolls offered as premiums by other companies during the decade. The Tastee-Freez dolls came in at least nine different costumes.

Besides the unusual variety of premium advertising dolls offered by companies during the 1950s, another advertising phenomenon occurred during the decade. Throughout the century several companies had lent their names to retail dolls to promote both the doll and the company. Included were the Campbell Soup Company (Campbell Kids), National Biscuit Company (Uneeda Kid), and the H.D. Lee Company (Buddy Lee). But during the 1950s, there was an increase in links between large corporations and doll companies that had never been experienced before. Perhaps it was because of the popularity of the glamour girl doll images of the era that went very well with the cosmetic and hair care product industry. Although these dolls were not premium advertising dolls, they did advertise various products and most of the corporations received royalties from the dolls that were sold which carried their name. The most popular of these dolls promoted the following products.

Tastee-Freez advertisement for doll premium offered at their stores in 1956. The dolls could be purchased for 99 cents and a filled punch card ($2.00 in products). The dolls came in different outfits but appeared to be the same inexpensive hard plastic dolls sold in dime stores to be dressed by their customers.

Coty Cosmetics

The Coty Girl doll was issued in 1957 by the Arranbee Doll Co. The vinyl doll was 10.5" tall, with feet molded for high heels, and was jointed at the waist. The doll appears to be a doll purchased by Arranbee from another firm as she is marked with a P in a circle like other dolls of lesser quality. Her finishing and clothing set her apart from these other cheaper dolls. She was made to compete with Vogue's Jill doll as well as the other dolls of this type and size from the era. (See chapter on Arranbee for more information).

Curity

First-aid products produced by Bauer and Black have been called Curity for many years. The company had used nurse dolls called Miss Curity to promote this line since a composition doll was issued in 1946. Because of the change in popular doll materials a new Miss Curity was produced in 1953 which was made of hard plastic. The doll was manufactured by the Ideal Toy Company. Her body was the same as that used on the Toni dolls from the same period. The 14" tall doll was dressed as a nurse with a blue cape. She came with a Bauer and Black Curity first aid kit and book. See the chapter on Ideal dolls for more information.

A smaller 7" Miss Curity hard plastic doll was also produced. The doll had a one-piece body and legs with a movable head and arms. She was probably used as a premium.

Another less desirable Miss Curity doll was issued in the late 1950s or early 1960s. This vinyl doll had feet molded to fit high heels and rooted hair. It was marked "AE 2006-2" on the back of the neck. It was also dressed in a nurse's uniform. (See the Ideal chapter for more information).

This advertisement from a catalog issued by Heibst in Fargo, North Dakota, in 1957 features the doll called the Coty Girl marketed by the Arranbee Doll Co. The doll was 10.5" tall and many different costume changes could be purchased for her. The basic doll sold for $2.98 while her costumes ranged in price from $1.49 to $4.98 each. Besides being a popular fashion doll, she also promoted Coty Cosmetics through the tie-in. (See Arranbee chapter). *Catalog from the collection of Marge Meisinger.*

This 1953 catalog page from the Dayton Co. in Minneapolis, Minnesota, featured three of Ideal's tie-in dolls. The Toni doll was priced at $12.75, the Harriet Hubbard Ayer doll at $11.95, and the 14" Miss Curity doll with her nurse's bag and accessories also at $11.95. Other Ideal dolls shown were Betsy McCall and Saucy Walker. (See Ideal chapter). *Catalog from the collection of Marge Meisinger.*

Hanes

During the early 1950s, vinyl baby dolls molded in the image of new babies were very popular. Most of these early dolls were made of a vinyl that became sticky with age. There was such a variety of these dolls that were produced that an interesting collection can be made with selections produced by the various doll companies. The babies which promoted Hanes sleepers were 21" tall, dressed in the famous pajamas (with feet), and were molded with the mouths open in a yawn and their eyes closed. The dolls were called "Sleepy" and were made by the E.I. Horsman Co. in 1951.

Harriet Hubbard Ayer

Ideal Toy Company combined with the Harriet Hubbard Ayer cosmetic company to produce the Harriet Hubbard Ayer doll in 1953. The doll came in sizes of 14", 15", 18.5", and 20.5". The doll had a vinyl head and arms, plastic body and legs, and an applied wig. The wig was glued on. The face of the doll was rather pale and the make-up that came with her was to be used to make the doll more attractive. The products were washable so the doll's face could be washed and the make-up re-applied. The doll also came with a vanity and curlers. (See chapter on Ideal dolls for more information).

This advertisement for the new Ideal Harriet Hubbard Ayer doll appeared in the Alden Christmas catalog for 1953. The 14" size vinyl doll sold for $11.29 and came with the cardboard vanity and accessories pictured with the doll. Special washable makeup came with the doll and was to be used to make the doll "beautiful." Ideal's Betsy McCall is also pictured. *Catalog from the collection of Marge Meisinger.*

Revlon, Inc.

One of the most successful partnerships between a doll company and a cosmetic corporation was the one that united Revlon, Inc. and the Ideal Toy Co. when the Miss Revlon dolls were produced. The dolls were first manufactured in 1956. The vinyl dolls came in several sizes including 15", 18", 20", and 22". The dolls were fashioned as glamour girls with feet molded to fit high heel shoes. Many different designs of costumes were made for the dolls. A smaller Little Miss Revlon doll was introduced in 1957. This doll was also designed to wear high heels and many fashionable outfits were produced which could be purchased to give the doll a glamourous wardrobe. The dolls were discontinued in 1960. (See chapter on Ideal dolls for more information).

10.5" Little Miss Revlon with her box and an original boxed dress circa 1958. The vinyl doll was made by Ideal as a tie-in to the Revlon cosmetic company. She has pierced ears, sleep eyes, rooted hair, and arched feet to wear high heel shoes. She is jointed at the waist as were Ideal's larger Revlon dolls which came in sizes of 15", 18", 20", and 22.5". The pictured outfit is one of many manufactured by Ideal for these small dolls. The number on its box is 53 and the costume cost $1.50 when new. (Boxed doll $125-150, boxed costume $40-45).

Lee (H.D.) Company

The Buddy Lee dolls which were produced to promote products for the H.D. Lee Company have been some of the most popular advertising dolls ever made. Although the dolls were never used as premium dolls, they were sold by the Lee company to advertise their clothing. The first dolls were composition dolls sent to dealers to place in store windows. When the dealers finished using the dolls, they were sold to consumers. They proved to be so popular the company began selling the dolls as part of their regular line of products. In 1949 the dolls were re-designed and were then made of hard plastic. These new dolls were 13" tall. Several different uniforms were made for the dolls in addition to cowboy and farm clothing. Eventually the hats and clothing for the dolls were contracted out to other companies. The dolls were discontinued in 1962.

13" hard plastic Buddy Lee doll first made in 1949. The dolls were used to promote clothing made by the H. D. Lee Co. Buddy Lee has molded hair and features and is jointed at the shoulders. He is marked on the back "Buddy Lee." He wears his original clothing except for the hat which has been replaced. ($200-250). *Doll and photograph from the collection of Jim Shivers.*

Toni

During the late 1940s and 1950s, the Gillette company marketed a home permanent called Toni. This product became very popular with women who could not afford a permanent wave from a beauty shop. The company also increased sales of the permanent with their ad campaign which pictured twins with curly hair styles and the tag line "Which twin has the Toni?" Ideal Toy Company combined with the Gillette company to produce the Toni dolls beginning in 1949. The dolls were a huge success and they continued to be sold until 1956. The hard plastic dolls came in various sizes including 14", 16", 19", and 21". Over a million of the dolls were sold. The dolls came with kits that included a bottle of wave-set, comb, and curlers. (See chapter on Ideal dolls for more information).

After Ideal discontinued their dolls, American Character began making vinyl Toni dolls in 1958. These dolls were modeled with feet to wear high heels and they came as small as 10.5" to as large as 20". Although these dolls met with some success, they did not attract the following experienced by the earlier Ideal dolls. These dolls also came with Toni wave lotion. (See American Character chapter for more information).

Ideal's Toni dolls also were successfully marketed as tie-ins to the Toni Home Permanent (a product of the Gillette Co.). This 15" hard plastic Toni is marked P-91 on its back. She is all original except for her hair bow. The Toni dolls were made with sleep eyes, wigs, and closed mouths. ($350-400). *Doll and photograph from the collection of Carol J. Lindeman.*

The Sears Christmas catalog for 1958 featured the 20" Toni dolls made by the American Character company. The vinyl walking dolls sold for $13.98 and $14.98 each in this ad. The vinyl dolls were made with the popular fashion doll bodies. (See chapter on American Character).

Comic and Cartoon Dolls

Blondie

The "Blondie" comic strip began on September 15, 1930. The comic was done by Murat (Chic) Young for King Features Syndicate. In the beginning, Blondie was a flapper and Dagwood Bumstead was the son of a railroad millionaire. When Dagwood and Blondie were married on February 17, 1933, the millionaire disinherited his son. Then Dagwood began work for Mr. Dithers to earn a living. Two children were born to the Bumsteads; Alexander in 1934 and Cookie in 1941. Daisy, the dog, completed the household.

For many years, "Blondie" was the most widely circulated comic strip in the world. The strip was also the basis for twenty-eight movies and a television show. In the films, Penny Singleton played Blondie and Arthur Lake was Dagwood.

Chic Young died in 1973 but his son and his assistants continued the strip.

Life magazine did a feature story on comic strip dolls circa 1953. The article pictured all of the dolls then on the market. The article stated that Cookie, the daughter of Dagwood and Blondie, was the first comic doll to appear on the market. The doll had a hard plastic head, molded hair, sleep eyes, and was dressed in a graduation cap and gown. The maker of the doll is unknown.

Another series of dolls pictured in the article included other dolls based on characters from the Blondie comic strip. These were all cloth dolls made by Columbia Toy Products. They first appeared on the market in 1947 but were apparently still being sold in the early 1950s. Dagwood was 18" tall with a mask buckram type face, painted features, fur-like hair, and two tuffs of straw type hair sticking up on each side of his head. A similar smaller doll represented Dagwood's son Alexander. Other dolls in the series included Popeye, Little Iodine, Olive Oyl, Wimpey, Snuffy Smith, Sweetpea, and Annie Rooney.

Dennis the Menace

"Dennis the Menace," by Hank Ketcham, first began as a single daily panel comic on March 12, 1951. A Sunday strip was added in 1952, and Dennis was syndicated by Hall Syndicate. It featured a young boy who was the terror of his suburban neighborhood. The character was based on Ketcham's own four-year-old son. Dennis' parents were Henry and Alice Mitchell. A neighbor, Mr. Wilson, a little girl called Margaret, and Dennis' dog Ruff also played a part in the story line. The strip became so popular that a "Dennis the Menace" television series was produced from 1959-1963 which aired on CBS. Actor Jay North played the part of Dennis.

Dennis the Menace dolls were sold during most of the last half of the decade of the 1950s. In 1954 the Niresk Ind. Inc. catalog sold a 17" tall vinyl doll dressed in overalls for $3.98. "Dennis the Men-ace" was printed on his overalls. The 1955 Sears catalog also pictured the same doll. By 1958 a 14" Dennis doll was being marketed wearing red overalls. He was priced at $2.89. The features on all of these dolls were painted and the hair was molded. Because the early dolls had bodies made of the latex magic skin material, they tended to fall to pieces after much use.

17" Dennis the Menace doll with vinyl head, molded hair, and stationary eyes. He has a one-piece latex body. He is wearing his original clothing. The doll sold originally for $2.98 circa 1955. The back of his neck is marked "Dennis the Menace." Because of the stuffed latex body, these dolls are hard to find in excellent condition. ($75-90).

Dick Tracy

The comic strip "Dick Tracy" was developed and drawn by Chester Gould for the Chicago Tribune-New York News Syndicate beginning in 1931. The comic was so successful that it appeared as a radio show, a television program (ABC-1950-51), and several motion pictures. In 1937, Republic did a fifteen episode Dick Tracy serial, and in 1945 RKO produced four full length movies. Dick Tracy was revived again as a film character in 1990 when Warren Beatty produced the first big budget Dick Tracy film.

The comic strip has undergone many changes through the years. After a long courtship, Tracy married girlfriend Tess Trueheart in 1949 and their daughter Bonny Braids was soon added as a character. The Chester Gould villains are very unusual and include such interesting types as Flattop, Shakey, Mumbles, and Pruneface.

Because of the popularity of the "Dick Tracy" comic strip the dolls based on its characters were best sellers. Sparkle Plenty arrived on the doll scene in 1947. She portrayed the baby born to characters Gravel Gertie and B.O. Plenty. This child was blessed with long flowing blonde hair and the doll duplicated this trait. The hair on the doll was made of a heavy thread or yarn. The 14" doll sold for $5.75 in the Sears catalog in 1950. It also came in 16", 18", and 20" sizes. Sparkle had a magic skin latex body that turned dark with age. Fortunately some of the dolls came dressed in a blue playsuit that had long sleeves and long pants so the discoloration is not as noticeable as it would otherwise have been. The head was hard plastic with sleep eyes. Sparkle Plenty was made by the Ideal Toy Co.

The second child to be marketed in doll form was the baby born to Dick Tracy and his wife Tess Trueheart. Ideal again produced a doll in its image. The character's name was Bonnie Braids. The doll was made in various forms from 1951 until 1955. The first model was a 14" baby with the body again made of latex magic skin. The head was early vinyl with painted features and hair except for tuffs on its head. The doll sold for $6.79 in the 1952 Sears catalog. By 1954 Bonnie Braids was being produced as a walker. This model had a vinyl head, hard plastic body, and sold for $5.99 in the Sears catalog in 1955. An 11" crawling Bonny Braids was also made which was made of plastic. The doll crawled through the use of a key wind mechanism and sold for $2.94.

14" Sparkle Plenty circa 1951 made by Ideal. The doll has a hard plastic head, latex stuffed body, yellow yarn hair, sleep eyes, and pierced nostrils. Sparkle was the daughter of B.O. Plenty and Gravel Gertie in the comic strip, "Dick Tracy." She is marked "Made in U.S.A. Pat # 2232077." She wears her original coveralls but her shoes have been replaced. Many of the bodies on these dolls deteriorated and/or turned brown with age. ($90-110). The *Baby Sparkle Plenty Paper Dolls* was published by The Saalfield Publishing Co. in 1948. It is #1510 and was copyrighted by *The Chicago Tribune*. ($40 and up).

Advertisement for the Sparkle Plenty and Bonnie Braids dolls from the Sears Christmas catalog from 1951. The 14" Ideal Sparkle doll sold for $6.49 and Bonnie was priced at $6.69 for the 14" size. Also shown is the Howdy Doody doll with a plastic head which cost $7.49 for the 20" size doll. *Catalog from the collection of Betty Nichols.*

11.5" Bonnie Braids circa 1951. She has a vinyl head, latex body, molded open mouth with one tooth, painted eyes, and molded hair except for two pigtails. This Ideal doll originally came with a toothbrush and Ipana toothpaste. Bonnie Braids was the daughter of Dick Tracy and Tess Trueheart. Her clothes are original and she has her tag as well. On her neck is "c 1951 Chi. Tribune/Ideal Doll/USA. ($125-150).

Eloise

Eloise was a character developed by Kay Thompson in her books for children. Eloise was a young girl who lived in New York's Plaza Hotel who became kind of a female "Dennis the Menace" for her urban existence as Dennis was for the suburbs. A large painting of the fictional Eloise graced the lobby of the hotel for many years.

The Eloise doll is currently a very collectible item. The all cloth doll had painted features, a mask type face, and yellow yarn hair. It was 22" tall and originally sold for $6.47 in the Sears catalog in 1958. It was marketed by the American Character Doll Co. and was designed by Bette Gould.

22" cloth Eloise doll marketed by the American Character Doll Corp. The doll was sold by Sears in 1958 for $6.47. The doll is cotton stuffed with a painted buckram face and yarn hair. She is all original with her box which is marked c Eloise Ltd. ($250 and up). Eloise was a character created by Kay Thompson for a series of children's books. Pictured is the book *Eloise in Paris* by Kay Thompson published by Simon and Schuster in 1957. ($20 and up).

Gasoline Alley

"Gasoline Alley" was first introduced as a comic strip on November 14, 1918. Frank King developed the strip for the Chicago Tribune-New York News Syndicate .

The strip began with the bachelor Walt Wallet as the main character. On February 14, 1921, he found a baby boy abandoned on his door step. He decided to adopt the child and named him Skeezix. In 1926, Walt married a girl named Blossom and they had two more children, Corky and Judy.

Skeezix grew up and did his part in the army in World War II. He married his girlfriend, Nina in 1944 and began his adult life.

Although King died in 1969, the strip was continued by others. Perhaps the longevity of "Gasoline Alley" was partly due to King's decision to allow the characters to age. Thus new generations of characters were "born", making Walt, Skeezix, and the others seem like real people instead of inhabitants of a comic strip.

Clovia, the daughter of Nina and Skeezix, was a character from the comic strip "Gasoline Alley." She was born in a taxicab in 1949. The doll made to represent this comic baby was also pictured in the *Life* magazine article circa 1953. The doll had a hard plastic head, sleep eyes, and appeared to have had a rubber body. She had what looks like a four leaf clover on one hand. She was dressed in a kimona. She looks similar to the early 12" American Character Tiny Tears babies or Ideal's Betsy Wetsy.

13.5" Bonnie Braids toddler walking doll circa 1953 made by Ideal. She has a stuffed vinyl head, hard plastic body, sleep eyes, molded open mouth with teeth, and molded hair except for two pigtails. She is all original. On her head is marked "Copr. 1951/Chicago Tribune/ Idea Doll." On her body is "Ideal Doll/14." ($100-125). *Bonnie Braids Coloring Book* published by The Saalfield Publishing Co., #2356-15. c 1951 by the Chicago Tribune. ($30-40).

Joe Palooka

"Joe Palooka" was a comic strip developed by Ham Fisher in 1928. Joe was a boxer with a manager named Knobby Walsh. The *The New York Mirror* syndicated the feature in 1931. It was so popular a movie based on the comic was made in 1933. Later both a radio program and a television series about Joe Palooka were produced. The television program was a syndicated show airing in 1954 which starred Joe Kirkwood, Jr. as Joe Palooka. The comic strip ended in 1984. The popular dolls from the series were spawned after Joe married his girlfriend, Ann Howe, in 1949.

The "Joe Palooka" comic strip was the inspiration for three different dolls during the decade of the 1950s. The first one was Joan Palooka made by Ideal in 1952. The doll represented the daughter of the famous comic character. The doll was 14" tall with a magic skin latex body and molded hair except a top knot on top of her head. She had a vinyl head and painted eyes. The body of these dolls tends to blotch or darken so few are found in excellent condition. Her brother, Buddy, was introduced in doll form in 1953. The vinyl doll was 16" tall and was made by Personality Doll Corp. Buddy had molded hair and features. According to Patricia Smith writing in her column in *The Antique Trader*, another Palooka doll was marketed in 1956 called Max Palooka. He was made by Juro and also had molded hair and painted features.

14" Joan Palooka made by Ideal in 1952. She has a vinyl head and stuffed latex body with jointed arms and legs. Her eyes are painted and her hair is molded except for a top knot. She represented the daughter of Joe Palooka and Ann Howe in the "Joe Palooka" comic strip. She is pictured with her original box and clothing. The dolls came with Johnson's baby soap, powder, and baby skin care. The box is marked "Made in USA by Ideal Toy Corp. Hollis 23, N.Y." with a price tag of $6.95. The doll is marked "c 1952/Ham Fisher/Ideal on the back of her head. ($125-150 boxed).

16" Buddy doll representing Buddy Palooka from the "Joe Palooka" comic strip. He has a vinyl head, painted eyes, molded hair and a one-piece vinyl body and limbs. The doll was made by Personality Doll Corp. circa 1953. Although this doll is unmarked, some of the dolls are marked "H. Fisher." This doll does not have his original clothing which consisted of a pair of boxing shorts and a terry cloth robe. ($75 and up this condition).

Li'l Abner

Li'l Abner was one of the most popular comic strips in America during the 1940s and 1950s. It started as a daily strip in 1934 for United Features. In 1935, a Sunday strip was added. Al Capp (Alfred Gerald Caplin) was the originator of the comic and the famous characters which included Li'l Abner, Daisy Mae, Pansy Yokum and her husband Lucifer Ornamental Yokum, Marryin' Sam, Hairless Joe, and Lonesome Polecat.

In order to take advantage of the popularity of the comic, two films were made. The 1940 movie was produced by RKO, and the 1959 picture by Paramount. Dogpatch and its inhabitants were also featured in a Broadway musical in 1957.

A wonderful set of dolls honoring the characters from "Li'l Abner" was produced in 1957. Mammy and Pappy Yokum were made of vinyl in both 13" and 21" sizes. The dolls had molded hair and features. Li'l Abner was also manufactured at the same time and was the same type of doll. It is thought that a Daisy Mae was also marketed but she had a wig instead of molded hair. The tag on the Yokum dolls reads "Al Capp/Dog Patch Family/Exclusive License/Baby Berry/Toy N.Y.C."

A doll in the image of Li'l Abner's son was produced by Ideal in 1953 but this doll did not meet with success. The doll was first called "Mysterious Yokum" because the comic strip character did not have a real name for some time. Later he was named Li'l Honest Abe. Abe had a vinyl head, latex body, painted features, and molded hair. The doll sold for $2.98. It is a very hard doll to locate today, perhaps because not too many of them were originally sold.

Left: 13" Mammy and Pappy Yokum dolls made by Baby Barry, circa 1957. The vinyl dolls have painted faces, molded hair, and hats and are dressed in their original clothing. The tag reads "Baby Barry Toy - NYC." On the doll "c B. B " ($100-125 each). The dolls also came in the 21" size. They were based on characters created by Al Capp for his "Li'l Abner" comic strip.

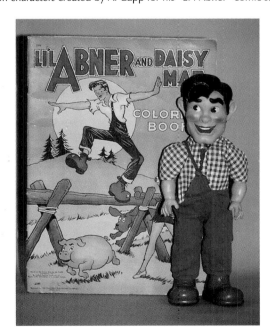

13" Li'l Abner vinyl doll made by Baby Barry. He is all original with molded hair and painted features. He is marked "Baby Barry Doll/25 c 1957. ($100-125). Also pictured is the *Li'l Abner and Daisy Mae Coloring Book* published by The Saalfield Publishing Co. #2391. ($50 and up). Both the doll and the book were based on the comic strip by Al Capp.

11" Mysterious Yokum doll based on Li'l Abner's son in the comic strip by Al Capp. The doll was made by Ideal in 1953 before the child was given the name Li'l Honest Abe. The doll has a vinyl head and a latex body. Its features and hair are painted. The doll is pictured with its original box and clothing. It still has the price tag of $2.98. ($100 and up).

Little Annie Rooney

"Little Annie Rooney" was a comic strip by Brandon Walsh that featured a twelve-year-old girl. It began as a daily strip in 1929 for King Features. The Hearst syndicate developed the comic to combat the popularity of "Little Orphan Annie." Several artists drew the character until it was taken over by Darrell McClure in 1930. A Sunday strip was also added at that time.

"Little Annie Rooney" was an orphan with a dog called Zero. The child, Annie, was eventually adopted by the Robins family. One of her favorite sayings, "Gloryosky" became a part of the language for a while. The strip ended in the mid-1960s.

A cloth doll was made in the image of Annie Rooney beginning in 1947 and apparently still on the market in the early 1950s. The doll had a buckram face, and painted features. It was made by Columbia Toy Products as a part of their series of "Comic Strip Dolls."

Little Iodine

The "Little Iodine" comic began as a Sunday feature in 1943. It was drawn by Jimmy Hatlo. Iodine was a mischievous little girl who lived in the suburbs with her father Henry and her mother Effie. She delighted in pulling pranks on her family and neighbors.

A Little Iodine doll was also produced by Columbia Toy Products as one of their "Comic Strip Dolls." These were all cloth dolls with painted features and buckrum type faces. They were on the market in the late 1940s and early 1950s.

Little Audrey

Little Audrey was a little girl comic character used by Harvey Films for cartoons distributed by Paramount. Many of these cartoons were shown on the television show, "Matty's Funday Funnies" on ABC from 1959 to 1962.

"Little Audrey" was also made in doll form. The doll had a vinyl head, molded hair and painted features. The rest of the doll was cloth. The tag on the doll reads "Little Audrey/Harvey Famous Cartoons." It is a very hard doll to locate today.

Little Lulu

"Little Lulu" had her beginning in June 1935 as a single panel cartoon in the *Saturday Evening Post*. The comic was drawn by Marge (Marjorie Henderson Buell).

In 1945, the character was featured in a comic book by Western Publishing Co. These Lulu comics were drawn by John Stanley.

"Little Lulu" became a newspaper strip for the New York News Syndicate from 1955 to 1967. Lulu and her boyfriend Tubby continue to be popular even today. Western Publishing Co. gained full ownership of the feature beginning in 1972.

Georgene Novelties held the rights to make Little Lulu dolls from 1944 until 1965. The company also produced Tubby and Alvin dolls. A cloth Little Lulu doll was marketed by the company during the later part of the 1950s. The 15" tall doll was advertised in the Sears catalog in 1958 for $3.79. The doll pictured in this book was purchased in 1955. The Sears Christmas catalog for 1959 featured two Little LuLu dolls. The smaller 14" doll was dressed in the traditional red dress while the larger 16" doll wore a western outfit made of felt and cotton. This doll also came with boots, guns, and a cowboy hat.

Nancy

Ernest Bushmiller began drawing a comic strip about Fritzi Ritz, a beautiful young woman, in the 1920s. In that comic, Nancy appeared as the heroine's eight-year-old niece. In 1940, Bushmiller made Nancy the star of her own strip, and by the 1950s and 1960s the comic really took off. "Nancy" was a kid strip with a boy named Sluggo as Nancy's friend. The comic was drawn very plainly and the two main characters remain popular today.

Characters from Nancy were produced in doll form in 1954. These dolls are very rare. The Nancy doll had a vinyl head with molded hair and hairbow and a vinyl body. She is marked "S&P/54/C 1954." The box for this doll is labeled "S & P Doll & Toy Co. Brooklyn." The Sluggo companion doll had molded hair and hat with set in plastic eyes.

15" Sluggo from the "Nancy" comic strip by Ernest Bushmiller. The doll dates from 1954 and was made by S & P Doll and Toy Co. in Brooklyn, New York. He has a vinyl head with a molded hat, set in plastic eyes, and a one-piece latex body. He is all original. He is marked on the back of his head "S & P/c 1954." A companion Nancy doll was also made. ($200-225).

15" Little Lulu cloth doll made by Georgene Novelties in 1955. The doll is cotton stuffed with a buckram face, thread hair, and painted features. Her shoes and socks are made as part of the body. She also is all original including her plastic purse. ($100 and up). Little Lulu was a comic character created by Marjorie Henderson Buell in 1935. The coloring book was published by Whitman Publishing Co. #1186 and carries a copyright by Marjorie Henderson Buell. ($20-25).

Popeye

Popeye began as part of the "Thimble Theater" comic strip which was started by Ekzue Crisler Segar for the W.R. Hearst chain in 1919. Popeye became a part of the strip in 1929. Other important characters were: Olive Oyl, Jeep, Swee'pea, and Wimpy. Paramount took advantage of the popularity of the characters by making animated movie cartoons beginning in 1932.

When Segar died in 1938 other artists continued to draw the strip. Popeye is still an important comic character, especially on television. A Popeye movie was made in 1980 which starred Robin Williams as Popeye.

A 13" Popeye doll was produced by Cameo during the late 1950s. The all vinyl doll had molded features, hat and clothing and came with a pipe. He was marked "Cameo K.F.S". He originally sold for $3.82 in the Sears catalog.

The Popeye characters had also been produced in doll form in 1947 and were still being sold circa 1950. These dolls were made of cloth with buckrum type faces. The dolls were marketed by Columbia Toy Products. Dolls representing Olive Oyl, Wimpey, Sweetpea, and Popeye were all part of the series.

Penny

"Penny" was one of the first Bobby-Soxer comic strips when it was begun in 1943. Harry Haenigsen was the originator of the strip. It was distributed by the Herald-Tribune Syndicate. The main characters were Penelope Pringle and her best friend Judy.

A large doll approximately 36" tall was made to represent Penny by the Alexander Doll Co. circa 1951. The doll had a vinyl stuffed head and limbs, wig, and a cloth body.

Poor Pitiful Pearl

"Poor Pitiful Pearl" was a cartoon character created by William Steig.

A Poor Pitiful Pearl doll was first marketed in 1958. It was 13" tall and was produced by the Brookglad Corp., Glad Toy Co. The doll came in two sizes, 13" or 16" and was sold with two outfits of clothing. She was dressed in a ragged dress but also was supplied with a party dress. The vinyl doll had rooted hair and painted features. The 13" model sold for $4.98 in 1958. Other versions of the doll were made by Horsman in later years.

The Sad Sack

"The Sad Sack" began as a World War II cartoon drawn by Sgt. George Baker for the Stars and Stripes newspaper and the army weekly magazine called Yank. These publications were both targeted to the G.I.s, but the feature was so popular it gained civilian attention as well. In 1946 it was issued as a Sunday comic distributed by Bell Syndicate. It was discontinued in the early 1950s. The comic was about the frustrations of being a G.I. in the army. A movie called The Sad Sack was made in 1957 with Jerry Lewis in the starring role.

A vinyl doll based on the character was featured in the Sears catalog in 1959. The 16" doll sold for $3.97. It had a one-piece vinyl body, painted features, and molded hair.

13" Poor Pitiful Pearl doll made by Gladtoy Toy Co., Brookglad Corp. The doll sold for $4.98 in the 1958 Sears Christmas catalog. The vinyl doll had sleep eyes, rooted saran hair, and was sold in a patched dress although a party dress was also supplied with the doll. The doll was based on a cartoon character created by William Steig. ($75-85).

16" vinyl Sad Sack doll based on the character created by Sgt. George Baker during World War II. The vinyl doll has molded hair, painted features, and a hard vinyl one-piece body. He is not marked. The doll was featured in the Sears catalog in 1959 when it sold for $3.97. The clothes on this doll have been replaced. ($50 and up). The Sad Sack comic is from July 1971 and was published by Harvey Publications. ($5).

13" Popeye vinyl doll. Marked "Cameo K.F.S." Circa 1950s. Pipe has been replaced. Made by Cameo based on the comic character carried by King Fisher Syndicate. ($40-50). Popeye Coloring Book #2834 was published by Samuel Lowe Company. c 1959 King Features Syndicate. ($20-25). Popeye Goes On a Picnic by Crosby Newell. Published by Wonder Books c 1958 by King Features Syndicate, Inc. ($5-8). From the collection of Suzanne Silverthorn.

Personality Dolls

Princess Anne

Princess Anne, the daughter of Queen Elizabeth II of England, was born August 15, 1950. A Princess Anne doll was marketed by Madame Alexander in 1957. The doll was one of the regular 8" hard plastic Wendy dolls dressed to represent the Princess. The doll had bending knees. A similar Prince Charles doll was sold at the same time. Prince Charles was born to Queen Elizabeth in 1948.

Annabelle

Annabelle was a little girl in Kate Smith's book *Stories of Annabelle*. Kate Smith was the star of her own television show for NBC from 1950 to 1954. The Madame Alexander Doll Co. marketed a Maggie doll as Annabelle in 1952. The doll wore a sweater with "Annabelle" stitched on the front. It came in sizes of 15", 18", and 23".

Gene Autry

Gene Autry was born in 1907 and he became a very famous western film star as well as a song writer. He began his career on radio and became a star on the "National Barn Dance." His first picture called *In Old Santa Fe* was made in 1934 and his last film was in 1953. Autry was usually teamed with Smiley Burnett, his sidekick, and his horse Champion in the movies he made for Republic. His national radio show began in 1940 and his career expanded even more when he recorded several hit records. Autry helped write his first hit song, "That Silver-Haired Daddy of Mine". Other well-known Autry recordings include "Mexicali Rose," "Here Comes Santa Claus," and "Rudolph the Red-Nosed Reindeer." After Autry served in the U.S. Air Force during World War II, he set up his own production company and continued to make western films. In 1950, Autry turned to television with "The Gene Autry Show" based at Melody Ranch.

A Gene Autry doll was marketed by the Terri Lee company in 1949 and 1950. The doll was a regular Terri Lee doll with painted hair and decal eyes. It is marked on the back "Terri Lee/Pat. Pending." Two different outfits were made for the doll. One had a yellow satin shirt and brown pants with fringe on the sides. The other one is pictured. The clothes were labeled with the Gene Autry name. (See Terri Lee chapter for more information).

16" plastic doll made by Terri Lee Inc. in 1949. He is wearing his original shirt and pants marked "Gene Autry." His belt and boots have been replaced. He is missing his hat and tie. His hair and features are painted. He is marked "Terri Lee/Pat. Pend." on his back. He originally sold for $10.95 through mail order. ($1300 and up). Also pictured is a *Gene Autry Coloring Book* (#1157) c 1949 by Gene Autry. Published by Whitman Publishing Co. ($35-50).

Lucille Ball

Lucille Ball appeared in nearly seventy-five motion pictures and was a famous movie star, but it is as the most popular television comedienne of the century that she will be remembered.

The famous redhead was born in 1911 in Celoron, New York. She began her career as a chorus girl in New York and was soon hired as a model by Hattie Carnegie. Lucy moved to California to make her first film, *Roman Scandals* in 1933. She continued her movie career with Goldwyn-United Artists, then Columbia and finally RKO. In 1940 she married Desi Arnaz who would become her co-star in the famous sitcom "I Love Lucy." After making several films for Metro-Goldwyn-Mayer from 1943 until 1946, Lucy turned to radio to play the leading role on the CBS show, "My Favorite Husband." The comedy star switched to television in 1951 and began filming the famous "I Love Lucy" with her husband Desi. The show aired on CBS and was an instant success. It continued on CBS until 1958. Other popular Lucille Ball television comedies include "The Lucy Show" (1961-1968) and "Here's Lucy" (1968-1974). Both programs aired on CBS.

Lucille Ball died in 1989 at the age of seventy-seven.

Because of the popularity of the "I Love Lucy" television program, many products were produced to tie-in to the show. The first doll was marketed by the American Character doll Company. It was called the "I Love Lucy Baby" and was made during Lucy's pregnancy circa 1952. It was similar to the Tiny Tears dolls made by the company. The doll was 16" tall, made of rubber with a hard plastic head. The doll could wet and blow bubbles. The hair was molded and the doll had sleep eyes. An all vinyl doll was made by American Character in 1953. This baby doll was a Little Ricky baby doll 20" tall with sleep eyes and molded hair. His mouth was open to take a bottle and he was dressed in a romper outfit with "Ricky Jr." embroidered on his belt. A third doll was marketed in a toddler model. American Character also produced this doll. This vinyl Ricky Jr. came in sizes of 17" or 21". He had rooted saran hair and still could take a bottle and blow bubbles.

An "I Love Lucy" doll was manufactured in 1953. The doll was 27" tall with a plastic face, orange yarn hair, and a cloth body. She is marked on the apron, "I Love Lucy/Desi."

21" vinyl Little Ricky doll made by American Character in 1953. He has sleep eyes, open mouth, and molded hair. He is wearing his original romper but is missing his shoes and socks. "Little Ricky" is embroidered on his belt. He is marked "Amer. Char. Dol." on the back of his head. ($150-175). Also pictured is the *Lucille Ball Desi Arnaz Cut-Out Dolls with Little Ricky* paper doll book (#2116). Published by Whitman Publishing Company, c 1953 by Lucille Ball and Desi Arnaz. ($85-100).

27" tall Lucy doll produced in 1953. The doll has a plastic face, orange yarn hair, and a cloth body. The apron is marked "I Love Lucy/Desi." ($140-160). *Courtesy of Dora Pitts and Al Pitts.*

A catalog issued by the Emporium in San Francisco, California, in 1954 pictured a Ricky, Jr. doll that came in both 17" and 21" sizes. He was made of vinyl and had rooted saran hair. The doll was made by American Character and sold for $10.95 for the smaller size and $15.95 for the larger model. *Catalog from the collection of Marge Meisinger.*

Advertisements for the American Character Doll Company from the early 1950s picture two dolls associated with the "I Love Lucy" CBS television show. The earliest doll, called the "I Love Lucy Baby" was produced during Lucy's pregnancy (circa 1952). It was similar to the Tiny Tears dolls made by the company. The doll was 16" tall, made of rubber with a hard plastic head. The doll could wet and blow bubbles. The hair was molded and the doll had sleep eyes. The second advertisement shows the doll that was made in 1953 after the birth of Little Ricky. Also pictured is a doll carriage labeled "Ricky, Jr." made by Play Time Products. A Trimble Doll Bath was also made for the 21" vinyl doll. Extra clothes for the doll could be purchased.

William Boyd (Hopalong Cassidy)

William Boyd was born in 1898 in Cambridge, Ohio. He was an actor in silent films beginning in 1920 before he made the first Hopalong Cassidy film in 1935. The character was based on fiction stories by Clarence E. Mulford. The original character had a limp which accounted for the name but William Boyd changed the characterization and did away with the limp.

There were sixty-six films made in the series which were syndicated for television in 1948. A half hour television show was begun in the same year. Ninety-nine episodes were used in the series. They were shown on NBC from June 1949 until December 1951. The part of Hopalong Cassidy was played by William Boyd and his partner, Red Connors, was played by Edgar Buchanan. Topper was the name of Cassidy's horse. The television show was so popular that numerous kid's products were made to tie-in to the program.

Included was the doll made by Ideal in 1949. It is a very good likeness of Boyd and has a vinyl head with painted features and molded hair. The body is stuffed cloth and the doll came in both 18" and 21" sizes. The doll was dressed in a satin jacket, necktie, belt with guns, and a black hat. The other clothing was made as part of the doll. This doll is very hard to find with all the original clothing pieces. Boyd died in 1972.

Champagne Lady

The Champagne Lady has always been associated with Lawrence Welk and his band. Welk was born in 1903 in North Dakota. He played the accordion and his organization was called "Lawrence Welk and His Champagne Music Makers." He had a very successful career, especially on television, and he died in 1992 at the age of eighty-nine. His original programs are still being run on PBS in most parts of the country. The shows were first aired on ABC beginning in 1955 and they continued on that network until 1971.

The programs always featured many singers and dancers but there have been only two "Champagne Ladies." Alice Lon held the title from 1955-1959 and then was replaced by Norma Zimmer. Alice Lon died in 1981.

The vinyl Champagne Lady doll was produced by the Effanbee Doll Co. during Alice Lon's tenure as the Champagne Lady. The doll was made in 1957 and came in 21" and 25" sizes. The Lady doll was a walker with feet molded to fit high heel shoes. She came with either blonde or brunette wigs, a red or green dress, and with gloves, a handbag, and a hat. The doll was jointed at the waist, knees, and ankles. She appears to have been marketed only one year and was priced from $15.95 to $18.95 depending on the size.

23" Hopalong Cassidy doll made in the likeness of William Boyd who played the part on television. The doll was made by Ideal circa 1950. He has a vinyl head, stuffed cloth body, molded hair, and painted features. He is missing his hat and necktie. ($350 and up). Also pictured is the *Hopalong Cassidy Coloring Book Starring William Boyd* (#1200). c 1950 by Doubleday and Company. Published by Samuel Lowe Company. ($40-50).

This advertisement for the new Hopalong Cassidy doll appeared in the *Playthings* magazine in July 1950. He came in two sizes: 23" which sold for $8.00 and 30" priced at $10. The doll was made by the Ideal Novelty and Toy Co.

19" "Lawrence Welk's Champagne Lady" doll. The doll was made in 1957 by the Effanbee Doll Company. Her arms and head are vinyl, and her body and legs are rigid vinyl. The legs are jointed at the knees and ankles and she wears high heel shoes. She is wearing her original clothing including a hat. She is marked "Effanbee" on the back of her head. ($200 and up).

Angela Cartwright

Angela Cartwright was born in 1952 and she became a television celebrity when she portrayed Danny Thomas' daughter on the "Danny Thomas Show" from 1957 to 1965.

Plastic Molded Arts Corp. produced a doll for General Food Corp. in 1959 in the young stars image. The doll was 14.5" tall and was used as a premium. It cost $2.00 plus two Post Toasties box tops to secure the doll. The doll had dark rooted hair, sleep eyes, and her head was marked "Linda Williams." In the early 1960s, the Natural Doll Company marketed an Angela Cartwright doll in several sizes.

15" Angela Cartright doll as Linda Williams from the ABC television program "Make Room for Daddy." The first Linda Williams dolls were made as premiums for General Foods Corp. in 1959. Later, another doll was issued by the Natural Doll company. Both dolls were approximately 15" tall with dark rooted hair, sleep eyes, and made of vinyl. This doll's head is marked "Linda Williams." ($50-75). Also pictured is a record called "An Evening with Danny Thomas." The recording was a premium from post Cereals and includes family members Marjorie Lord, Rusty Hamer, and Angela Cartwright. Columbia LP recording ($8-10).

Dick Clark

Dick Clark, the eternally young host of "American Bandstand," was born in 1929. The famous show began as a local Philadelphia program in 1952. It premiered on the ABC network in the fall of 1957. The series remained on the air for decades, with several format and name changes.

One of the most sought-after products from the early years of "American Bandstand" is the Dick Clark doll. It was made by Juro Novelty Co. in 1958. The doll was 27" tall, with a stuffed body and vinyl head and hands. It was called an autograph doll and was made for older teens so they could collect autographs on the doll's jacket.

Dorothy Collins

Dorothy Collins was born in Canada in 1926 and she became a well-known television personality when she starred in "Your Hit Parade" from 1950 until 1959. According to John Axe in his book *The Encyclopedia of Celebrity Dolls*, the Star Doll Co. marketed a Dorothy Collins walking doll in 1954. The head was marked "14" and the back "Made in USA 14". The doll was all hard plastic and she had a blonde wig, open mouth, and teeth.

Davy Crockett

Davy Crockett, the American Frontiersman, was born in 1786. He died defending the Alamo in 1836. The "Davy Crockett" television show was originally shown as part of the "Disneyland" series in 1955 on NBC. Fess Parker played the part of Davy. The show was a hit with kids and many products were produced as tie-ins. Several dolls were also marketed in the Davy Crockett image during the mid-1950s. Both the Madame Alexander and Vogue doll companies produced these dolls. Both companies dressed their regular Wendy and Ginny dolls in Davy Crockett outfits to achieve the Crockett look. (See Vogue chapter). Several other companies also made Davy Crockett dolls.

33" Davy Crockett doll with plastic mask face and cloth body. Circa 1955. Maker unknown. The doll was apparently made to take advantage of the Davy Crockett boom which came about because of the popularity of the program shown on the "Disneyland" series in 1955 on NBC. ($25-30). Many other companies also produced Crockett dolls during the mid-1950s. See Vogue chapter.

27" Dick Clark doll portraying the host of "American Bandstand" the popular ABC television show. The doll has a vinyl head and hands, molded hair, painted features, and a cloth body. He is wearing his original clothes. The head is marked "Juro." It was made in 1958 by Juro (Eegee). Sears sold the doll for $7.49 in 1959. ($225-275).

Arlene Dalton

Arlene Dalton was the Story Princess on the Howdy Doody show which began on NBC in 1947. In 1954 the Alexander company marketed a Story Princess doll using the Margaret face for the 15" doll. The doll was also issued in 1955 and 1956. The 18" size was made with the Binnie Walker face.

18" hard plastic Story Princess from 1954. The doll came in a 15" size as well. She was based on Arlene Dalton, the NBC television star who played the "Story Princess" on the "Howdy Doody" program during the early 1950s. The doll uses the Binnie Walker face. She is in mint condition and all original. ($700-800). *Doll and photograph from the collection of Marge Meisinger.*

Elizabeth II

Elizabeth II, Queen of England, was born in 1926 to the Duke and Dutchess of York. Her father became King George VI in 1936 when Edward VII abdicated in order to marry "the woman he loved." Elizabeth became the heir to the throne at the age of ten. In 1947 Elizabeth married Phillp Mountbatten, formerly Prince Philip of Greece. Elizabeth became Queen of England in 1952 at the death of her father. She was twenty-five years old. She was crowned Queen in 1953.

The Madame Alexander Doll Co. produced several different Queen Elizabeth dolls during the decade of the 1950s. In 1953 an 18" hard plastic Margaret faced doll was used to represent the new queen. The doll was dressed in a white brocade dress with a blue sash and was included in the "Glamour Girl" series. The same doll with an added long velvet robe trimmed in white fur was included in the series called "Beaux Arts Creations" the same year. She was identified as Queen Elizabeth. A similar doll was issued in the "Me and My Shadow" series in 1954. The description says she is wearing a white orlon ermine cape over her white court gown. A similar doll was also made in the 7.5" size that year. In 1955 the 7.5-8" Queen Elizabeth doll #499 was issued by the Alexander Company. The doll was the regular Alexander-Kins doll dressed in a gown of white brocade with a scarlet velvet robe. The new Alexander 20" Cissy was also marketed dressed as Queen Elizabeth in 1955. She was part of the "A Child's Dream Come True" series. She wore a court gown of white brocade with a garter sash and star. Her costume also featured a tiara, earrings, bracelets, and long white gloves. In 1956 as part of "Cissy Fashion Parade" another Cissy Queen Elizabeth doll was issued. She wore a hoop skirt petticoat of taffeta. By 1957 the Cissy Queen was no longer being identified as Queen Elizabeth. This doll was part of the series called "Cissy Models Her Formal Gowns." Her gown in 1957 was made of gold brocade. Another version of this doll dressed in gold brocade was offered in 1958. In both 1958 and 1959 the 10" Cissette doll was dressed as a queen in a gown of gold brocade in 1958 and in white brocade in 1959. She was just labeled a queen and was not called Queen Elizabeth. (See also Alexander chapter).

10.5" Madame Alexander hard plastic Cissette doll dressed as Queen Elizabeth marketed in 1959. Her crown has been replaced. Although the doll is called only "Queen" in the company catalog, this Cissette costume was much like dolls produced throughout the decade that were labeled "Queen Elizabeth." See Alexander chapter for pictures of several of these dolls. ($200 and up). Also pictured is the *Coronation Coloring Book* (#2415). Published by The Saalfield Publishing Co., 1953. ($20-30).

Dale Evans (see Roy Rogers)

Haleloke

Haleloke was a Hawaiian dancer who was featured on Arthur Godfrey's television show, "Arthur Godfrey and Friends" on CBS. A doll was made in her image in 1954. The hard plastic walking doll was 18" tall and came dressed in a grass skirt and top. She was available from the Cast Distributing Corp. The doll was sold with a trunk which included an extra outfit and a guitar.

18' hard plastic doll representing Haleloke, a performer on the Arthur Godfrey show (CBS). The doll has sleep eyes, open mouth with teeth, and an applied wig. She was made in the USA in 1954 by the Cast Distributing Corp. and is a jointed walker. She is pictured with her extra dress. Her grass skirt is replaced. She originally came with a guitar. ($200-250).

Rusty Hamer

Rusty Hamer was another television personality from the 1950s. He played Danny Thomas' son on the "Make Room for Daddy" series beginning in 1953 on ABC. His character's name was Rusty Williams. According to Patricia Smith in her book *Effanbee Dolls That Touch Your Heart* a Rusty doll was made by Effanbee which was in the television character's image in 1955. The vinyl doll had molded hair and sleep eyes.

Mary Hartline

Mary Hartline (born 1926) got her title as "Queen of the Super Circus" because of her role on the "Super Circus" television program. The show aired on ABC from 1949 until 1956. It featured circus variety acts with Claude Kirchner and Jerry Colonna as ringmasters. Mary Hartline acted as bandleader.

Ideal first marketed their Mary Hartline doll in 1952. At first the doll was strung but later it was made as a walker. The hard plastic doll came in sizes of 16" and 23". It used the Toni bodies. Two versions of a smaller Mary Hartline doll were made. They were both a little over 7" in height. One model was made by Ideal while the other cheaper version was a Lingerie Lou Doll. All the dolls were dressed in majorette outfits. The larger dolls came in green costumes as well as the more popular red. (See Ideal chapter for more information).

16' Mary Hartline doll made by the Ideal Toy Company. She represented the star of the "Super Circus" television program which aired on ABC. She dates from 1952. She has a blonde nylon wig, closed mouth, and blue sleep eyes. She is marked on her back "Ideal Doll/P-91" and is wearing her original clothing although she is missing her baton. ($300 and up). Also pictured *Mary Hartline Cut-Out Dolls Coloring Book (#2104)*. c M.H.E. Published by Whitman Publishing Co., 1951. ($30-40).

8" hard plastic Mary Hartline doll. Her back is marked "This is an original/ Lingerie Lou/Doll." The doll has sleep eyes and blonde hair. She is wearing her original outfit from "Super Circus." ($25-35). Also shown is the book *Super Circus* by Helen Wing. Rand McNally and Company. C 1955 American Broadcasting Company. ($5-10).

Sonja Henie

Sonja Henie made her way to the Hollywood screen in a very unique way. She traveled the road to fame and fortune on ice skates.

Born in Oslo, Norway, in 1912, Sonja began skating at the age of six and by fourteen was declared the ice skating champion of Norway. In 1927, she was awarded the world skating championship, a title she held for ten years. In 1928 she won her first Olympic gold Medal in figure skating and went on to win again in 1932 and 1936.

After the 1936 Olympics, Sonja and her father went on a skating tour in the United States. Darryl Zanuck from Twentieth Century-Fox saw the show and signed Sonja to a five year contract with his studio. Sonja's first film, *One In a Million*, was released in 1936 and became an immediate success. Sonja continued to make skating pictures for Fox for several more years.

In addition to doing films, Sonja began the Hollywood Ice Revue. The show was to become an annual touring event. She skated in the revue until 1952. Sonja Henie died from leukemia in 1969.

The Alexander company had been successful marketing Sonja Henie dolls made of composition so in 1951 the firm issued a new Sonja doll with a vinyl head. This model had a hard plastic body and her vinyl head was stuffed with cotton. The doll came in sizes of 15", 18", and 21". The doll came with a glued on wig and used a Madelaine face.

18" Sonja Henie doll made by Alexander in 1951. The doll has a vinyl head, applied wig, and sleep eyes. The hard plastic body is fully jointed and is the same design that was used on the Madelaine dolls. She is wearing her original clothing. ($750 and up). *Doll from the collection of Jo Ann and Jason Walters. Photograph by Kelly Anderson.*

Sherry Jackson

Sherry Jackson was born in 1947 and gained fame for her child role on the Danny Thomas television show, "Make Room for Daddy." She played Thomas' daughter Terry on the program beginning in 1953.

According to Patricia Smith in her book *Effanbee Dolls That Touch Your Heart* a doll was manufactured in Sherry's image by the Effanbee company in 1955. The Sherry doll had a vinyl head, rooted hair in pigtails, and perhaps a hard plastic body. It was issued at the same time as the Rusty doll which was made to honor Rusty Hamer who played her brother on the ABC show.

Bob Keeshan (Capt. Kangaroo)

Robert (Bob) Keeshan was born in 1927. He began his television career playing the part of Clarabell on NBC on the "Howdy Doody" show. In 1955 he changed networks and characters and became Captain Kangaroo for CBS. The show became the longest running show on television.

Many dolls have been produced in the Captain's image but one of the best was manufactured by Baby Barry in the late 1950s. This doll was 21" tall and had a vinyl head and hands with a stuffed cloth body. The doll featured molded grey hair and a molded moustache.

Richard Keith (Little Ricky)

Richard Keith played Little Ricky on the very popular television program, "I Love Lucy." The show, starring Lucille Ball and Desi Arnaz, aired on CBS in several formats from 1951 until 1958. Several dolls as well as a puppet were made in the image of Little Ricky. (See Lucille Ball for more information).

Emmett Kelly

Emmett Kelly was the most popular clown the circus has ever known. During the high point of his career the "Willie the Clown" character was recognized everywhere. Kelly was born in 1898 and he began his life as a circus clown in 1931. Kelly's clown character even made appearances in the movies (*The Greatest Show on Earth*) and on television. Kelly died in 1979.

A Willie the Clown doll was produced by Baby Berry in 1958. The doll came in both 15" and 24" sizes. It was sold by Sears in 1958 in the 15" size for $2.79.

13" Emmett Kelly doll made in the image of the famous clown he played called Willie. The doll has a vinyl head with molded hat, hair, and features and a vinyl body. The doll was made by Baby Barry Toy in the late 1950s. A larger 21" doll was also made. The clothing on this doll has been replaced. ($35-40).

Pinky Lee

Pinky Lee, the popular star of children's television, was born Pincus Leff in 1916. He played the burlesque circuit for many years before his career was revived with his television show. "The Pinky Lee Show" was a children's program that aired on NBC from 1950 until 1955. The show included music, circus acts, and comedy, with Pinky Lee as host.

A 25" tall doll was produced by Juro (Eegee) in the early 1950s. The doll had a vinyl head and a molded hat. The body was cloth. The back of the head was marked "A/Juro/Celebrity/Product.

Vivien Leigh

Vivien Leigh was an English actress born in 1913, who had the good fortune to play the part of Scarlet O'Hara in the movie *Cone With the Wind*. The film premiered in Atlanta, Georgia, on December 14, 1939. The movie was based on the best selling novel by Margaret Mitchell which had skyrocketed to success in 1936. David O. Selznick bought the film rights for $50,000 and began shooting the movie in January 1939. The public had insisted that Clark Gable play the role of Rhett Butler, and a nation-wide search was launched by Selznick to find a girl to play Scarlet. Selznick's brother Myron introduced him to Vivien and she won the role. The film was awarded ten Academy Awards including Best Actress for Leigh. The movie also captured the Best Picture award.

Vivien Leigh also appeared in many more films in both England and the United States from 1934 until the 1960s. She was married to famous English actor Laurence Olivier and the couple appeared in several plays together. Leigh died in 1967.

Many Scarlet dolls were produced by the Madame Alexander company from 1940 until the present time. Although the dolls don't really represent Vivien Leigh, they are usually dressed in costumes modeled after those the star wore in the famous film. Hard plastic Scarlets were produced in the 7.5" size in 1955, 1956, and 1957. The dolls were from the regular Alexander-Kins line but dressed in Scarlet costumes.

Shari Lewis

Shari Lewis was a ventriloquist who worked with puppets and entertained millions of children on her various television shows. She was born Shari Hurwitz in 1934.

After two successful local New York children's programs, Shari had her first national program for NBC in 1957. The show featured her famous puppets, Lamb Chop, Charlie Horse, and Hush Puppy. She continued to do various shows for NBC until 1963. Shari Lewis currently appears on the PBS network in her own children's program.

The Madame Alexander company produced a doll to honor Shari Lewis which was marketed in 1959. The doll came in two sizes, 14" and 21". Her feet were modeled to fit high heel shoes. The 21" doll used the Cissy body. Both sizes came in various outfits. (See Alexander chapter for more information.)

Princess Margaret Rose

Margaret Rose was born in 1930 to the Duke and Dutchess of York. Her father became King George VI in 1936. Princess Margaret was just as famous as her sister, Elizabeth, during the 1930s and 1940s. Paper dolls and dolls were modeled after the two sisters during this time. After Elizabeth became Queen of England in 1952 (Coronation in 1953) Margaret was no longer as important but her life still remains of interest to the public.

The Madame Alexander company marketed several dolls honoring Princess Margaret Rose. In 1946 a Margaret composition doll was sold in 15", 18", and 21" sizes. During the late 1940s the firm produced other Princess Margaret Rose dolls in the 15" size using the Margaret face. The earliest doll (circa 1948) was hard plastic and had a mohair wig. The later doll (circa 1949-1950) had a synthetic wig. The most sought after Princess Margaret doll was made in 1953 as part of the Beaux Arts Creations group. The doll was #2020B and was 18" tall. She wore a gown of pink faille taffeta which came with jeweled tiara, bracelet, pearl necklace, and earrings.

21' and 14" Shari Lewis dolls representing the famous ventriloquist. They were produced by the Madame Alexander Doll Co. in 1959. The hard plastic dolls have sleep eyes, applied wigs, fashion bodies with arched feet, and closed mouths. They are all original in their yellow satin dresses and flowered hats. The dresses are tagged "Shari." Some of the dolls are marked "19 c 58/Alexander." (13" $400-500, 21" $700-750). *Dolls and photograph from the collection of Carol J. Lindeman.*

Mary Martin

Mary Martin was born in Texas in 1913. She had a long career as an actress-singer both on Broadway and in films. She began her screen career in 1939 and continued to make pictures through the early 1940s. She also had a cameo role in 1953 in *Main Street to Broadway*. She will best be remembered for her Broadway roles in *South Pacific*, *Peter Pan*, and *The Sound of Music*.

In 1949 and 1950 Madame Alexander produced a doll to honor Mary Martin in her role of Nellie Forbush in *South Pacific*. The doll came in two sizes, 14.5" and 17". The doll was all hard plastic with a caracul wig. She was dressed in several different outfits including the popular sailor suit, a long white gown, and an overall costume. The hair color was originally a red-brown but some wigs have faded over time. (See Alexander chapter for more information).

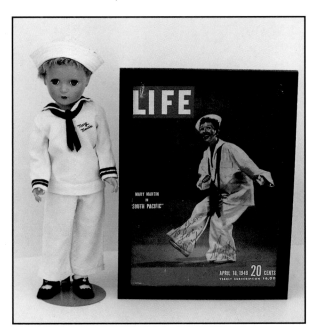

17" hard plastic Mary Martin doll made by the Madame Alexander Doll Co., circa 1950. She is wearing her original sailor costume based on the one Mary Martin wore in her hit Broadway show *South Pacific*. The doll has sleep eyes, closed mouth, and a caracul wig. Her name is embroidered on the front of her shirt. The doll was also made in a 14" size. ($700 and up). Also shown is an autographed *Life* magazine cover picturing her in her sailor costume from the *South Pacific* show. (See also the chapter on Alexander for another photograph).

Annie Oakley

Annie Oakley was born Phoebe Anne Oakley Mozee in 1860 in Ohio. In 1885 she joined "Buffalo Bill's Wild West Show." She became famous as a sharp shooter and traveled with the show for seventeen years. Eventually a television program, a Broadway show (*Annie Get Your Gun*), and movie were made to tell her story. She died in 1926.

The television program called "Annie Oakley" was a show for children that aired on ABC from 1953 until 1958. Annie was played by Gail Davis. When the show began attracting lots of tie-in attention because of its popularity, American Character produced a hard plastic doll named Annie Oakley. The 1954 doll was really a hard plastic Sweet Sue doll dressed in western clothing.

GiGi Perreau

GiGi Perreau was a child actress who made thirty-six movies from the 1940s through the 1960s. She was born in 1941 and started her career at the age of two in M-G-M's *Madame Curie* in 1943.

The Goldberger Doll Manufacturing Co. Inc. produced a doll in the image of the young star in 1952. The doll had a vinyl head and a plastic body. It was 20" tall and wore a dark wig. The doll is seldom seen and would be hard to identify without a tag or box.

Prince Philip

Philip Mountbatten, formerly Prince Philip of Greece, married Princess Elizabeth of England in 1947. He was born in 1921 and was a Lieutenant in the Royal Navy when he married the Princess.

Madame Alexander produced an 18" male hard plastic doll with the Margaret face in the early 1950s. Collectors call the doll Prince Philip although he is not pictured in the catalog that features the Queen Elizabeth and Princess Margaret dolls in 1953 which honored the Coronation of the Queen. The doll was more likely intended to be a groom to accompany the Alexander bride dolls of the era.

Elvis Presley

Elvis Presley was born in 1935 in Tupelo, Mississippi. Times were hard for the Presley family during those years of the Depression and the family never did achieve economic success. His father bought Elvis a guitar when he was twelve and he began to make music. After his high school graduation in 1953, while recording some records for his mother, he met Sam Phillips of the Sun Record Co. Phillips helped Elvis get his start by recording his first records, "That's All Right (Mama)" and "Blue Moon of Kentucky." By 1955 Elvis had a recording contract with RCA and Colonel Tom Parker as his manager. He began making television appearances and soon was also making films through a contract with Twentieth-Century-Fox. His first picture, *Love Me Tender* was released in 1956. The Elvis career was put on hold in 1958 when he was drafted into the army. In 1960 when his army stint was over, he continued his successful career in movies and recordings. By 1968 his career had slowed but it was revived with his television special for NBC in December of that year. In 1969 he began his successful appearances in Las Vegas and also made personal appearances around the country. Although these new shows added several more years of success for Presley, his career had again taken a downward turn by the time he died in 1977 of reported heart failure.

18" Annie Oakley hard plastic walker made by American Character in 1954. She has sleep eyes, a closed mouth, applied wig, and is all original complete with tag. The doll was really a Sweet Sue costumed in Annie Oakley clothing. ($500-600). *Doll from the collection of Jan Clanton. Photograph by Darek Clanton.*

An Elvis Presley vinyl doll was marketed in 1957. The 16" doll came in a box labeled "Licensed by Elvis Presley Enterprises/ c 1957/ All Rights Reserved/Sole Distributor Acme Merchandise Co., Inc. New York, NY. The doll had molded, painted hair and eyes and was dressed in a plaid shirt and blue pants.

16' Elvis Presley vinyl doll. Box labeled "Licensed by Elvis Presley Enterprises/C 1957/all rights Reserved/Sole Distributor Acme Merchandise Cc, Inc. New York, N.Y." Doll has molded hair and painted features and wears his original clothing. ($1200 and up). *From the collection of Bob and Elaine Ehnisz. Photograph by Bob Ehnisz.*

The new composition Jackie Robinson doll was advertised in the Alden Christmas catalog in 1950. It was tied to the new movie called *The Jackie Robinson Story*, marketed at the same time. The doll could be purchased with a blue warm up jacket, small bat, and Jackie Robinson baseball game for $2.98.

Jackie Robinson

Jackie Robinson was born in 1919 and he became the first black major league baseball player in 1947 when he played for the Brooklyn Dodgers. He had a very successful career with the Dodgers and he retired in 1956. In 1962 he was elected to the Baseball Hall of Fame. In 1997, as part of the fifty year celebration of Robinson's first appearance as a major league baseball player, all major league teams wore commemorative patches on their uniforms. The sport also donated one million dollars to the Jackie Robinson Foundation which provides scholarships to minorities.

In 1950 he played himself in the film *The Jackie Robinson Story*. At this time a composition doll was marketed in the athlete's image. The doll was sold by the Allied-Grand Manufacturing Co. in 1950. The doll was 13" tall and could be purchased with a ball, bat, and jacket. Aldens catalog sold the doll itself for $1.98, but for $2.98 the doll came with a jacket, bat, baseball game, and booklet.

13.5" composition Jackie Robinson doll with molded hair and painted features. He is in his original clothing but is missing his cap. ($500 and up).

Roy Rogers and Dale Evans

Roy Rogers took over the "Number One Cowboy Star" role from Gene Autry in 1943. He was born in Cincinnati, Ohio, in 1912 and Rogers began his movie career in 1935 with the singing group Sons of the Pioneers. In 1938 he made *Under Western Stars*, the first of his starring Westerns for Republic Pictures. Rogers made forty-two pictures for Republic, and remained the number one star of "B" Westerns until 1951.

Dale Evans was born in 1912 and she began making films with Rogers in 1944. She and Roy Rogers were married in 1948 and they made a total of twenty Western films together.

Some of Rogers' best pictures include: *In Old Caliente* (1939), *King of the Cowboys* (1943), *Yellow Rose of Texas* (1944), *San Fernando Valley* (1944), *Man From Oklahoma* (1945), and *Springtime in the Sierras* (1947).

In 1951, Rogers turned to television where he and Dale did "The Roy Rogers Show" for CBS until 1964. In the show, the action took place on the Double R Ranch in Mineral City. Rogers' horse, Trigger, and dog, Bullet, shared in the adventures. From September 1962 until December 1962 Rogers and Evans hosted a musical variety show on ABC.

During the early 1950s, Nancy Ann Storybook Dolls, Inc. marketed a pair of 8" tall hard plastic Roy Rogers and Dale Evans dolls. Both dolls had sleep eyes and Roy's hair was molded while the Dale doll featured a wig. The dolls were dressed in western clothing and each also came with a set of guns in holsters.

Matching 8" Dale Evans hard plastic doll also by Nancy Ann Storybook Dolls, Inc. Wearing original clothing and pictured with original box. Has sleep eyes and a wig. ($175 and up). *Doll and photograph from the collection of Jackie Robertson.*

Roxanne

Delores Rosedale used the stage name "Roxanne" on the television program called "Beat the Clock" that aired on the CBS network beginning in 1950. The game show host was Bud Collyer and Roxanne was his assistant.

A 21" hard plastic walking doll was issued which collectors call the Roxanne doll. The tag indicated the doll was advertised on the show and viewers should "See Roxanne walk this doll every week on 'Beat the Clock.' " The tag also states it is a Mona Lisa exclusive by Valentine Dolls. Another doll made of vinyl was also made in several sizes.

8" Roy Rogers hard plastic doll marketed by Nancy Ann Storybook Dolls, Inc. Wearing original clothing and pictured with original box. Has sleep eyes and painted hair. ($175 and up). *Doll and photograph from the collection of Jackie Robertson.*

21" Roxanne doll with a tag reading "Beat the Clock Roxanne's T.V. Walking Doll." Back of tag reads "See Roxanne Walk this doll every week on 'Beat The Clock', Sylvania's outstanding T.V. show." A Mona Lisa Exclusive by Valentine Dolls, Inc. Head and body are marked "210." The doll has sleep eyes, a Saran wig and is circa 1953. Roxanne (born Dolores Rosedale) was hostess on the show ($150-175). Also pictured is a "Beat the Clock Game" by Lowell Toy Corp. c 1954 by Beat the Clock, Inc. A Goodson-Todman Production in association with CBS Television. ($20-25).

Lu Ann Simms

Lu Ann Simms was born in 1932 and her professional career reached its peak when she was a member of the cast of the television program called "Arthur Godfrey and His Friends" in the early 1950s. The show aired on CBS from 1952 until 1955. Simms was a singer along with cast member Julius Larosa, who gained unwanted fame for being fired by Godfrey during a live program.

A Lu Ann Simms hard plastic walking doll was issued circa 1953. The doll was made by the Roberta Doll Company and came in 16", 18", and 21" sizes.

Shirley Temple (see Shirley Temple chapter)

16" Lu Ann Simms walking doll made of hard plastic. The doll represents a regular singer on the "Arthur Godfrey and His Friends" television program aired on CBS. Made by Roberta Doll Company, Inc., circa 1953. Her tag reads "One of Arthur Godfrey's Friends/Lu Ann Simms Walking Doll/CBS television Star/Mfg. by Roberta Doll Company, Inc." The number "170" appears on the back of her head. The doll has a ponytail, wears a red dress trimmed in rick rack, and carries a purse with her name on it. The doll also came in larger sizes. ($400 and up).

Shirley Temple

In 1934, during the midst of the worst Depression this world has ever known, America fell in love with a tiny golden haired moppet: Shirley Temple. Now, nearly sixty years later, some people are still actively pursuing their love affair with Shirley by collecting Shirley Temple memorabilia.

Shirley was born on April 23, 1928, in Santa Monica, California. Her parents, George and Gertrude, had already been blessed with two sons, so the addition of a darling little girl to the family was most welcome.

Shirley was enrolled in dancing school in Los Angeles when she was only three. It was while Shirley was a pupil at the school that the movie scout Charles Lamont from Educational Studios chose her to appear in short films to be made by that studio. Shirley was paid $10 per day for four days of work on each short in the series called "Baby Burlesk."

Shirley's charm in these films caught the attention of Leo Houch, who was an assistant director for Fox Film Corp., and he gave her a starring role in *Stand Up and Cheer* in 1934. Shirley's golden curls and her pleasing personality made her an instant hit with the public so she was signed to a seven-year contract with Fox for $150 per week.

The studio took advantage of their tiny star's success and she made eight movies in the year of 1934 alone. Because of Shirley's popularity many new products were produced with Shirley's endorsement. These included dolls, toys, books, and clothing.

By 1935, Shirley Temple was in the number one position among the top ten box office stars of the country. She would retain that spot through 1938. Her fan mail averaged 5,000 letters each week.

From 1935 to 1940 Shirley appeared in sixteen motion pictures but her popularity had slipped by 1939. In 1940 Shirley had outgrown her curls and little girl parts and was not quite ready for adolescent roles so Fox terminated her contract.

After a brief rest Shirley continued her film career during the 1940s by making movies for other companies. She starred in thirteen more pictures before leaving the world of film in 1949.

Shirley was only seventeen when she married Sgt. John Agar in 1945. The couple had one child, Linda Susan, born in 1948. The marriage was not a happy one and Shirley and Agar were divorced in 1950. Shirley soon married Charles Black and they had two children, Charles born in 1952 and Lori born in 1954.

In 1957 Shirley Temple began another show business career when she agreed to do the "Shirley Temple Storybook" series on television. Shirley acted as mistress of ceremonies on the program and also starred in some of the episodes. The publicity generated by the series rekindled fans' interest in dolls depicting Shirley as a child. Many products were produced to take advantage of this publicity. In 1958 the Ideal Co. issued new Shirley Temple dolls, this time made of vinyl and plastic instead of composition. The dolls were made in sizes of 12", 15", 17", and 19". In 1960 a large 36" model was made. The most expensive of these dolls today is the 36" doll. Vinyl Shirley Temple dolls were still being advertised in 1962 in the Sears Christmas catalog. The 12" doll with four outfits and accessories was priced at $9.89 and a 15" doll dressed in a Heidi costume was priced at $6.98. The basic 12" doll in a slip sold for from $3.00-4.00 during the late 1950s. Costumes for these dolls could also be sewn at home and several commercial patterns were manufactured to supply designs for clothing for these popular Shirley dolls.

"Shirley Temple's Storybook" ran on NBC from January until September 1958 and then was shown on ABC from January to June 1959. Finally it was returned to NBC as "The Shirley Temple Show" from September 1960 until it finished its run in September 1961.

Beginning in 1960 Shirley Temple became active in politics. She campaigned for the Republicans in the presidential elections of 1960, 1964, and 1968. She was also in an unsuccessful campaign of her own when she ran for Congress in 1967. Her political work earned her a new job when President Nixon appointed her to be a U.S. delegate to the United Nations. Later, President Ford named her as the Ambassador to Ghana in Africa. After the completion of this job, she was appointed as Chief of Protocol in Washington. Shirley continued her government work when she was assigned to be Ambassador to Czechoslovakia in 1989.

Most of Shirley's child-star contemporaries grew up to face problems they could not overcome, while Shirley Temple Black has continued to grow and succeed as an adult. No wonder Shirley Temple collectors continue to multiply. These collectors pay homage to a delightful child of the past, as well as the admirable woman she became.

12" vinyl Shirley Temple dolls first marketed by Ideal in 1958. The dolls have sleep eyes, rooted hair, and open mouths. They are marked on the back of the head "Ideal Doll/ST-12," and on the shoulder "ST-12N." The doll on the left is the basic doll wearing her tagged slip and with her original tag. The other doll is wearing a tagged Shirley Temple dress. (Tagged doll $150-175, other $135-150).

12" Shirley Temple modeling the Wee Willie Winkie costume, one of the many outfits made for the doll. The box is marked "Shirley Temple Doll Clothes /#9560 $3.00/Ideal Shirley Temple Doll Clothes." The box for the MIB cowgirl costume is marked "Shirley Temple Doll Clothes/Ideal Hollis, N.Y. #9718." (MIB special outfits $75 and up).

Fifteen different Shirley Temple outfits are pictured on the back of the clothes box for the Wee Willie Winkie costume. Besides the more usual outfits, an ice skating costume is pictured.

Hutzler's of Baltimore, Maryland, advertised the 12" Shirley Temple dolls priced at $3.98 for the basic doll. The cost of her outfits varied from $1.50 for pajamas to $2.50 for the overalls, shirt, and hat. *Catalog from the collection of Marge Meisinger.*

Boxed 12" Shirley Temple red felt coat, striped tam, and purse circa 1960. ($55-65). *From the collection of Mary Stuecher. Photograph by Werner Stuecher.*

The Montgomery Ward Christmas catalog from 1959 featured three sizes of the vinyl Shirley Temple dolls: 12" priced at $3.87 for the basic doll, 15" dressed for $7.29, and 17" for $9.88 for a dressed doll. *Catalog from the collection of Marge Meisinger.*

12" Shirley modeling the Scotch Outfit as pictured in the Montgomery Ward catalog in 1959. It sold for $1.87 originally. (Outfit only $40-45).

This Rain Outfit was also pictured in the Montgomery Ward catalog in 1959 and sold for $1.49. It was also for the 12" doll. (Outfit only $35-40).

12" Shirley Temple vinyl doll, mint with tags and box. May be from the early 1960s. ($225-250). *Doll and photograph from the collection of Marge Meisinger.*

This 12" Pajama Outfit came in several different colors. The one pictured in the 1959 Ward catalog had a red top. It was priced at $1.49. (Pajama set only $25-30).

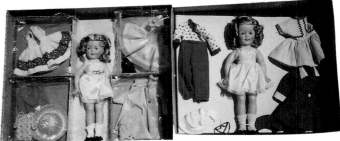

12" vinyl Shirley Temple dolls in mint gift sets circa 1959. Most sets included a doll and four outfits and sold for $11.98. ($350 and up). *Dolls and photograph from the collection of Marge Meisinger.*

12" Shirley Temple is pictured with her wardrobe and trunk circa 1959. The dress she is wearing also was made in different prints and was called a "Heidi Outfit" in the Wards 1959 catalog and was priced at $1.87. The purse shown at the right also came with the dress. (Dress and purse $40-45, doll and wardrobe $350 and up).

Right: The May Company in Los Angeles featured a page of Shirley Temple items in their 1959 catalog. Included were dolls in the 12", 15", 17", and 19" sizes as well as clothing for the 12" dolls, and a gift set 12" Shirley Temple. The Shirley Temple dishes are also pictured. *Catalog from the collection of Marge Meisinger.*

15" Ideal vinyl Shirley Temple dolls shown in original costumes. Included are Red Riding Hood, Cinderella, Little Bo Peep, and apparently Alice in Wonderland. ($250-300 each). *Dolls and photograph from the collection of Marge Meisinger.*

15" Shirley Temple marked "Ideal Doll/ST-15N/" on the back of her neck. On her back is "Ideal Doll/ST-15." She has rooted hair, sleep eyes, and an open mouth. She is wearing her original dress with an added bow and probably replaced shoes. ($135-150). Also shown is one of the many clothes patterns made to fit the Shirley Temple dolls. This one is #3217 and was issued by Simplicity. The finished clothes were to fit a 19" doll. ($30-40).

17" mint Ideal Shirley Temple complete with curlers, tote case, pin, and tag. She has flirty sleep eyes and wears her original nylon dress. ($300-350). *Doll from the collection of Mary Stuecher. Photograph by Werner Stuecher.*

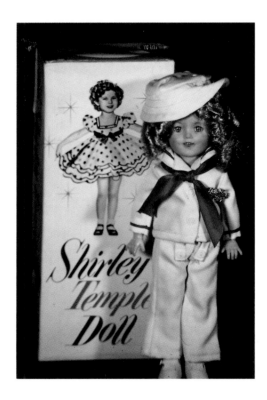

35" vinyl Shirley Temple Playpal doll circa 1960. Has sleep eyes, rooted hair, and jointed wrists. She is all original. The Shirley Temple locket dates from the 1930s. ($1200-1500). *Doll from the collection of Mary Stuecher. Photograph by Werner Stuecher.*

12" Ideal Shirley Temple doll complete with her original box in mint condition with pin. ($225-250). *Doll and photograph from the collection of Marge Meisinger.*

Miscellaneous Dolls

A & H Doll MFG. Corp.

A & H Doll Mfg. Corp. was located in Woodside, New York. They were responsible for making the 7.5" hard plastic **GiGi** walking dolls in the early 1950s. The dolls came in both straight leg and bending knee models. By 1955 the dolls were being made with vinyl heads. Many different outfits were also marketed for the dolls.

The company also made 7.5" hard plastic **Marcie** Dolls dressed in different costumes. The dolls had wigs and sleep eyes and were the type that were used by many companies as premium dolls or for women to dress in crocheted outfits during the early 1950s.

7.5" hard plastic Gigi Walking Doll in a more elaborate costume. Circa 1954. ($65-85). *Doll from the collection of Marge Meisinger.*

7.5" mint Gigi doll with original box. The doll is made of hard plastic, has sleep eyes, and is a walker. It was produced by the A. & H. Doll Mfg. Corp. The doll came in both straight leg and bending knee models. In 1955 Gigi was made with a vinyl head. ($65-85). *Doll from the collection of Marge Meisinger.*

Brochure picturing clothes produced for the Gigi doll. There were at least thirty-six different outfits made for the doll. The dolls sold for $1.98 while the clothes were priced at $1.00 for each costume. *From the collection of Marge Meisinger.*

Active Doll Corp.

The Active Doll Corp. from Brooklyn, New York, made the 8" hard plastic walking **Mindy** dolls in the early to mid-1950s. These dolls were produced in both a straight leg and bending leg model. Lots of costumes were also manufactured for these dolls.

The company also produced a line of hard plastic Beau Art Dolls in inexpensive costumes during the 1950s. These dolls were only 5.5" tall.

8" hard plastic head turning Mindy dolls produced by Active Doll Corp. The doll on the left has bending knees while the doll on the right has straight legs. Their clothes and trunks are original. The outfits were packaged in round plastic containers. The one pictured is an ice skating costume with hat and skates. The package is labeled "Mindy's Ensembles." Circa mid-1950s. (Dolls $25-30, suitcases $10-15, MIP outfits $15-20). *Dolls and accessories from the collection of Marge Meisinger.*

This Mindy brochure pictures several of the outfits and the trunk. The doll alone was priced at $1.98 while most of the costumes were $1.00 each. The brochure says the doll was also available in an 11" size. The dressed doll, trunk, and one other costume was priced at $2.98. *Brochure from the collection of Marge Meisinger.*

Twenty-four of the Mindy costumes are shown in this brochure. The company also issued a baby sister named Minnette made of vinyl. *Brochure from the collection of Marge Meisinger.*

Advance

Advance had two successful dolls on the market during the early 1950s. One was called **Wanda the Walking Wonder**. The doll was made of hard plastic and was approximately 18" tall. She had a glued on wig, sleep eyes, and she walked by means of a key wind mechanism. Her shoes had rollers on the bottom so she could move. Wanda's head turned and her arms moved as she walked.

Because of the success of Wanda, the company produced another doll called **Winnie the Wonder Doll**. This doll was 24" tall and could both walk and talk. She had a keywind mechanism for walking and a record to make her talk. Winnie was first made with a hard plastic head and body but by the mid-1950s her head was vinyl.

19" hard plastic Wanda the Walking Doll circa 1949-1950. She has sleep eyes, closed mouth, and an applied wig. She is a key wind walker and walks with the aid of rollers on the bottom of her shoes. She is wearing her original dress. ($125-150).

26" Winnie the Walking and Talking doll was advertised in Aldens Christmas catalog in 1953. The doll sold for $19.95. The hard plastic doll walked in the same manner as the earlier Wanda but she also had a record to make her talk. She performed both functions after only one key was wound. Later the doll was made with a vinyl head as pictured here. ($150-200). *Doll from the collection of Jan Clanton. Photograph by Darek Clanton.*

Beehler Arts Ltd.

Beehler Arts Ltd., of New York City, marketed many dolls during the decade of the 1950s. The boxes used for Virga dolls sometimes give the Beehler name as the manufacturer. It is likely that **Virga** was a trade name used by Beehler Arts. Both hard plastic 8" Ginny Vogue type dolls, as well as 8.5" high heel plastic dolls were sold by the company during the early 1950s.

In the late 1950s, the famous French designer Madame Schiaparelli was engaged to design clothing for a line of Virga dolls. The clothes were tagged "Schiaparelli." These dolls had vinyl heads. The company was also marketing a vinyl high heel type doll in the 10.5" size to compete in the Miss Revlon (made by Ideal) market.

The dolls sold by Beehler were usually of poorer quality than other dolls of their type but some of their 8" hard plastic dolls look like the Cosmopolitan Ginger dolls and are the same quality. Many times the clothing of the Beehler dolls was inferior to the outfits made by the larger firms.

Right: 8" hard plastic Virga doll mint with box circa 1954-1955. These dolls were manufactured by Beehler Arts Ltd. in New York City. They were made to compete with the Vogue Ginny dolls. ($75-85). *Doll from the collection of Marge Meisinger.*

8" hard plastic Virga Play-Mates doll. Information on the box states that the doll was "Manufactured by Beehler Arts Ltd." She is labeled as a "Camp Girl with Bending Knee." None of the dolls are marked. Like the other dolls, she has sleep eyes, molded eyelashes, closed mouth, applied wig, and she is a walker. Many other costumes were also made for these dolls. ($55-65).

8" hard plastic Virga walker mint in her original box with extra clothing. It is inscribed "My Name is Lucy I Walk." ($125-150). *Doll from the collection of Jan Clanton. Photograph by Darek Clanton.*

8.5" hard plastic Virga Hi-Heel 'Teen. She was also made by Beehler Arts Ltd. The doll has sleep eyes, closed mouth, an applied wig, bending knees, and arched feet. Although these dolls were sold cheaply when they were new, they are quite nice dolls when found in mint condition as this one is. She is not marked. Many fashions were also made for this doll. Circa 1956-1957. ($75-100).

8" Go Go doll with a vinyl head, hard plastic body, and bending knees. This was one of the Virga dolls with clothes designed by Mme. Elsa Schiaparelli in 1956. The tag reads "Schiaparelli Dolls, LTD/New York, 10, New York/ Created especially for you by Mme Elsa Schiaparelli, world famous designer." The pictured doll is wearing roller skates. Another of her special dresses is shown. (Doll and box $125-140, costume $25-30). *Doll and costumes from the collection of Marge Meisinger.*

Belle Doll and Toy Corporation

The Belle Corporation, located in New York City, marketed many different inexpensive dolls during the 1950s. Although some of the dolls were quite nice, many times the doll's clothing was made more cheaply than dolls from better companies.

The firm sold a nice newborn infant doll in 1950 for $4.98 for a 20" size. The doll had a vinylite head, arms and legs and a cloth body. This doll was made to compete with other dolls of this type. Many of these infant dolls became sticky with age because of the material used in their manufacture. Another doll added to the company line in 1952 was Belle's hard plastic walking doll called **Heddi Stroller**. Her head turned when she walked.

Belle also marketed hard plastic little girl dolls as well as vinyl high heel type dolls later in the decade. The adult dolls came in sizes as small as 10" and as large as 20".

14" hard plastic girl doll made by the Belle Doll and Toy Corporation and featured in the 1953 Herpolsheimer's catalog from Grand Rapids, Michigan. The store was selling the doll called Heddi Stroller for $9.98 complete with suitcase and wardrobe. The doll is mint with her original suitcase and clothing. She is dressed in a taffeta formal and her other clothing includes a coat and hat, sundress, jeans and top, and a dress with a pinafore. Her tag reads "A Belle Doll has a Saran Wig." ($200-250).

Block Doll Corporation

The Block Doll Corporation of New York City sold inexpensive hard plastic dolls throughout the 1950s. In 1951 the firm advertised **"The Answer Doll"** a hard plastic toddler doll 12" tall that could nod its head "yes" and shake its head "no." The company also marketed a hard plastic walking doll similar to Arranbee's Littlest Angel. The doll was sold with a wardrobe or without.

11" hard plastic doll made by Block in her original trunk with wardrobe. These dolls competed with Arranbee's Littlest Angel dolls. They had sleep eyes, closed mouths, applied wigs, and were walkers. Circa mid-1950s. ($150-175).*Doll from the collection of Jan Clanton. Photograph by Darek Clanton.*

Doll Bodies, Inc.

Doll Bodies was another lesser known company, located in New York, that competed in the inexpensive doll market in the decade of the 1950s. They specialized in selling small undressed 7.5" or 11" hard plastic dolls that were to be dressed by the customer. Many of these dolls were to be dressed in hand made crochet outfits. Patterns were printed in various crochet booklets and women seemed to enjoy dressing these dolls during the early years of the 1950s.

Besides these small dolls, the company also marketed some nice quality hard plastic walking dolls in 1955. These **Mary-Lu Walker** dolls were 18" tall and had sleep eyes and glued on wigs. Sixteen different dresses were also available for the dolls.

17" hard plastic Mary Lou Walker by Doll Bodies circa 1955. Although this company is better known for its inexpensive smaller dolls, this doll is very collectible when found in mint condition. She has sleep eyes, open mouth with teeth, her original clothing, and her tag. ($150-175). *Doll from the collection of Jan Clanton. Photograph by Darek Clanton.*

Eegee (Goldberger Doll Mfg. Co.)

The trade name Eegee came from the founder's name, E. Goldberger. The Goldberger company had been in business since before 1920 and it was still active in the doll market in the 1950s. Although they followed the trend of other doll makers of the time, the firm also produced one unique doll. It was a personality doll called **Gigi Perreau** made in 1952. The doll was made in the image of the child movie star and was 20" tall, had rooted hair, a vinyl head, and jointed body. The doll is very hard to find for today's collector.

Other more ordinary dolls made by the company included a **Susan Stroller** head turning walker doll made in 1953. The doll originally had a hard plastic head but later she was made with a vinyl head. Another doll made by Goldberger circa 1953 was **Baby Gurglee** with a hard plastic head and a latex body. He was 13" tall and sold for $2.69 in the Aldens catalog in 1953. A later vinyl baby doll only 8" tall was marketed to compete with Vogue's Ginnette doll. The doll was called **Baby Susan**.

Many of the high heel type dolls made by the firm were made of stuffed vinyl. Goldberger also produced toddler dolls in the same material during the late 1950s.

In 1958 the firm marketed a 10" vinyl doll called **Little Miss Debutante** to compete against Vogue's Jill doll. The doll had pierced ears and a jointed waist. An 8" stuffed vinyl doll was also sold at about this same time. Many costumes were also available to fit these dolls. Larger high heel type dolls of vinyl were also made. Some of these dolls were dressed as ballerinas.

17" Susan Stroller doll made by Eegee (Goldberger Doll Mfg. Co.) in the mid-1950s. The first Susan Stroller dolls were produced with hard plastic heads in 1953. This doll is a later version made with a vinyl head. The doll still retains the hard plastic body and she has bending knees. She is marked on the back "EEGEE" and has rooted hair, sleep eyes, a closed mouth, a grill in her stomach, and she is a pin hipped walker. She is all original. ($55-75).

13" Baby Gurglee doll made by Eegee in 1953. The doll has a hard plastic head and a latex body. He is all original with his tag. When his tummy is squeezed, he makes a noise. The baby has molded hair, sleep eyes, and a closed mouth. He is not marked. His tag reads "Baby Gurglee/Squeeze Me Now/Plastic Head/An EE-GEE Product/Brooklyn, N.Y." The Baby Gurglee doll was advertised in the Aldens Christmas catalog in 1953. The doll sold for $2.69 in his basic outfit. ($50-60).

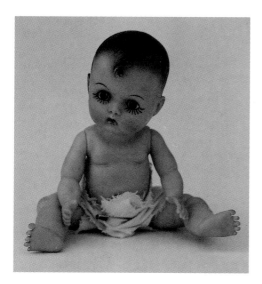

17" vinyl fashion doll made by Eegee in the late 1950s. The doll has a soft vinyl head and rigid vinyl body and arms and legs. She is marked "Eegee" on the back of her head. The doll has pierced ears, sleep eyes, closed mouth, rooted hair, and a turning waist. She is wearing her original clothing and hat but has replaced shoes. ($50-75).

8" vinyl Baby Susan made by Eegee in the mid-to late 1950s. She was a cheaper doll to compete with Vogue's Ginnette. She has sleep eyes and is marked on the back of her head "Baby Susan." ($15-20).

20" vinyl ballerina doll with hard plastic body and vinyl head and arms. She has sleep eyes, closed mouth, rooted hair, and is jointed at the waist, knees, and ankles. She is marked "20 HH" on the back of her head. She came with two ballerina outfits, a strapless dress, shoes, tights, and a leotard. Thought to be made by EEGEE circa late 1950s. (Set $50 and up).

Fortune Toys Inc.

Fortune Toys was located in Jamaica, New York. The firm was another of those small companies that competed in the 8" and 10.5" doll market of the 1950s. The company's 8" doll was called **Pam**. The doll was a walking doll with a vinyl head, rooted hair, and sleep eyes. Her different characteristic was the modeling of her feet which were made to wear Cuban heel shoes. The doll sold for $1.98 and each of her twelve outfits was priced at only $1.00. The doll is marked "Pam" on her back. The Fortune's 10.5" vinyl doll was named **Miss Pam**. This grown-up model wore high heel shoes and earrings. She also could bend at the waist. Miss Pam was priced at $2.98 and each of her twelve outfits also sold for $1.00.

Eight of Pam's twelve outfits are pictured as shown in her original brochure. Her costumes were priced at $1.00 each.

8" hard plastic and vinyl Pam walking doll with Cuban heel shoes. The doll was manufactured by Fortune Toys Inc. The doll has a vinyl head, hard plastic body, sleep eyes, a closed mouth and rooted hair. She is marked "Pam" on the back of her head. She originally sold for $1.98. Her clothing is not original. Circa 1957-1958. (Doll $25, brochure $20).

Miss Pam was also made by Fortune. This 10.5" vinyl doll had sleep eyes, rooted hair, arched feet, pierced ears, and turning waist. Twelve costumes were made for the doll. Pictured are six of them from the original brochure. Her outfits were also priced at only $1.00 each.

Hollywood Dolls

Dominick Ippolite was the founder of Hollywood Doll Manufacturing Co. which was located in Glendale California. He marketed dolls under this name from 1941 to 1956. The earlier dolls were made of composition or painted bisque. The later hard plastic 5.5" dolls were sold during the 1950s. The dolls came in many different costumes and were meant to be a cheaper doll to compete with the Nancy Ann Storybook Dolls.

Mary Jane, see Togs and Dolls, Inc.

Mollye

Dolls known as "Mollye" were blank dolls purchased and dressed by Mollye Goldman. Goldman played a part in the doll industry for many years having earlier helped design Ideal Shirley Temple clothes in the 1930s. She also worked for several other doll companies besides marketing dolls under her own name. Mollye dolls have included those made of composition, cloth, hard plastic, and vinyl. Since most of her dolls are not marked, it is very difficult to know which dolls Mollye dressed unless they are tagged. She was known for making lovely doll clothes with lots of details. Mollye was especially fond of making bridal costumes.

5.5" hard plastic Hollywood Doll all original with her box and brochure. The dolls were made by the Hollywood Doll Manufacturing Co. of Glendale, California. The doll has sleep eyes, applied wig, and is jointed at the neck, shoulders, and hips. Her wrist tag says "Queen Titania." She was one of the Sweetheart Series. Circa 1954. ($25-35).

18" hard plastic doll attributed to Mollye. This firm purchased blank dolls which were to be dressed by Mollye Goldman. The doll has sleep eyes, a closed mouth, and is beautifully dressed with a hoop skirt. Circa mid-1950s. ($450 and up). *Doll from the collection of Jan Clanton. Photograph by Darek Clanton.*

17" hard plastic doll attributed to Mollye. The "Coronation Queen" is circa the mid-1950s. She is also beautifully dressed. ($450 and up). *Doll from the collection of Jan Clanton. Photograph by Darek Clanton.*

Roberta Doll Co., Inc.

In 1950, the Roberta Doll Co. of New York City was marketing hard plastic girl dolls and baby dolls with hard plastic heads and latex arms and legs.

Most of these dolls are not marked so it is difficult to identify the company's dolls unless they are tagged. One of their most collectible dolls is the **Lu Ann Simms** hard plastic doll. The doll portrayed Lu Ann who was a singer on the Arthur Godfrey television show (see personality section).

Although, for the most part, the Roberta dolls were aimed at a cheaper market, when the hard plastic dolls are found in mint condition they make a very desirable addition to a hard plastic doll collection. Besides the hard plastic dolls, the firm also marketed baby dolls of stuffed vinyl and vinyl high heel type dolls in the 1950s.

14" hard plastic Roberta doll known as "Roberta Princess." She has sleep eyes, a long curl wig, and an open mouth with teeth. She is all original. Circa early to mid-1950s. ($150-200). *Doll from the collection of Jan Clanton. Photograph by Darek Clanton.*

14" hard plastic little girl doll made by Roberta. The information on the box reads "Roberta Doll/Quality Products/Of Roberta Doll Co., Inc. New York U.S.A." The doll has sleep eyes, a closed mouth, and an attached wig. She is all original and mint with her box. Probably dates from the early 1950s. ($275 and up). *Doll from the collection of Jan Clanton. Photograph by Darek Clanton.*

21" doll with stuffed vinyl head and stuffed vinyl one-piece body. The doll was made by the Roberta Doll Co. She has sleep eyes, a closed mouth, and is all original with her box. Both the tag and box read "Roberta Doll/Quality Products/Of Roberta Doll Co. Inc. New York U.S.A." Her original price as marked on the box was $16.98. Circa 1957. ($100-125).

Left: 15" vinyl fashion doll made by Roberta. Although the doll is unmarked, the box contains the following information "A/Toby-Teen/Fashion Doll Set/Mfg. By/Roberta." The doll has sleep eyes, closed mouth, and arched feet. Her wardrobe includes underwear, strapless short formal, skirt and top, nightgown, hat, and jewelry. All of the items are cheaply made. Circa 1957-1958. (Set $100-125).

Sayco Doll Corp.

Sayco Doll Corp. of Brooklyn, New York, also competed in the lower cost doll market. During the 1950s, the firm produced the 10.5" **Miss America Pageant Doll**. The doll had a hard plastic body and a vinyl head. The firm also seemed to specialize in baby and boy and girl dolls made of latex with molded hair.

Later the firm made high heel type dolls with soft vinyl heads and hard bodies. One of these dolls was called **Miss America**. Some of the company's dolls are marked "Sayco" on the back of the heads but many are unmarked.

11" Miss America Pageant Dolls as pictured in the Montgomery Ward Christmas catalog in 1956. The dolls had vinyl heads and hard plastic bodies. They were made by Sayco Doll Co. The dolls had sleep eyes, closed mouth, rooted hair, and jointed knees. The dolls have a small "s" on the back of the head and they came in many different costumes.

21" Sayco Baby with head made of stuffed vinyl and body of stuffed latex. She has molded hair, sleep eyes, and open-closed mouth. Her box is still marked with a $9.95 price tag. She is mint and all original. Circa 1956. ($100-125).

Sun Rubber Co.

The Sun Rubber Company of Barberton, Ohio, was very active in doll production during the 1950s. At the beginning of the decade their dolls were really made of rubber. During the mid-1950s the dolls had vinyl heads but continued to have rubber bodies, but by the end of the era, the company dolls were being made entirely of vinyl. Because of the materials used by the firm in making dolls, they relied heavily on baby and toddler dolls.

The two most famous dolls made by Sun Rubber were the **Amosandra** doll made in 1949 which portrayed the baby on the "Amos and Andy" CBS show and the **Gerber** baby doll offered both as a premium and as a regular store offering during much of the decade.

Other dolls of interest include a doll with molded hair with a hole for a hair ribbon from 1953 and the 10" **Tod-L-Dee**, and **Tod-L-Tim** dolls with molded on clothes. The twins had inset glassene eyes and molded hair. The 10" **"So Wee"** dolls of the period, made of vinyl with molded hair and stationary eyes, were popular for young children. The dolls had been modeled by Ruth Newton and were made in 1957.

20" Sunny tears doll made by The Sun Rubber Co. in 1957. The all vinyl doll has sleep eyes, open mouth, and rooted hair. She is pictured with her original accessories: a bubble pipe, bottle, washcloth, dress, panties, and booties. The information on the box reads "drinks-wets-sleeps-coo voice-movable arms and legs/Sun tear baby cries HAPPY tears/c The Sun Rubber Co. 1957." ($100-125).

Togs and Dolls, Inc.

The **Mary Jane** dolls were made in two different models and had several names attached to them. In an early ad which appeared in *Playthings* magazine in June 1953 the name Kathryn Kay Toy Kreations Inc. appears to be the maker of the new dolls. Also associated with the project was the firm of G.H. and E. Freydberg, Inc., a leading children's dress maker, who was responsible for designing and producing the clothing for the dolls. Kathryn Kay Fassel was also involved with the Cosmopolitan Co. which made Ginger dolls. The hard plastic Mary Jane dolls were walkers with flirting eyes (closing) and were advertised as having complete wardrobes. Some of the clothes included a sailor dress and hat, pajamas, robe, shirt and jeans, cardigan sweater and beret with a pleated skirt, taffeta and net formal and cowgirl outfit. The doll sold for $9.95 in 1953.

The doll looked very much like the Terri Lee doll and that company sued to prevent the making of the new dolls. After the law suit was settled in Terri Lee's favor in 1954, the dolls were redesigned with vinyl heads on the hard plastic bodies. These dolls had sleep eyes and rooted hair. They were marketed by Togs and Dolls, Inc. until 1956.

This advertisement for Mary Jane dolls appeared in *Playthings* magazine for June 1953. The dolls were very similar to the Terri Lee dolls and a lawsuit was brought by the Terri Lee Company to stop production of the dolls.

Two tagged Mary Jane outfits include a sport set made very much like the Terri Lee clothes and a bathrobe with the "Mary Jane" tag showing. The belt is replaced. (Robe $20, shorts set $35.)

17" hard plastic Mary Jane dolls made in 1953 with sleep eyes, closed mouths, and attached wigs. They are wearing a five-piece tagged Mary Jane outfit (shoes replaced). A halter top is under the terri cloth jacket. The eyes on these dolls frequently do not function. The clothes were made by G.H. and E. Freydberg, Inc. Kathryn Kay Toy Kreations, Inc. was also involved in the enterprise. The dolls are unmarked. (Doll on left $150 and up, doll on right $200 and up).

17" hard plastic Mary Jane doll on the right. She is wearing a tagged outfit with replaced boots and hat. ($275 and up). The doll on the left is the doll that replaced the earlier Mary Jane when the court case was settled in Terri Lee's favor. She has a vinyl head, hard plastic body, sleep eyes, closed mouth, and tagged outfit. The doll is a head turning walker and was still called Mary Jane. She was made by Togs and Dolls, Corp. of New York circa 1955. The doll had thirty-six outfits that sold separately. ($300 and up). *Dolls and photograph from the collection of Carol L. Linderman.*

Uneeda

Uneeda of Brooklyn, New York, has been in business since before 1920. During the 1950s, the company scored a hit with their **Dollikins** doll. The lady doll mannikin had sixteen flexible joints on a body made of hard plastic. The doll's head was vinyl. She wore high heel shoes and could be costumed as a ballerina or an adult fashion doll. A baby doll was produced later using a similar jointed style body.

Other popular dolls for the company included a set of 10.5" vinyl **Tinyteen** dolls called **Suzette** and **Bob** circa 1957. Both dolls have the "Uneeda" mark on the backs of their heads. **Pri-thilla**, a 12" vinyl doll who sucked her thumb, was also a success when it was sold in 1958.

In addition Uneeda produced many of the same types of dolls as other companies were making in the 1950s. These included the high heel style dolls that were dressed as ballerinas as well as in other types of costumes.

17" vinyl doll with sleep eyes, closed mouth, rooted hair, pierced ears, turning waist, and arched feet. Although she is not marked her dress snap is one that was used by the Uneeda firm. It is marked "RAU SKLIKITS." She is original except for her shoes. Circa late 1950s. ($50-75).

10.5" Suzette and Bob Tinyteen vinyl dolls made by Uneeda Doll Co., Inc. circa 1957. The dolls have soft vinyl heads, rigid vinyl bodies, sleep eyes, and she has rooted hair while he has molded hair. She has arched feet to wear high heel shoes. Both dolls are marked "Uneeda" on the backs of their heads. (In played with condition $35-45 each). *Dolls from the collection of Marge Meisinger.*

Right: 19" Dollikin made of vinyl and hard plastic by Uneeda circa 1959. The doll has a vinyl head, hard plastic body, sleep eyes, closed mouth, and rooted hair. Her appeal came from her sixteen movable joints. She is marked "Uneeda 2 S" on the back of her head. She is all original with her box. ($150 and up).

19" Dollikin made by Uneeda dressed in her original ballerina costume. Since the doll had so many different joints, she was ideally suited for a dancing doll. ($125 and up). *Doll from the collection of Jan Clanton. Photograph by Darek Clanton.*

This advertisement for Uneeda dolls appeared in the Montgomery Ward Christmas catalog in 1959. Besides the Dollikin priced at $5.49, the ad also features the "Wee Three Family" set of dolls. Included were a 20" Mama, 13" Toddler, and 8" Baby Brother. The dolls were all made of vinyl with sleeping eyes. The mother and daughter had rooted hair while the baby had molded hair. The set sold for $9.29. *Catalog from the collection of Betty Nichols.*

Valentine Dolls, Inc.

Many of the dolls marketed by Valentine Dolls were sold in the mail order catalogs of the time. Their ballerina dolls were especially popular. Many of these dolls wore marked Capezio ballerina slippers. The dolls had vinyl heads, rooted hair, hard plastic bodies, and came in several sizes. The high heel type doll in the larger sizes was also a popular model for the Valentine company.

Valentine was also responsible for one of the personality dolls marketed during the 1950s when they produced **Roxanne**, a hard plastic doll made to tie-in with the "Beat the Clock" television show (see personality chapter).

12.5" "Prithilla" doll made by Uneeda circa 1958-1959. The vinyl doll has sleeping eyes, rooted straight hair, open mouth, and was able to suck her thumb. In the 1958 Sears Christmas catalog she was priced at $3.89. She was designed to be a tomboy. She is wearing her original clothes. *Doll from the collection of Carolyn Sharp. Photograph by Mark W. Carpenter.*

Far left: 17" doll with vinyl head and arms, hard plastic body, sleep eyes, closed mouth, rooted hair with joints at the waist, knees, and ankles. She is marked "17 VW" on the back of her neck. She came with her original box which says "Valentine High Heel Doll." Her original tag is from Armstrong's in Cedar Rapids and she was priced at $10.98. Her shoes are replaced. Circa 1956-1957. ($75-100).

Left: 10.5" vinyl and hard plastic ballerina by Valentine. The doll has a vinyl head, hard plastic body, sleep eyes, closed mouth, jointed knees, and rooted hair. She is marked "11 VW" on the back of her head. She has molded slippers under the added ballet shoes. Her arms are curved. Circa 1959. ($75-85).

Walkalon Mfg. Co.

Another unusual doll that appeared during the decade first came on the market in 1950. The doll was called **Betsy Walker** and was made by the Walkalon Mfg. Co. Betsy was 21" tall and was a keywind walker whose head and arms moved as she walked. The doll originally sold for $19.95. She had sleep eyes and molded hair and was made of hard plastic.

21" Betsy Walker doll with sleep eyes, closed mouth, and molded hair. She is made of hard plastic and is a key wind walker. She walks with the aid of rollers attached to her shoes. She is wearing replaced clothing. ($75 and up).

The new Betsy Walker doll was advertised in *Playthings* magazine in August 1950. The doll was made by the Walkalon Mfg. Company and sold for $19.95.

Miscellaneous

18" hard plastic doll with sleep eyes, closed mouth, and a real hair wig in all original mint condition. She was made by the Welsh-Morris Corp. of Mishawaka, Indiana. She is "Darling Daughter." Circa early to mid-1950s. ($200 and up). *Doll from the collection of Jan Clanton. Photograph by Darek Clanton.*

12" hard plastic "Squeezums" doll made by Royal in New York. When her tummy button is pushed she moves her head up and down for yes. When her back button is pushed she shakes her head for no. The toddler doll has sleep eyes, a closed mouth, molded hair, and is all original in her box. She also has a bracelet and rattle in an original package. Her back is marked "Patent Pending." Circa mid-1950s. ($100-125).

18.5" hard plastic Hawaiian doll dressed in her original clothing. She has sleep eyes, open mouth with teeth, and a coarse black wig. She is marked on the back of her neck "200". Her dark color is painted on. Circa early 1950s. ($175-200).

18" mint unmarked beautiful hard plastic girl doll with sleep eyes, closed mouth, and applied wig. She is wearing a formal with hat and gloves. Although not marked, she looks similar to the dolls dressed by Mollye. Circa early to mid-1950s. ($300-400). *Doll from the collection of Jan Clanton. Photograph by Darek Clanton.*

14" unmarked doll in original suitcase with extra clothes. The doll's head is stuffed vinyl while the body is made of latex. She has sleep eyes, closed mouth, and rooted hair. Her extra outfits include a sundress and robe. She also has sunglasses, and a comb, mirror, and brush. Circa 1956. ($75 and up).

Pair of unmarked vinyl and latex dolls all original in their original box. The larger doll is 16" tall while the smaller doll is 10.5" tall. The heads are made of stuffed vinyl and their bodies and limbs are latex. The larger doll has plastic eyes while the eyes on the other doll are painted. Both dolls have molded hair. There are no markings on the dolls or the box. Probably date from around 1950. ($100 and up).

19" unmarked vinyl fashion doll with sleep eyes, closed mouth, pierced ears, and rooted hair. Her arms seem to be too close to her body. She bends at the waist. She is a very heavy doll. She is all original and is pictured with her original box. This box is the same design as that used with a smaller fashion doll which came with a Mary Hoyer flyer (see Mary Hoyer chapter). Circa late 1950s. ($75 and up).

10.5" high heel fashion dolls called Miss Marie. They are all original in their boxes. The printing on the boxes states that the dolls were sold only at Woolworths with the Cat. No. 50-198. The dolls are marked with a P in a circle on the backs of their heads. Neither doll has painted eyelashes. The dolls likely sold for $1.98 each. They have sleep eyes, closed mouths, arched feet, and rooted hair. Circa 1958-1959. ($30 and up each).

Bibliography

Alexander Doll Company, Inc. Catalogs. New York, 1952-1959.

Anderton, Johana Gast. *Twentieth Century Dolls From Bisque to Vinyl*. North Kansas City, Missouri: The Trojan Press, 1971.

Axe, John. *The Encyclopedia of Celebrity Dolls*. Cumberland, Maryland: Hobby House Press, Inc., 1983.

_____. "Portraits of Ginny—The 1950s." *Doll Reader*. November 1982, pp. 6-10.

_____. "Tribute to the Grand Madame Madame Beatrice Alexander." *Doll Reader*. December 1990-January 1991, pp. 180-182.

_____. "William Boyd as Hopalong Cassidy." *Doll Reader*. June-July, 1983, pp. 134-135.

American Character Doll Corp. Catalogs. Showroom 1107 Broadway, New York, Factory 5112 Second Avenue, Brooklyn, New York. 1952, 1956.

Arranbee Doll Company. Various brochures.

Casper, Peggy Wiedman. *Fashionable Terri Lee Dolls*. Cumberland, Maryland: Hobby House Press, Inc., 1988.

Cosmopolitan Toy and Doll Corp. New York. Various brochures.

Cruse, Marvin. "Loss in Terri Lee Doll Plant Fire is $291,500." *Lincoln Evening Journal*. Lincoln, Nebraska: December 17, 1951.

Effanbee Doll Company Catalogs. New York, 1950, 1952.

Foulke, Jan. *Blue Book Dolls and Values*. Volumes Three-Twelve. Cumberland, Maryland: Hobby House Press, Inc.

Franklin, George. "Lincoln Woman's Plant Puts Out Modern Doll." *Lincoln Sunday Journal and Star*. Lincoln, Nebraska: July 11, 1948.

Gibbs, Patikii. *Horsman Dolls 1950-1970*. Paducah, Kentucky: Collector Books, 1985.

Guyette, Barbara. "Betsy McCall: A Look at a Doll Who Worked for a Living." *Doll Reader*. November 1984, pp. 114-116.

Hencey, Naomi. "American Character's Beautiful Betsy McCall." *Doll Reader*. February 1993, pp.198- 204.

Hoyer, Mary. *Mary Hoyer and Her Dolls*. Cumberland, Maryland: Hobby House Press, Inc., 1982.

Ideal Toy Corp. New York. Various company brochures.

Izen, Judith, and Carol Stover. *Collector's Encyclopedia of Vogue Dolls*. Paducah, Kentucky: Collector Books, 1998.

Izen, Judith. *Collector's Guide to Ideal Dolls*. Paducah, Kentucky: Collector Books, 1994.

_____. "Saralee—The First Anthropologically True Mass-Produced Negro Doll." *Doll Reader*. July 1992, pp. 92-96.

Jensen, Don. "Lawrence Welk's Champagne Lady." *Doll Reader*. October 1992, pp. 142-146.

Judd, Pam, and Polly Judd. "Coca Cola and Santa Claus Dolls—A Long Tradition." *Doll Reader*. December 1992- January 1993, pp. 38-40.

_____. "Diminutive High Heeled Fashion Dolls." *Doll Reader*. December 1983, January 1984, pp. 178- 181.

_____. "Fashions for Virga Dolls by Elsa Schiaparelli." *Doll Reader*. March-April, 1993, pp. 24-26.

_____. *Glamour Dolls*. Cumberland, Maryland: Hobby House Press, 1988.

_____. *Hard Plastic Dolls Identification and Price Guide*. Cumberland, Maryland: Hobby House Press, 1990.

_____. *Hard Plastic Dolls, II Identification and Price Guide*. Cumberland, Maryland: Hobby House Press, Inc., 1990.

_____. "Raving Beauty Dolls." *Doll Reader*. August 1992, pp. 44-46.

_____. "Worldwide Doll Club." *Doll Reader*. September 1993, pp. 22-24.

Lincoln Journal. "Doll Plant May Reopen In January." Lincoln, Nebraska: December 20, 1951.

Lincoln Journal and Star. "Terri Lee Co. Moving West." Lincon, Nebraska: March 1, 1953.

Lincoln Sunday Journal and Star. "Thriving Doll Factory in Lincoln Refutes Early Warnings." Lincoln, Nebraska: November 11, 1951.

Lincoln, Nebraska Sunday Journal and Star. "Mrs. Gradwohl, Doll Firm Founder, Dies." Lincoln, Nebraska: July 23, 1972.

Loder, Venice. E. "In Search of the Elusive Gigi." *Doll Reader*. December 1987-January 1988, pp. 131-135.

Maciak, Heather. "Identifying Muffie." *Doll Reader*. December 1986-January 1987, pp. 120-124.

Manderville, A. Glenn. "Betsy McCall Revisited." *Doll Reader*. December 1988, January 1989, pp. 178-185.

_____. "Ideal Dolls...The End of an Era." *Doll Reader*. November 1986, pp. 114-120.

_____. "Celebrity Dolls of the 1950s." *Doll Reader*. September, 1991, pp. 104-108.

_____. *Ginny...An American Toddler*. Grantsville, Maryland: Hobby House Press, 1994.

_____. "A Honey of a Doll—Effanbee's Honey Family." *Doll Reader*. October 1987, pp. 136-141.

_____. "35 Years with Betsy McCall." *Doll Reader*. October 1986, pp. 106-111.

_____. "The Many Faces of Ginny." *Doll Reader*. June-July 1989, pp. 206-213.

_____. "The Mary Hartline Story..." *Doll Reader*. May 1986, pp.156-159.

_____. "So Beautiful Her Name Just Had to be...Revlon." *Doll Reader*. December 1987-January 1988, pp. 106-113

_____. "The World of Alexander Kins. *DollReader*. August-September 1987, pp. 206-211.

Mary Hoyer Doll Mfg. Co. Reading, Pa. Various company booklets and brochures.

Miller, Marjorie A. *Nancy Ann Storybook Dolls*. Cumberland, Maryland: Hobby House Press, 1991.

Millhouse, Peggy. "Doll Clothes Cleaning and Restoration," "Doll Wig Restoration." Self Published: 510 Green Hill Road. Conestoga, Pa. 17516

Montgomery Ward Catalogs. Chicago, Illinois. Various issues.

Nagley, Richard Ashton, and Tracy Sexton Davis. "Little Lulu, I Love You, Lu." *Doll Reader*. December 1988, January 1990. pp.177.

Nancy Ann Storybook Dolls, Inc. Brochures. San Francisco, CA. Various issues.

Nettleingham Roberts, Sue, and Dorothy Bunker. "Ginny's Formative Years." *Doll Reader*. April 1991, pp. 86-89.

_____. "Ginny's Birth." *Doll Reader*. February-March 1991, pp. 146-151.

_____. "Ginny's Triumphant Years." *Doll Reader*. December 1992-January 1993, pp. 198-203.

Niswonger, Jeanne. "Ginny's Little Sister—Ginnette and the Baby Ginnys." *Doll Reader*. May 1987, 130-132.

Robison, Joleen Ashman, and Kay Sellers. *Advertising Dolls*. Paducah, Kentucky: Collector Books, 1992.

Roth, Lillian, and Heather Browning Maciak. *The Muffie Puzzle*. Santa Monica, California: Roth and Maciak, 1993.

Schmuhl, Marian. "The Richwood Toy Co." *Doll Reader*. October 1991, pp. 112-118.

Sears Catalogs. Chicago, Illinois. Various issues.

Smith, Patricia. *Doll Values Antique to Modern*. Volumes Two-Twelve. Paducah, Kentucky: Collectors Books.

_____. *Effanbee Dolls That Touch Your Heart*. Paducah, Kentucky: Collector Books, 1983.

_____. *Madame Alexander Collector's Dolls*. Paducah, Kentucky: Collector Books, 1977.

Terrace, Vincent. *The Complete Encyclopedia of Television Programs 1947-1979 Vol. I, Vol. II*. New York: A.S. Barnes and Co., 1979.

Thompson, Deborah Adam. "Ideal's Revlon Dolls." *Doll Reader*. October 1993, pp. 82-85.

Vogue Dolls, Inc. Medford, Massachusetts. Various company brochures.

Webster, Edna Robb. "Doll House in Apple Valley." *Independent Woman*. December 1954, pp. 452-454.

Zillner, Dian. *Collectible Coloring Books*. West Chester, Pennsylvania: Schiffer Publishing Ltd., 1992.

_____. *Collectible Television Memorabilia*. Atglen, PA: Schiffer Publishing Ltd., 1996.

Index